Defending
Human Dignity

Defending Human Dignity

John Paul II and Political Realism

Derek S. Jeffreys

Brazos Press

Grand Rapids, Michigan

© 2004 by Derek S. Jeffreys

Published by Brazos Press
a division of Baker Book House Company
P.O. Box 6287, Grand Rapids, MI 49516-6287
www.brazospress.com

Printed in the United States of America

Library of Congress Cataloging-in-Publication Data
Jeffreys, Derek S., 1964
     Defending human dignity : John Paul II and political realism / Derek S. Jeffreys.
          p.   cm.
     Includes bibliographical references and index.
     ISBN 1-58743-092-4 (pbk.)
     1. John Paul II, Pope, 1920- 2. Catholic Church and world politics—History—20th century. I.
Title.
     BX1378.5.J4165 2004
     261.7′092—dc22   2004000447

For Celestine

Contents

Acknowledgments

I first became interested in political realism at the University of Chicago and owe a great deal to my teachers at this institution for my intellectual formation. I began this book while teaching at California State University, Chico, and would like to thank its religious studies faculty for encouraging me to undertake it. I owe much to Paul J. Griffiths, teacher and friend, who exemplifies Christian scholarship, and whose witness to the Christian faith I deeply admire. I have also benefited greatly from wonderful conversations with W. Norris Clarke, S.J., who has shown me the power of Thomistic personalism.

For their support and advice, I also want to thank Armand Antommaria, John F. Crosby, David Walsh, Franklin I. Gamwell, Samuel Gregg, Bruce Grelle, Harvey J. Kaye, Charles Mathewes, Gilbert T. Null, Jerrold C. Rodesch, and Joel Zimbelman. I am also grateful to Rodney Clapp and Rebecca Cooper at Brazos Press, who have offered excellent comments and advice about this book.

Finally, God has graced me with a wonderful family. Becoming a father to my sons, Zachariah and Caleb, has been one of the most beautiful experiences of my life. My wife, Celestine, has supported me as I worked on this book, and she never ceases to amaze me with her vibrant, outgoing spirit. It is to her that I dedicate this book.

Sources and Abbreviations

Pope John Paul II has given an extraordinary number of addresses, speeches, and other public presentations. Fortunately, the Vatican has a website that contains most of them. Unless otherwise indicated, I have taken all of John Paul II's speeches and other writings from this website, which can be found at http://www.vatican.va/holy_father/john_paul_ii/index.htm.

I have used the Joseph Donders translation of the following encyclicals: "Redemptoris Hominis," "Dives in Misericordia," "Laborem Exercens," "Dominum et Vivificantem," "Sollicitudo Rei Socialis," "Centesimus Annus," "Veritatis Splendor," and "Evangelium Vitae."

Throughout the text, I use the following abbreviations:

1999America	"Ecclesia in America," January 22, 1999.
1999Asia	"Ecclesia in Asia," November 6, 1999.
CA	"Centesimus Annus," May 1, 1991.
2002Celebration	"Celebration of the World Day of Peace," January 1, 2002.
1994Clinton	"Letter to President Clinton," April 5, 1994.
1999Culture	"Address to the World of Culture," November 9, 1999.
DM	"Dives in Misericordia," November 30, 1980
DV	"Dominum et Vivificantem," May 19, 1986.
EV	"Evangelium Vitae," March 25, 1995
1993Food and Agriculture	"Address to the United Nations Food and Agriculture Organization," November 11, 1993.

FR	"Fides et Ratio," September 14, 1998
LE	"Laborem Exercens," September 14, 1981.
"Letter to Families"	"Letter to Families from Pope John Paul II," February 2, 1994.
1986Liberation	"Instructions on Certain Aspects of the 'Theology of Liberation,'" March 22, 1986.
1996Lichtenberg and Leisner	"Beatification of Bernhard Lichtenberg and Karl Leisner," June 23, 1996.
1999Love	"Message of Love to Confront the Loss of God in Society," December 15, 1999.
1999Migration	"Message of the Holy Father for World Migration Day," November 22, 1999.
NMI	"Novo Millennio Ineunte," January 6, 2001
2000Peace	"Message of Pope John Paul II for the Celebration of the World Day of Peace," January 1, 2000.
2001Peace	"Message for World Day of Peace," January 1, 2001.
RH	"Redemptor Hominis," March 25, 1987
RP	"Reconciliatio et Paenitentia," December 2, 1984
2000Science	"Address of John Paul II to the Pontifical Academy of Sciences," November 13, 2000.
SD	"Salvifici Doloris," Feburary 11, 1984
SR	"Solicitudo Rei Socialis," December 30, 1987.
TMA	"Tertio Millennio Adveniente," November 10, 1994
1996Truth	"Truth cannot contradict truth," October 22, 1996.
1979UN	"Address to the United Nations General Assembly," October 2, 1979.
1995UN	"Address to the United Nations General Assembly," October 5, 1995.
2000UN	"Audience with the Secretary General of the United Nations," April 7, 2000.
VS	"Veritatis Splendor," August 6, 1996
2000Workers	"Jubilee of Workers," May 1, 2000.

Introduction

For you know as well as we do that right, as the world goes, is in question only between equals in power, while the strong do what they can and the weak do what they must.[1]

Thucydides

"I know for certain, though, that I have chosen the greater freedom."[2]

Adam Chmielowski

The great Athenian historian Thucydides records a famous episode during the Peloponnesian Wars that illustrates the logic of political realism.[3] Melos, a small island in the Mediterranean, rebelled against the Athenian empire. During an interlude in the conflict, delegates from Melos and Athens met to discuss their disagreement. In his celebrated style, Thucydides records their speeches during the conference. The Athenians maintain that matters of justice and right play no role in the brutal world of international politics. They present the Melians with simple calculations of consequences: they can surrender and avoid destruction, or they can continue to fight and face certain annihilation. Ruthlessly, the Athenians reject the Melians' suggestion that a world governed by justice benefits all nations. Instead, they argue, all nations pursue their self-interest, legitimizing it with "specious pretences" like appeals to justice and equity (Thucydides 1982, bk. 5, 89). In this environment, weak nations are well advised to avoid turning to "the invis-

ible, to prophecies and oracles," and should acknowledge the realities
of power politics (ibid., 103). They should submit to stronger nations,
making the best of their poor natural and cultural endowments. Otherwise, they have only trust in the gods and hope, both unreliable guides
for statecraft. Repeatedly, the Athenians appeal to the visible, evoking
short-term calculation of interests as the sole consideration in politics.
They present power as the central currency of politics, maintaining that
we cannot ignore or wish it away. Unfortunately, the Melians refuse to
recognize such realities, choosing instead to battle for their freedom.
Thucydides records their fate in a terse but frightening sentence. The
Melians, he says, "surrendered at discretion to the Athenians, who put
to death all the grown men whom they took, and sold the women and
children for slaves, and subsequently sent out five hundred colonists and
inhabited the place themselves" (ibid., 115).[4]

Introducing Political Realism

In emphasizing power, violence, and the measurable consequences
of action, the Athenians embody political realism.[5] A host of political
realists have repeated and developed their arguments, including St.
Augustine, Machiavelli, John Calvin, Thomas Hobbes, Max Weber,
Hans Morgenthau, Reinhold Niebuhr, George F. Kennan, Kenneth
Waltz, Paul Ramsey, and Henry Kissinger. At first blush, putting all
of these thinkers into one category called political realism seems odd.
They inhabit very different historical contexts and have diverse and
competing philosophical and theological visions. However, they are all
realists because they share the perception that politics is characterized
by "givens," phenomena that we can never eliminate.[6] The first of these
givens is the pursuit of power. In politics, realists maintain, people continually try to impose their will on others. Some realists posit a natural
drive toward power, and thus argue that people pursue power as an end.
Others, however, particularly Christian realists, describe how political
actors use power to achieve material or ideological ends. Nevertheless,
either as an end or a means, the pursuit of power is always present in
politics. The second given realists presuppose is group loyalty. They focus
on how our commitment to a group shapes our thoughts and actions.

They often describe how group symbols, ethos, and language become vehicles for pursuing power. Social structures support drives for power, often making political actors oblivious to criticism. Finally, political realists assume that politics is conflictual. Some realists depict a state of war in which continual violence reigns. Others focus on non-violent conflict, recognizing that although violence is frequent, other forms of conflict such as economic conflict can be deeply destructive.

In reading political realists, however, we discover different explanations of the pursuit of power, group loyalty, and conflict. For example, St. Augustine describes how pride generates an endless pursuit of power. For him, pride is a "longing for a perverse kind of self-exaltation" leading us to turn our minds and wills away from God (Augustine 1986, bk. 14, ch. 13). In his famous nineteenth chapter of *The City of God,* he describes how pride infects every aspect of social life, including the family, friendship, and political life.[7] In contrast, Hobbes describes a physiological drive for power that disrupts social life. In his famous words, without government, this drive makes life "solitary, poor, nasty, brutish, and short" (Hobbes 1991, 89). Similarly, in considering group loyalty, Thucydides focuses on the balance of power within and among societies. When this balance is upset, groups compete viciously, undermining the conditions for social order.[8] On the other hand, Reinhold Niebuhr describes how groups become idols. For Niebuhr, we have a capacity to transcend our finitude, yet often direct our loyalty narrowly toward groups, trusting in them excessively.[9] Finally, when accounting for conflict, contemporary realists in international relations analyze structural constraints in politics. International politics encourages violent competition, primarily because no power exists that is strong enough to prevent it. Brilliantly, political scientists like Kenneth Waltz articulate this form of realism.[10]

These "givens" render politics a dangerous and ambiguous enterprise in which doing the right thing is extremely difficult. Often, realists depict conflicts between values. Should we prefer order to freedom? Can democracy create dangerous disorder? Do we sometimes have to harm the innocent in order to combat tyranny? Historically, political realists have addressed these and other issues. In reading their work, one gets a sense of the tragic character of political life. As Morgenthau puts it, political realism "knows that political reality is replete with contingencies and systemic irrationalities" (Morgenthau 1985, 10). Not only is the political world a struggle for power and resources, but it is also an arena of intractable conflicts between values.

Realists also offer different *prescriptions* for how we should respond to these conflicts. Often, realism is mistakenly identified with amoralism. Realists, it is said, think that politics is the realm of necessity in which moral claims have no relevance.[11] Undoubtedly, some realists have been amoralists; Hobbes was certainly one, some nineteenth-century realists were also amoralists, and the British historian E. H. Carr in the mid-twentieth century could also be classified as such.[12] Yet, other realists are decidedly not amoralists. For example, St. Augustine never divorces morality from politics. For him, a proper understanding of ordered love is essential in political life. Likewise, Calvin always maintains that despite chaos, the moral law binds political leaders. His sermons and commentaries are filled with eloquent denunciations of tyrants who disregard moral norms.[13] Thucydides also pays attention to the moral dimensions of politics. As classicist David Grene noted many years ago, he subtly expresses his horror at acts of political violence, such as the massacre of schoolchildren during the Athenians' Sicilian campaign.[14] Therefore, we should not identify political realism with amoralism. Realists agree that politics is disorderly and dangerous, yet ethically, they respond to this chaos differently, depending on historical circumstances and philosophical and theological visions.

Realism and Consequentialism

Despite this diversity, however, many realists share a concern with calculating the consequences of our actions. From Thucydides to Henry Kissinger, they have insisted that the statesperson guide his action by considering its foreseeable consequences. In his famous essay "Politics as a Vocation," Max Weber articulates one of most compelling examples of this political ethic.[15] He distinguishes between an "ethic of ultimate ends" and an "ethic of responsibility." With an "ethic of ultimate ends," a moral agent locates value in intentions, seeking purity of intention and character, showing little or no concern for the consequences of his action. In contrast, with the "ethic of responsibility," he accepts the foreseeable consequences of his action. Recognizing that purity of intention is a dangerous political aspiration, he overrides moral principles binding the conscience of those outside of politics. In Weber's vision, the statesman is a heroic figure. He understands the brutality of the political arena, bravely confronting its moral ambiguities. Unlike a private citizen with the luxury of cultivating moral purity, he knows that in politics, one inevitably incurs guilt for moral wrongdoing. Instead of ignoring what must be done or denying political realities, he courageously does what most of us consider morally repugnant. Those outside of politics often forget that without this courageous action, political order would degenerate into chaos.

Undoubtedly, Weber's portrait of statesmanship rests on his controversial understanding of rationality and morality. Nevertheless, his ethic of responsibility articulates a central theme in realist political thought. One does not have to look far to find similar ethics in Machiavelli's *The Prince,* Hobbes's *Leviathan,* Morgenthau's *Politics among Nations,* or Kissinger's *White House Years.* These thinkers share what in modern ethics is known as consequentialism, the "doctrine that the moral value of any action always lies in its consequences, and that it is by reference to their consequences that actions, and indeed such things as institutions, laws, and practices, are to be justified if they can be justified at all" (Smart and Williams 1973, 79). To be more precise, consequentialism maintains, as philosopher Bernard Williams notes, that the only things that have value are "states of affairs, and that anything else that has value has it because it conduces to some intrinsically valuable state of affairs" (ibid., 83). Usually, political realists restrict consequentialism to politics. They assert gaps between interpersonal and political morality, urging politicians to sacrifice their personal integrity to serve the common good. For example, Morgenthau states that "the individual may say to himself: *'Fiat justitia, pereat mundus'* (Let justice be done, even if the world perish), but the state has no right to say so in the name of those in its care" (Morgenthau 1985, 12). Others echo him, restricting consequentialist reasoning to the political arena, while allowing religious or other values to shape private choices.

In the twentieth century, the realist emphasis on measurable consequences gained considerable power and cultural support in many countries. Technological and scientific developments enabled statespeople, diplomats, and bureaucrats to claim that they could calculate the consequences of actions precisely. Philosophical positivism, the rapid development of medical and other technology, and confidence in scientific and pseudo-scientific measurements made it seem that the visible was all that really mattered in politics. Other arenas of modern life reinforced this trend toward measuring consequences. Generals and politicians calculated probable battlefield causalities, using intricate strategic bombing analyses. Economists promised to calculate the precise consequences of economic policy, measuring the outcome of complex market transactions. In the beginning of this century, geneticists and health researchers hailed scientific developments like the Human Genome Project as an opportunity to end suffering and manipulate human nature. Those fighting terrorism promise to bring terrorists to justice using technological innovations that minimize civilian casualties.

The al-Qaeda terrorist attacks against the United States and other nations illustrate the deep attraction of consequentialist reasoning. They created tremendous insecurity, and predictably, people responded to it by clamoring for instant action against al-Qaeda. Gradually, governments developed policies to respond to terrorism. For example, in its 2002 document "The National Security Strategy of the United States," the United States government articulated a controversial doctrine of preemptive war. Appealing to a venerable concept in political realism, the document's introduction states that the United States will "seek instead to create a balance of power that favors human freedom: conditions in which all nations and all societies can choose for themselves the rewards and challenges of political and economic liberty" (National Security Strategy of the United States, introduction). However, it also calls for a strategy relying on preemption, rather than deterrence. During the Cold War, the United States threatened the Soviet Union with massive retaliation if it invaded Western Europe. Deterrence was successful because the Soviet Union was a rational adversary weighing costs and benefits of its strategy. However, with its suicide attacks, al-Qaeda demonstrated that massive retaliation would not deter it. Instead, it deliberately created wanton destruction, welcoming a response creating further chaos and destruction. Consequently, in its 2002 document, the U.S. government embraced a different strategy, stating that it "has long maintained the option of preemptive actions to counter a sufficient threat to our national security. The greater the threat, the greater is the risk of inaction—and the more compelling the case for taking anticipatory action to defend ourselves, even if uncertainty remains as to the time and place of the enemy's attack. To forestall or prevent such hostile acts by our adversaries, the United States will, if necessary, act preemptively" (ibid., part 5). The shift from deterrence to preemption represented an important change in American military strategy.

Preemptive action raises many difficult ethical questions about the justification of war, but I think it also places great weight on calculating consequences.[16] Preemption requires leaders to make political judgments based on imperfect intelligence and incomplete information. Considering the September 11 attacks on the United States, many people argue that even under such constraints, acting preemptively is the best defense against ruthless terrorists. Critics of preemption argue that it will have disastrous consequences for the international political order. Others appeal to national sovereignty or some other value that renders preemption immoral. However, these voices appear politically irresponsible, for they are willing to risk terrible consequences if terrorists use nuclear or biological weapons.

Those who resist calculating consequences, however, will likely find little support among populations terrified by terrorism. Such fear makes the allure of the visible very powerful. Armed with data about the probable consequences of action, modern-day Athenians often dismiss appeals to religious values, insisting that they are irrelevant and immeasurable distractions. Those presenting alternatives to technocratic reasoning often find little public support, their voices drowned out by the appeals to the tangible. Confronting large-scale global changes and terrible threats of violence, what right-thinking person would resist measuring the foreseeable consequences of our action? If we have the technology to make such measurements, it would seem that only Luddites and reactionaries would oppose using it. All of these developments have bolstered the realist argument that calculating consequences should be at the heart of a political ethic.

The Dilemmas of Political Realism

Those who are uneasy with political consequentialism respond to this cultural climate in several ways. Some reject the political realist's *descriptive* account of politics, maintaining that the pursuit of power and security are not key factors driving political actors. Groups and individuals do not always pursue power, and reason and moral sentiment can move them. Nonviolent political action can also effectively counter terrorism and oppression. Others reject realism's *normative* claims by playing the consequentialist game, arguing that moral rules have positive consequences for political life. Like the Melians, they insist that pursuing justice is in the long-term interest of all countries, and they embrace technocratic reasoning as a way of furthering it. Finally, others adhere strongly to moral rules, maintaining that ethics has nothing to do with calculating consequences. They acknowledge that the pursuit of power characterizes politics, yet reject any kind of consequentialism.

Each of these responses presents significant difficulties. Thucydides and Machiavelli expose the naïveté of those who reject the pursuit of power in politics. Repeatedly in the last century, Reinhold Niebuhr, Morgenthau, and Kennan attacked political "idealists" who denied that politics is an arena of conflict and disorder. Many today have foolishly forgotten this critique, but it remains very powerful nevertheless, militating against any easy rejection of political realism. If anything, developments since the end of the Cold War have strengthened the realist case against idealism, dashing the hopes of many who longed for a more peaceful world. The war in the Balkans, the Persian Gulf Wars, the genocide in Rwanda, and terrorist attacks against the United States are only a few of the horrors that have greeted those harboring aspirations for a more humane globe. These developments have made it increasingly difficult to deny the pursuit of power in international relations.

Similarly, those who respond to realism by playing the consequentialist game provide only flimsy support for justice and human rights. In conflict situations, calculating that a moral rule will produce long-term beneficial consequences is notoriously unreliable. The certainty attached to such calculations "is usually pretty low; in some cases, indeed, the hypothesis invoked is so implausible that it would scarcely pass if it were not being used to deliver the respectable moral answer" (Smart and Williams 1973, 100). For example, let us consider noncombatant immunity, a key element of the just war tradition. The just war tradition is a centuries-old way of thinking about warfare, and includes a strict prohibition against intentionally killing the innocent, usually called noncombatant immunity. Does adhering to this principle serve the common good? In discussions of the just war tradition in the last decades of the twentieth century, some theologians and philosophers defended restraint in warfare by arguing that it has positive consequences for the international community. For example, theologian Richard A. McCormick, S.J., argued that "direct attacks on noncombatant civilians in wartime, however effective and important they may seem, will in the long-run release more violence and be more destructive to human life than the lives we might save by directly attacking noncombatants" (McCormick 1978, 31).[17] Yet he never tells us how to make this calculation. Over what period of time do we consider the consequences of action? How can we predict with any confidence the precise effects of action over extended periods of time? Despite our capacity to measure, such a judgment requires knowledge of consequences that few possess.

The end of the Soviet empire in the last century provides another example of the notorious difficulties in making predictions about consequences. As historian John Lewis Gaddis carefully shows, few specialists in international relations or military strategy came anywhere close to predicting that the Soviet Union would fall when it did (see Gaddis 1992/1993). Many expected that it would collapse, but few foresaw that it would so dramatically and peacefully disintegrate in the space of a few years. Similarly, in the 1990s, some intelligence experts warned that al-Qaeda terrorists represented a significant threat to the United States, but few came anywhere close to predicting that in 2001 they would crash civilian aircraft into New York City's World Trade Center. Witnessing these and other predictive failures, the long-range measurements McCormick and others confidently make carry little epistemological weight.

Finally, rejecting an ethic of consequences in favor of moral rules holds considerable promise, but often appears moralistic and legalistic. Williams's well-known critique of utilitarianism illustrates this danger. Williams recognizes that those adhering to rules seem guilty of a "kind of self-indulgent squeamishness" (Smart and Williams 1973, 102). Anglo-American ethics is full of thought experiments that invite the charge of self-indulgence. When considering if sheriffs should hang an innocent man to prevent riots, or whether the conductor of the untracked trolley should kill one or five people, those who hold fast to rules appear heartless, lovers of abstractions over people.[18] Moreover, even if we carefully defend these rules, a world that values science and measurement often dismisses such arguments, relegating them to the political sidelines. Those who cling to them are labeled "irrelevant" and seen as anachronistic minds out of step with right-thinking moderns or postmoderns.

Perhaps we can resist these charges by emphasizing moral integrity. In discussing his oft-cited example of a person ordered to kill one person or witness twenty others killed, Williams insists that it is morally significant that the choice to kill is something a person *does*. For the utilitarian, he argues, whether I do or allow something is irrelevant for evaluating the morality of my act, and I am responsible for failing to prevent the deaths of twenty people if I refuse to kill one person. This, Williams maintains, undermines a moral agent's pursuit of projects that are distinctive to her identity. She becomes an "agent of the satisfaction system who happens to be at a particular point at a particular time" (Smart and Williams 1973, 115). Whether or not she succeeds depends on other causal forces, and has nothing to do with her character or projects. Williams sees this account of moral agency as a direct challenge to moral integrity. Moral integrity values our deepest commitments, but if they conflict with maximizing good consequences, the utilitarian insists that we surrender them. Williams thinks this is an absurd demand of a person because it alienates "him in a real sense from his actions and the source of his action in his own convictions" (ibid., 116). It is an intolerable attack on integrity, and gives us good reason to reject consequentialism.

Williams makes a powerful and persuasive point that a consistent consequentialism undermines a certain kind of moral integrity. Unfortunately, without a deeper account of what is valuable in life, his argument begs too many questions to be of use against political realism. At most, Williams demonstrates that moral integrity is important, yet does little to show that it is *more* important than good consequences. What is so valuable about the inner life of persons? Without addressing this question, Williams leaves himself vulnerable to the charge of self-indulgence. Furthermore, people may achieve moral integrity by pursuing projects harmful to others. Some limitations to our integrity must, therefore, be permitted, and if so, why not define acceptable character development by calculating the consequences of our actions? Finally, political realists have always presented a picture of *political* integrity that celebrates the politician who puts his moral scruples aside in order to do distasteful acts for the sake of the common good. For Machiavelli, Morgenthau, and many others, a statesperson who refuses to do so lacks the moral character to be a leader and should retire to private life. In this world, the refusal to accept consequentialism is what undermines moral integrity.

Obviously, such considerations may not sway those who reject the realist normative analysis of politics, but they do point to difficulties in appealing to integrity to counter consequentialism. Moreover, they reveal the dilemmas political realism creates. The political realist uses his dark descriptive account of politics to support his normative prescriptive, arguing that those who fail to adopt consequentialism are guilty of underestimating human evil. Those opposing this challenge seem to have only a few options. On one hand, they can maintain that despite appearances, the pursuit of power and political disorder are really not constitutive of political life. However, this approach flies in the face of the self-evident, and must confront the powerful witness of the political realist tradition. On the other hand, they can accept political realism but cling to moral rules that put brakes on political consequentialism. However, this approach seems excessively legalistic and selfish, a self-centered act of someone who, in political philosopher Michael Walzer's phrase, wants to avoid "the problem of dirty hands."[19] In a technocratic and scientistic atmosphere, it is also unlikely to attract public support and will be relegated to political irrelevance. Both of these responses to political realism are dissatisfying and come nowhere near meeting its challenges.

Pope John Paul II and Political Realism

However, there is another possible response to political realism. We might endorse its descriptive account of power and disorder, acknowledging that human beings have powerful tendencies to dominate others for selfish reasons. Yet, in confronting power, we might reject political realism's normative project, refusing to adopt an ethic of consequences. Instead, we might rigorously challenge its basic assumptions and propose and embody an alternative ethic that values the dignity of the person over calculating consequences. In this book, I argue that Pope John Paul II offers this kind of nuanced response to political realism. For most of his adult life, he has opposed ethics based on calculating consequences. As a young priest and later Bishop of Krakow, he confronted both the Nazi and Soviet regimes, two of the twentieth century's most powerful totalitarian governments, both of which repeatedly appealed to consequences to justify their crimes. In plays and philosophical works, he subtly criticized the Marxist materialism that played such a big part in Soviet reasoning. As pope in the 1980s, John Paul II attacked the utilitarian reasoning justifying abortion, euthanasia, and population control. Adopting the memorable phrase, "the culture of death," he warned that crass appeals to consequences undermine our modern concern for human rights. Finally, in the 1990s, John Paul II turned his attention to nationalism and the free market. Powerfully, he criticized nationalists who at the end of the Cold War justified horrific crimes as necessary for achieving nationhood. Confronting the explosive growth of the global market, he warned against uncritically endorsing a free-market economic system. Responding to terrorism, he unequivocally condemned those who use it to correct social injustices. In each of these discussions, John Paul II has been an important voice opposing consequentialist reasoning.

However, his opposition has not been merely negative. He has also offered a compelling ethical alternative grounded in the dignity of the person. Developed in conversation with modern philosophy, it rejects any attempt to dehumanize human persons. This vision, I will argue in this book, is a particularly effective response to political realism, because John Paul II shares some of political realism's insights. He often emphasizes the power of sin, focusing on structures of sin in international politics. In writing about abortion, euthanasia, and suffering, he presents a dark vision of human life that bears strong resemblance to a Niebuhrian conception of politics. Moreover, he is fully aware of the powerful pull of scientistic and technocratic reasoning that supports an ethic of consequences. In fact, much of his work focuses on how modernity has negatively affected culture. Finally, John Paul II not only reflects theoretically about ethics, but also embodies his ethic visibly. Although he commands no military, he exerts an extraordinary influence on international politics. As an actor on the political stage, he wields power in ways that any realist would admire. For example, many scholars recognize his influence in weakening the Soviet empire in Eastern Europe. Among others, Jonathan Kwitny and George Weigel detail how he masterfully wielded rhetorical, symbolic, and institutional power to respond to the Soviet domination of Poland (see Kwitny 1997 and Weigel 1999). However, Poland is only one place where he has employed such power. For example, Weigel describes how John Paul II used his 1998 visit to Cuba to promote religious liberty. Deftly navigating a complex situation in which American politicians demanded he denounce Castro, and critics insisted that he call for an end to the American economic embargo against Cuba, he successfully communicated with hundreds of thousands of Cubans in huge rallies normally forbidden in Cuba. Hobbes would marvel at such a display of power.[20]

John Paul II's Philosophical Project: The Philosophy of Being and the Philosophy of Consciousness

John Paul II interests so many people not only because of such extraordinary public displays, but also because he brings to the public arena a philosophical and theological vision. Rarely do we encounter someone who has been both a philosopher and a powerful public figure. Public figures often completely ignore philosophical issues. When they do consider them, they are frequently dilettantes who pervert the philosophical treasures of the past with superficial analyses. Likewise, many philosophers eschew any serious involvement in public life. When they consider political matters, they often ignore their complexity, authoritatively pronouncing on difficult issues in an ignorant and arrogant manner. Thus, although he exercises power very differently than do statespeople, John Paul II represents a unique link between philosophy and power that has much to teach both philosophers and politicians.

Despite the many works on John Paul II's political ethics, however, few have adequately considered his political thought in its larger philosophical context. John Paul II is a complex thinker whose work attracts people with diverse interests. Often, we find excellent works on one element of his thought that fail to link it to others. For example, George Weigel and Jean Bethke Elshtain illuminate John Paul II's ethic and uses of power, yet say little about his attempt to retrieve a philosophy of consciousness. Robert P. George and John M. Finnis carefully consider his response to consequentialism, but neglect his understanding of sin and power. Andrew Woznicki details his extraordinary treatment of love, but says little about what it implies about political life.

Recently, however, a group of thinkers has begun to explore John Paul II's philosophical project. Kenneth L. Schmitz, Jaroslaw Kupczak, Rocco Buttiglione, and John F. Crosby maintain that John Paul II develops a philosophical project that is grounded in a philosophy of being but that retrieves elements of a philosophy of consciousness. Schmitz has been particularly eloquent in discussing this project. He maintains that John Paul II appreciates modernity's emphasis on the interiority of the person and is particularly drawn to modern phenomenology. However, the pope is deeply worried that subjectivism and relativism are gradually undermining modernity's positive elements. Many modern and postmodern philosophers refuse to affirm that reality exists independently of our capacity to think about it. Instead, they argue that it is socially constructed or a product of language. This refusal to link subjectivity with a realist ontology threatens to destroy our noble aspirations toward human rights and equality. John Paul II, Schmitz argues, insists that if we want to salvage these ideas, we must link modern philosophy to a Thomistic realism. He can be described, therefore, as a Thomist who critically and cautiously retrieves elements of modern phenomenology.

Both phenomenologists and Thomists have criticized this project, charging that it is an incoherent hybrid. Phenomenologists maintain that phenomenology comports ill with Thomism's metaphysic of being. Thomists maintain that modern phenomenology often embraces philosophical idealism, thus failing to provide the mind with adequate access to reality. Complicating matters is the unfortunate fate of the pope's central work in phenomenology, *The Acting Person.* Controversies over its translation into English make it difficult for scholars to fully engage this work. These difficulties and criticisms have prompted Schmitz, Crosby, and others to develop John Paul II's project in greater detail, focusing on areas he has had little time to consider. Schmitz has carefully defined the conditions that must obtain in order for John Paul II's project to succeed, focusing on subjectivity and objectivity, interiority, metaphysical realism, and the unity of human action (Schmitz 1993, 138–46). Kupczak also affirms the coherence of John Paul II's philosophical project, while noting that his "method requires further specifications and needs some more precise formulations" (Kupczak 2000, 80).

These careful discussions establish the importance of John Paul II's philosophical project, while also revealing important questions about the relationships between Thomism and phenomenology. I believe that its attempt to appreciatively use phenomenology within a Thomistic metaphysic constitutes an important philosophical development. However, it will not be fully developed until scholars explore more carefully how John Paul II uses phenomenology. Too often, Thomists eager to establish his Thomistic credentials neglect his creative use of philosophies of consciousness. Carelessly, they identify phenomenology with its idealist strands, ignoring the realist phenomenology that originated in Germany in the early twentieth century. Max Scheler, Adolf Reinach, Dietrich von Hildebrand, Edith Stein, and others reject the charge that phenomenology leads to idealism, yet many Thomists ignore their careful arguments. Similarly, phenomenologists interested in John Paul II's work fail to understand his deep commitment to Thomism. John Paul II has always argued that a Thomistic metaphysical framework is indispensable, maintaining that without it, phenomenology is deficient. We should reject any interpretation of his work that implies that he is not a Thomist. Finally, in ethics, few contemporary scholars consider John Paul II's engagement with phenomenology when exploring the disputed ethical issues that have emerged during his papacy. For example, discussions of his views on euthanasia focus almost entirely on his Thomistic theory of action, ignoring how he uses phenomenology to analyze suffering. Similarly, debates about his sexual ethic fixates on the sexual act and procreation, ignoring how he uses phenomenology to analyze the relationships between men and women.

In this book, I present an account of John Paul II's engagement with political realism that emphasizes his philosophical project. Focusing on several key areas where John Paul II critically retrieves the phenomenologist Max Scheler's work, I argue that this engagement reveals the radical character of his critique of contemporary ethics. Scheler is a central presence in John Paul II's writings. Many know that the pope wrote his habilitation thesis on him and rehearse his criticism that Scheler's work cannot be reconciled with a Christian ethics. Others note how his Thomistic commitments lead him away from Scheler's emphasis on the emotions. All of these claims are correct, but John Paul II's disagreements with Scheler are in no way the whole story of his engagement with the phenomenologist and, in my mind, have received too much attention in the contemporary literature. Few have detailed the full extent of Scheler's influence on John Paul II's thought, ignoring how in key areas such as love, value theory, and political life, John Paul II draws on Scheler's work. This neglect prevents us from fully understanding him as a thinker and impedes a clear evaluation of how he uses phenomenology.

In ethics and political thought, those who ignore John Paul II's engagement with Scheler also misunderstand John Paul II's critique of contemporary thought. A central issue in this book will be political consequentialism, an important feature of political realism. Undoubtedly, the role of consequences in ethics has received extensive treatment in contemporary Christian ethics, and, in fact, some believe that the debate about this topic has run its course. However, for those familiar with John Paul II and Scheler, this debate seems impoverished. For example, basic goods theory is an important movement in contemporary Roman Catholicism. It emphasizes the importance of respecting basic goods like life and knowledge, strongly rejecting practices like abortion that denigrate them. Basic goods theorists like Germain Grisez and John Finnis agree with John Paul II's opposition to consequentialism, arguing that it attempts to calculate incommensurable goods. Basic goods like life and health, they argue, cannot be measured or played off against one another, and any attempt to do so is incoherent. Proportionalists, in contrast, argue that John Paul II adopts a rule-based ethic that ignores important goods. They maintain that when confronting ethical dilemmas, we must proportion the good and evil an act produces and choose the act that yields the greatest good. They also maintain that John Paul II takes an absolutist approach to ethics that has detrimental social consequences. Both these schools of thought yield important insights into the debate about consequences. Nevertheless, in light of John Paul II's philosophical project, they represent a superficial tinkering with modern thought. Basic goods theorists reject the idea of a hierarchy of value, insisting that basic goods are of equal value. However, this kind of argument disregards John Paul II's hierarchy of value, developed in conversation with Scheler, one of the twentieth century's most eloquent proponents of a value hierarchy. Proportionalists ignore John Paul II's insistence that spiritual values cannot be measured, an argument he draws directly from Scheler. In both cases, we see important contemporary thinkers who fail to understand the sophisticated way John Paul II uses modern thought. By focusing on Scheler, this book corrects such shortcomings, illustrating why his philosophical project is important for understanding international politics.

A Word about Karol Wojtyla and John Paul II

In writing about John Paul II, a scholar confronts a significant hermeneutical issue. Prior to becoming pope in 1979, Karol Wojtyla wrote numerous articles and contributed to writing ecclesial documents. During his papacy, his output has been enormous, yet much of it involves collaborating with others. Thus, researchers in the last twenty years have wrestled with how to approach such a complex set of texts. Some, like Rocco Buttiglione, focus only on Karol Wojtyla's work, arguing that we should exclude papal works when analyzing Wojtyla's work (see Buttiglione 1997). Others, like Samuel Gregg, carefully explore Wojtyla's work within the context of twentieth-century magisterial social teaching (see Gregg 1999). Finally, most thinkers depart from these two approaches by considering both Karol Wojtyla's work and the documents of John Paul II's papacy. In doing so, they trace continuities between these texts, without establishing definitively that John Paul II is the author of all works issued under his name.

I admire scholars like Gregg for carefully focusing on how John Paul II's work relates to magisterial teachings, and I understand the hermeneutical difficulties in ascribing individual authorship to ecclesial documents. Nevertheless, I will take the conventional approach of considering both pre-papal and papal documents together, tracing themes that have been central for both Karol Wojtyla and Pope John Paul II. Often, when considering a papal document, thinkers try to ascertain exactly which passages come directly from the pope himself, and this becomes a way for them to reject ideas they find disturbing. I will not engage in this kind of text parsing and do not pretend to be competent to establish precise relationships between the pre-papal and papal documents. Nevertheless, a working hermeneutical assumption of this book will be that there is continuity in John Paul II's thinking that spans more than fifty years.

Outline of the Book

John Paul II is a complex thinker who draws on numerous sources in his work. In this book, I will not offer a complete account of his philosophical anthropology. Schmitz, Buttiglione, and Kupczak all present comprehensive accounts of his thought that I use. I will also be very selective in my analysis, focusing on how John Paul II uses Scheler in his political thought. I will take several key concepts he critically retrieves from Scheler and show how they enable him to seriously engage political realism. I will rely heavily on non-Christian variants of realism, because they provide the clearest contrast to John Paul II's work. Finally, I forgo judging the accuracy of John Paul II's treatment of Scheler, providing exegesis of Scheler's work but relegating critical comments to an occasional footnote.

In chapter 1, I develop the conceptual framework I use throughout the book, focusing on intentionality, love, and the hierarchy of value. John Paul II develops each of these elements of his thought through a careful and critical engagement with Scheler. This chapter includes a great deal of Scheler's exegesis and analysis of complex philosophical concepts, but I ask the reader to bear with me as I explore how John Paul II interprets Scheler.

With the conceptual framework clear, in chapter 2 I argue that John Paul II largely accepts the realist descriptive account of politics as characterized by the pursuit of power. I argue that it is precisely his engagement with Scheler that enables John Paul II to astutely analyze how people turn against God and their neighbors, leading them to use others merely as means to an end. I show how sin creates a drive for power that distorts relations among political communities. Focusing in particular on John Paul II's analysis of "structures of sin" in economics and politics, I explore it through the lens of distorted intentionality and a perverse ordering of values. This analysis of sin, I argue, shows clear traces of Scheler's insights into the solidarity of sin. I then illustrate this influence by considering John Paul II's analysis of distortions in globalization and nationalism in a post-Cold War world. I close by noting that in its sense of depravity and tragedy, the pope's understanding of sin and politics rivals that of any of the great political realists.

In chapter 3, I maintain that despite his dark vision of human relations, John Paul II refuses to endorse an ethic of consequences. Instead, he offers a compelling ethic based on the personalistic norm and a hierarchy of value. I show how this ethic undermines consequentialism, arguing in particular that we cannot divide and measure spiritual values. Consequently, political consequentialism either arbitrarily ignores them or commensurates material and spiritual values using ad hoc or subjectivist criteria. Here, I again demonstrate Scheler's influence, discussing how he is deeply concerned with how utilitarianism elevates lower values to the highest value, a concern John Paul II shares. Considering objections to John Paul II's critique of consequentialism, I argue that both basic goods theorists and proportionalists misunderstand it. Their criticisms, I maintain, have little merit and reveal significant ignorance about John Paul II's philosophical project.

In the final chapter, I consider how John Paul II applies his philosophical project to international politics, using humanitarian intervention as a test case. After outlining his concept of participation, I show how he uses it to consider the rights of nations, a civilization of love, and a duty of humanitarian intervention. After considering how John Paul II can address conflicts between these ideas, I argue that he fails to apply his conception of sin consistently to the United Nations. In recent years, the United Nations has exhibited precisely the forms of sin John Paul II identifies, but he largely ignores them. Political realists are skeptical of the United Nations' capacity to structure international politics, and I argue that John Paul II should apply his own political realism more consistently.

In the book's conclusion, I emphasize how John Paul II's philosophical project enables him to respond to political realism. Recognizing that he is that rare thinker who links philosophy and global action, I endorse his philosophical project as an important guide for international politics in this century.

1

John Paul II and the Experience of Values

The first impression Scheler made was fascinating. Never again did I encounter the "phenomenon of genius" so purely in a human being.

Edith Stein[1]

Most people who met Max Scheler (1874–1928) recognized him as an undisciplined but extraordinary thinker who had his finger on the pulse of the issues of his day. He wrote about topics philosophers rarely treat, yet always demonstrated that they were worth exploring. For example, Scheler considered love, repentance, *ressentiment,* shame, and sympathy, drawing on thinkers like Blaise Pascal, Edmund Husserl, Franz Brentano, and St. Augustine. In retrospect, Scheler seems like a natural interlocutor for Karol Wojtyla. In his dissertation on St. John of the Cross, Wojtyla had already explored experience, and began linking his reflections to Thomism.[2] In 1951, Wojtyla's professors assigned him the task of writing his habilitation thesis on Scheler, and some have speculated that they did so because they saw in Scheler a natural ally against Kantianism.[3] Nevertheless, whatever the contingent reasons for Wojtyla's choice of thesis topics, the future consequences of this work were far-reaching.

Many scholars detail John Paul II's differences with Scheler, but overlook just how much he is indebted to him. They correctly note that he criticizes Scheler for neglecting norms in ethics, misunderstanding conscience, and failing to comprehend essential elements of Christian ethics.[4] Undoubtedly, in his habilitation thesis, Wojtyla resists reconciling Christian ethics with Scheler's work.[5] Nevertheless, he also writes frequently and appreciatively about Scheler. Unfortunately, many contemporary interpreters of the pope's work ignore the nuances of this complex discussion.

In this chapter, I explore John Paul II's creative engagement with Scheler, focusing on our intentional relation to values, love, and hierarchies of value. I argue that with each of these ideas, he retrieves Scheler's thought, but alters it by emphasizing the will and cognition. First, drawing on Schmitz's work, I briefly outline John Paul II's philosophical project, showing how it uses elements of a philosophy of consciousness within a philosophy of being. Second, I consider intentionality, arguing that despite John Paul II's reservations about it, he agrees with Scheler that we are intentionally related to values. However, he departs from him by emphasizing the cognitive and volitional dimensions of this relationship, arguing that people alter their personhood by willing to relate to particular values. Third, I show how this emphasis on will and cognition shapes John Paul II's analysis of love. Like Scheler, he grounds his ethic in love, maintaining that it is a movement of the person toward values. Yet, unlike Scheler, he argues that we must *will* to give ourselves to others and accept them as a gift. Fourth, I show how John Paul II uses this capacity to love to establish a hierarchy of values. Appreciative but critical of Scheler's idea of an *ordo amoris,* he defends a hierarchy of value that makes spiritual values preeminent. I close by emphasizing that what John Paul II and Scheler share distinguishes them significantly from contemporary thinkers.

The Philosophy of Being and the Philosophy of Consciousness

Those encountering John Paul II's philosophical writings for the first time often find them confusing. He employs different philosophical idioms, sometimes beginning with a formal definition of personhood, the human experience of value, or Thomas Aquinas and human action. At first glance, these various philosophical and theological concepts seem incompatible. Yet, as Schmitz carefully details, they reflect a narrative about the history of thought linking the philosophy of being with modern philosophies of consciousness (Schmitz 1993).[6] John Paul II, Schmitz argues, recognizes that by exploring the subject, modern thought deeply illuminates our interior life. However, it often rejects metaphysical realism, devolving into relativism and subjectivism. John Paul II, Schmitz notes, wants to salvage modern insights about the subject by locating them within a Thomistic conception of being (Schmitz 1993, ch. 1).

To develop this project, John Paul II embraces elements from twentieth-century philosophy he thinks are undeveloped in Thomism. He is, as Schmitz writes, "seized with a properly modern sense of interiority, experience, and subjectivity" and sees modernity's focus on interiority as a positive addition to Thomism (Schmitz 1993, 140). His early poetry and plays, *Love and Responsibility, The Acting Person,* and "Salvifici Doloris," are just a few writings emphasizing experience. From Scheler, he also learned that "the fact that ethics is a normative science can in no way obscure the fact that it is deeply rooted in experience" (Wojtyla 1993, 22).[7] Thomism, John Paul II notes, provides a "point of departure" for the study of the person but pays insufficient attention to lived experience (Wojtyla 1993, 166–67). Thomas discusses the person largely within the context of the Trinity and Incarnation, and when it comes to consciousness, "there seems to be no place for it in St. Thomas' objectivist view of reality" (Wojtyla 1993, 170).[8] In fact, "it must be conceded" that aspects of human consciousness were "not developed in the Scholastic tradition" (Wojtyla 1993, 226). In a clear assessment of Thomas and consciousness, John Paul II maintains that while "St. Thomas gives an excellent view of the objective existence and activity of the person," it "would be difficult to speak in his view of the lived experience of the person" (Wojtyla 1993, 171).[9]

Despite these critical comments about Thomism, however, John Paul II maintains that lived experience cannot ground moral norms unless it *presupposes* a Thomistic metaphysic. He makes this point repeatedly in his Lublin lectures, given during the early 1950s in Poland. For example, writing on Kant and Scheler, he concludes that "phenomenology can indirectly assist us in overcoming certain errors in views of the will that arise from an improper relation to empirical facts, but it cannot serve as a tool for the sort of ethical experience upon which ethics as a normative science is based" (Wojtyla 1993, 21). Discussing the same two thinkers on experience, he says, "I am convinced that the ethics of Aristotle and St. Thomas Aquinas is based on a proper relation to experience, and, moreover, that their view of the ethical act is the only proper and adequate description of ethical experience" (Wojtyla 1993, 43). Finally, discussing hierarchies of value, John Paul II notes that "the concept of a norm is justified in a system of moral philosophy that proceeds from an existential view of the good and is not really justified in a system of a philosophy of values" (Wojtyla 1993, 93). Clearly, then, John Paul II never rests content solely with an ethic grounded in lived experience. Left to its own devices, it leads to dangerous subjectivism and relativism. Reflection on lived experience must always occur *within* a metaphysical framework acknowledging the reality of being.[10]

I will make one final point about this larger philosophical project, and it concerns the *kind* of philosophy of being John Paul II uses. Thoroughly conversant with different kinds of Thomism, he uses Thomistic concepts like conscience, act and potency, being, the relationship between faith and philosophy, and natural law.[11] He wrote his dissertation on John of the Cross with Reginald Garrigou-Lagrange, who clearly influences his thought. However, he often draws heavily on the work of Etienne Gilson, Jacques Maritain, and other existential Thomists.[12] Kupczak documents how existential Thomism influenced John Paul II in the 1950s, particularly when he gave his Lublin lectures.[13] Years later, in "Fides et Ratio," his interest in Gilson reappears when he praises him for integrating faith and reason.[14] Because John Paul II combines many intellectual influences, we cannot simplistically identify his Thomism with that of Gilson and Maritain. Nevertheless, I think they have exerted a significant influence on his philosophical project.

To summarize the elements of John Paul II's philosophical project: he resists creating a hybrid of two complex philosophical systems.[15] Instead, within Thomism's dynamic structure of being, he retrieves elements of phenomenology critically and carefully. As a result, he is open to developments in modern philosophy, while remaining firmly rooted in a premodern metaphysic.

John Paul II and the Intentional Relation to Value

With this philosophical project in mind, I now turn to John Paul II and Scheler, focusing on intentionality and value, love, and the hierarchy of values.[16] I begin with Scheler's conception of feeling and value. In an essay written in 1974, John Paul II notes that for Scheler, we experience values in feeling, and that the "structure of that experience is set up by the intentional acts which Scheler reveals to us as a constituting human morality in its own essence" (Wojtyla 1976, 271). Scheler maintains that we experience values through value-feelings (*Wert-fuhlen*), meaning that feelings take values as their *objects.* He carefully distinguishes between values and goods. Goods are things or collections of things presenting themselves to us as valuable. Although given to us in goods, values are independent from them. Goods are given to the person, and she feels the values in them. Alfons Deeken describes this important distinction well, noting that "goods, according to Scheler, are the bearers of value in a similar way as things are the bearers of colors. Values are qualities experienced *in* things, but they are not identical with them" (Deeken 1974, 14). Beauty, for example, differs from the landscape that manifests it.

John Paul II admires Scheler's understanding of the *experience* of values, noting that it constitutes a "basic step in the direction of empirical reality and, in particular, in the direction of the reconstruction of the very contours of the ethical act" (Wojtyla 1993, 34). Many of John Paul II's criticisms of Scheler, in fact, *presuppose* this experience of values. We never stand outside of values, deciding at some point to relate to them. Instead, we *find* ourselves related to them. Like Scheler, John Paul II rejects narrow understandings of experience that arbitrarily reject the idea of moral experience. Both thinkers maintain that much of modern philosophy embraces a defective account of experience based on the idea of sense impressions. For example, Hume, Kant, and others give us a picture of knowledge that begins with sense impressions that bombard the mind. The mind organizes these incoming impressions through induction, cognitive categories, or social devices. Systematically, Scheler dismantles this position, denying that pure sense impressions exist. Instead, he argues that the mind is confronted with objects that are already wholes, requiring little or no mental or cultural construction. Attacking Kant, he argues that "no presumptive construction of the contents of intuitions out of 'sensations' could *ever* be a philosophic task" (Scheler 1973, 59). Pure sense impressions are a dangerous fiction that undermines moral realism, and Scheler issues a clarion call to dispense with it.

John Paul II agrees entirely with Scheler in rejecting this picture of perception, observing that with it, "the concept of experience of morality does not and cannot have any meaning" (Wojtyla 1993, 114). Experience, he argues (following Scheler), is "not limited to the perception of purely sensory contents alone, but includes the particular structure and essential content of that perception" (ibid.). Its first element is a "sense of reality," an awareness of the fact that "something exists with an existence that is real and objectively independent of the cognizing subject and the subject's cognitive act, while at the same time existing as the object of that act" (ibid.). This sense of reality is accompanied by a sense of knowing "what really and objectively exists with an existence independent of the cognitive act and, at the same time, in contact with the act" (ibid., 115). The mind shows a dynamism toward the truth of the object. In doing so, it apprehends more than simply sense impressions.

This analysis of perception is absolutely essential for understanding John Paul II's ethic, for it enables him to argue that we directly perceive values. I will have more to say about value perception in a later chapter, but let me make a few general comments about its emotional component. Undoubtedly, John Paul II draws on Thomistic resources to emphasize the mind's contact with being, and Kupczak suggests that Maritain is the primary influence on his account of perception.[17] However, John Paul II also agrees with Scheler, who attacked misguided views of perception that ignore the emotions. He accepts *"in full its emotional character and emotional depth* of which Scheler gave a notable expression in his analysis" (Wojtyla 1976, 275). Brilliantly, Scheler describes phenomena like sympathy, and John Paul II has no intention of negating "all that is penetrating and apt in Scheler's analysis" of such topics (ibid., 276). For example, he notes, "there is no way to deny that human acts, precisely in terms of their moral value, i.e., the good or evil contained in them, are accompanied by very deep emotional experiences: by joy and spiritual contentment in the case of good and by depression and even despair in the case of evil" (Wojtyla 1993, 124). Our lived experience of morality, therefore, contains an important emotional component.

Intentionality: A Brief Interlude

How, exactly, can we have an emotional relationship to values? Do they really exist, or are they just a product of our subjective desires? These and other questions naturally arise for those unfamiliar with the philosophical idiom John Paul II and Scheler use. For many thinkers in Anglo-American ethics, a direct and emotional contact with values is a foreign concept. They arbitrarily ignore its possibility, assuming that it is impossible. For example, for many years, ethicists have dismissed any appeal to a direct relationship to values by associating it with intuitionism, a prominent movement in twentieth-century ethics. Intuitionists claimed that we could directly intuit moral norms. Even though intuitionism has long passed from the philosophical scene, it still exerts a powerful influence on many ethicists. For example, for many years, John Rawls wrote about rational intuitionism as an important option in ethics.[18] Utilitarians often describe a chasm between "is" and "ought," rehearsing the old "facts-values" distinction. This distinction presupposes that what we perceive are valueless facts from which we cannot draw normative conclusions. For example, we cannot argue that heterosexuality is a moral ideal simply by describing the compatibility of the male and female sexual organs. This is a fact that tells us nothing about the moral value of heterosexuality. Other contemporary ethicists insist we begin ethical reflection with a general skepticism about values and then "justify," "validate," or "construct" norms. For example, Jürgen Habermas validates moral norms by establishing the necessary conditions for communicative action (see Habermas 1990). He exerts considerable effort demonstrating that skepticism about ethics is self-defeating. In response to this approach to ethics, some contemporary thinkers refuse to justify their positions, appealing instead to cultural practices or pragmatism. For example, Rawls denies that his ethical claims are universal, arguing instead that they are "political, not metaphysical."[19] Pragmatists like Richard Rorty argue that all knowledge, including ethical knowledge, is socially constructed. Consequently, demands for justifying ethical norms beyond the confines of a particular community make little sense.[20] Thus, in contemporary ethics, thinkers taking very different approaches nevertheless repudiate or simply ignore the idea that we have direct contact with values.[21]

The origins of these developments are complex, and I would have to write a history of modern ethics to explain them. However, I think we can account for some of them by noting how contemporary thinkers neglect intentionality, the hallmark of twentieth-century phenomenology. For both Scheler and John Paul II, this concept is central for their argument that we directly experience values. Intentionality refers to the "aboutness" of cognition, the way it is directed toward objects. As Robert Sokolowski puts it, "the core doctrine in phenomenology is the teaching that every act of consciousness we perform, every experience that we have is intentional: it is essentially 'consciousness of,' or an 'experience of' something or other" (Sokolowski 2000, 8). Intentionality differs from "intention." An intention is a purpose we have in mind when acting, whereas intentionality is the general orientation of consciousness toward objects. Philosopher Daniel Dennett calls intention a "false friend" of intentionality that has a voluntary element often absent from intentionality (Dennett 1997, 34–36).[22] To put matters simply, our minds focus on thousands of objects (intentionality), often in an involuntary way, many of which have absolutely nothing to do with purposes for action (intention). In twentieth-century phenomenology, intentionality was an important means of linking consciousness and reality. Many strands of modern philosophy depict consciousness as a private affair, creating serious conceptual problems for relating mind and external reality. Intentionality "shows that the mind is a public thing that acts and manifests itself out in the open, not just inside its own confines" (Sokolowski 2000, 12).[23] By connecting us to objects and a social world, it allows us to escape egoism. Intentionality also enables us to explore how objects present themselves to us, revealing the structures shaping consciousness.

These features of intentionality have always attracted Roman Catholic thinkers, leading to strong historic ties between Catholic thought and phenomenology. This should come as no surprise, because intentionality was a central concept in medieval philosophy. In fact, Franz Brentano, a Catholic for a good part of his career, retrieved and developed medieval conceptions of intentionality, shaping modern phenomenology significantly.[24] Edmund Husserl was one of Brentano's students, and in a seminal part of his *Logical Investigations,* he criticizes and develops Brentano's ideas.[25] In turn, Catholic thinkers responded to Husserl's careful treatment of intentionality. For example, Scheler had a complex and not always positive relationship with Catholicism. Edith Stein was one of Edmund Husserl's students, and he influenced her work significantly. At one point in her career, she wrote a fascinating essay comparing the thought of Husserl and Aquinas.[26] Dietrich von Hildebrand also studied with Husserl, developing his thought in important ways. Finally, some Thomists have engaged in careful dialogue with phenomenologists. André Hayen, S.J., and other twentieth-century Thomists developed rich conceptions of intentionality, engaging phenomenology both critically and appreciatively.[27] As Sokolowski puts it, Thomism "shares with phenomenology the conviction that reason is ordered toward truth," and Thomists concerned about subjectivist conceptions of truth have found much to appreciate in modern phenomenology (Sokolowski 2000, 206).[28]

John Paul II and Intentionality

John Paul II uses intentionality carefully and critically. At first glance, he seems very critical of the concept, and his first worry is that it misrepresents how consciousness functions. He acknowledges that cognitive acts have an "intentional character, since they are directed toward the cognitive object" (Wojtyla 1979, 32). Yet this intentional character is not consciousness's essential property, and "contrary to the classical phenomenological view" the "cognitive reason for the existence of consciousness and of acts proper to it does not consist in the penetrative apprehension of the constitutive elements of the object" (ibid.). Consciousness also includes a "mirroring" function, which understands what has been constituted and comprehended. Kupczak notes that for John Paul II, "consciousness only mirrors the outcome of the cognitive process of knowledge and self-knowledge" (Kupczak 2000, 97). Likewise, Schmitz suggests that rather than constituting "objects and their meaning, consciousness reflects them" (Schmitz 1993, 70).[29] He argues that John Paul II "reverses the usual modern order between consciousness and cognition" by refusing to derive the functions of consciousness from the intentional act, arguing instead that this act *serves* consciousness (ibid.).

John Paul II also worries that intentionality reifies consciousness, making it an autonomous subject rather than part of the "dynamism and efficacy of the person" (Wojtyla 1979, 33). Consciousness is not a substance, but part of the person. Without recognizing this point, John Paul II thinks, we risk endorsing a dangerous idealism.[30] Therefore, he accentuates the person's active movement toward objects. The personality, he insists, "possesses also a rational intentional structure," but is "not to be reduced to the intentional act no matter how complex" (Wojtyla 1976, 269). Thus, for John Paul II, intentionality is not the "hallmark of consciousness in its entirety, and, so to speak its essential property" (Schmitz 1993, 69).[31] By focusing exclusively on it, we ignore important elements of the person, including all of the things that happen to her body and in her subconscious.[32]

These comments reflect John Paul II's commitment to Thomism. Repeatedly, he uses the phrase *operari sequitur esse* (operation follows being), indicating that conscious action originates in persons. A phenomenologist may treat consciousness as an *aspect* of the person, "bracketing" the analysis of being. This is a useful "cognitive method," that "can and does bear excellent fruit," and there is "no doubt" that it "should be used extensively in the philosophy of the human being" (Wojtyla 1993, 226). However, we must always presuppose the truth of the philosophy of being, lest we fall prey to the subjectivism and relativism characterizing much of modern philosophy. This emphasis on being also explains why John Paul II maintains that by itself, intentionality tells us little about the perfection of the person. Contrasting intentionality and self-determination, he says:

> Intentionality points as though outward—toward an object, which, by being a value, attracts the will to itself. Self-determination, on the other hand, points as though inward—toward the subject, which by willing this value, by choosing it, simultaneously defines itself as a value: the subject becomes "good" or "bad." (Wojtyla 1993, 191–92)

Although intentionality links the subject to reality and undermines solipsism, by itself it does little to explain how the self develops. Therefore, it provides an insufficient basis for a philosophical anthropology.

These critical comments about intentionality, however, in no way detract from John Paul II's affirmation that we are intentionally related to values. Instead, they indicate caveats about reifying consciousness and express a concern that twentieth-century philosophy ignores important elements of the person.[33] Scheler shares these same worries. He resists excessively focusing on consciousness, always emphasizing the entire person.[34] For him, the person is the unity of being of all acts. Manfred Frings notes that for Scheler, "the person suffuses every act with its uniquely individual traits and, reciprocally, every act is suffused with the individual person" (Frings 1997, 42). He argues that by emphasizing the person this way, Scheler moves away from intentionality as the primary way to understand him.

Unfortunately, scholars like Rocco Buttiglione misunderstand what John Paul II says about intentionality. Buttiglione argues that his understanding of intentionality differs fundamentally from what we find in phenomenology. Intentionality in the Aristotelian and Thomistic sense, he argues, involves an "intentional" form, an "essential attribute of an object" made present through thought (Buttiglione 1997, 274). In contrast, the phenomenological idea of intentionality "connotes not a real object but the object as it is constructed in one determinate way" (Buttiglione 1997, 274). Therefore, Buttiglione concludes, we cannot maintain that John Paul II uses intentionality in a phenomenological way. Buttiglione is a very careful scholar who knows a great deal about John Paul II's relationship to phenomenology. However, I think he misses a central point about both Scheler and phenomenology. Whatever interpretation one adopts of Husserl, Scheler remained interested in the Scholastic notion of *esse intentionale* (intentional being). Thomists maintain that when the subject knows, the objects of knowledge have a particular kind of mental existence or being, *esse intentionale*.[35] Although an opponent of Scholasticism, Scheler embraces this idea, particularly in his later writings on realism and idealism.[36] He thus confounds Buttiglione's clear distinction between a phenomenological and a Scholastic understanding of intentionality. Similarly, Dietrich von Hildebrand uses intentionality to defend a realist epistemology and axiology. He maintains that phenomenology includes an "unambiguous refutation of psychologism, subjectivism, and all types of relativism" (von Hildebrand 1960, 223).[37] For von Hildebrand, intentionality is precisely the means by which we connect to real objects. The story of phenomenology, Thomism, and intentionality is, therefore, far more complex than Buttiglione recognizes.[38] It is historically inaccurate to argue that phenomenological understandings of intentionality differ fundamentally from those in medieval philosophy. Given what Scheler, von Hildebrand, and others have written, we cannot sustain a clear distinction between Thomist and univocal "phenomenological" conceptions of intentionality.[39]

Another misunderstanding of what John Paul II says about intentionality and value involves the distinction between values and goods. As I noted earlier, Scheler carefully distinguishes between these two concepts. When he compares Scheler and Aquinas, John Paul II suggests that one important difference between them is that Aquinas emphasizes goods over values. However, like Scheler, John Paul II often discusses values and clearly thinks they are as important as goods. For example, in *Love and Responsibility,* he carefully defines the term *value,* insisting that many values are independent of our desires. In fact, we aspire to moral values because they draw us toward them. Like Scheler, he distinguishes between an object representing a value and the value itself. A value "constitutes a specific object-subject or subject-object relationship, an expression of a particular correspondence (of some-one to some-one, of something to some-one, or of something to something as it affects some-one)" (Wojtyla 1960, 304 n.52). Thus, John Paul II differentiates between goods and values, insisting that we explore our intentional relation to values. Thomas D. Williams notes how many contemporary thinkers are uneasy with the term *value* (Williams 1997). To them, it implies ethical relativism, particularly because twentieth-century social scientists describe different "value-systems." Yet, as Williams notes, we cannot credibly accuse John Paul II of promoting relativism. I would add that we could say the same about Scheler, who was deeply concerned with relativism. Therefore, I see no reason to worry about using the term *values* and see little merit in attempts to distinguish John Paul II from Scheler by emphasizing goods over values.

To summarize how John Paul II and Scheler approach lived experience, intentionality enables both thinkers to affirm that we have a direct and emotional contact with values. They deny any gap between the person and values that we must close through mental representation or social construction. They also resist identifying intentionality with the entire person, arguing instead that it is only one part of her.

Cognition and Our Intentional Relation to Value

Despite these agreements, however, John Paul II sharply criticizes Scheler for his "emotionalism," maintaining that Schelerian values are "not the same as principles of practical reason" (Wojtyla 1993, 11). Scheler depicts the intentional grasping of values as having a cognitive content, but it is not a cognitive experience "in the first place" (ibid., 35). In fact, John Paul II maintains, Scheler ignores the "intellectual insight" accompanying our powerful feelings of value (ibid., 125). Through our emotions, we undoubtedly experience value; however, "the emotional stirrings and the emotions themselves point to values, but as such they have no cognition or desire of values" (Wojtyla 1979, 248). Emotions may signal value, but by themselves they lack cognitive content.

In contrast to Scheler, as a Thomist, John Paul II insists on a complex interplay between emotion and cognition in our intentional relations to values. The truth about objects and values "crystallizes this or that moment of the good," involving the entire person, not just her emotions (Wojtyla 1979, 141).[40] In this context, John Paul II makes one of his strongest charges against phenomenology, asserting "the concept of intentional act is a kind of timid reference to the structure of Aristotelian philosophy" (Wojtyla 1993, 41). By itself, it is incapable of fully capturing our experience of the ethical life. Contrasting Thomas and Scheler, John Paul II argues that for Thomas, "the moral life consists in attaining the truth in all our actions and behavior" (ibid., 91). The cognitive element of values and goods enters into our consciousness of all of our human acts. Part of lived experience, it becomes an object for both the intellect and will. For Scheler, in contrast,

> the moral life consists in the emotional experience of moral value. Moral value, in turn, arises spontaneously upon the occasion of our emotional involvement in the world in some world of values or other and becomes the object and content of a separate experience precisely because the emotional involvement in our world of values is connected with the experience of a certain hierarchy of values. (Wojtyla 1993, 91)

In this discussion, John Paul II stays *within* lived experience, emphasizing that we *experience* the cognitive element of value. This experience "reaches immediately and simultaneously to the potentiality of the human intellect, and with its aid, evokes the distinctive perception of reality that is morality" (Wojtyla 1979, 117). John Paul II thus argues that Scheler is not phenomenological enough because he ignores an important element of lived experience.

Values and the Will

John Paul II also stays within lived experience when criticizing Scheler for neglecting the will. Once someone apprehends a value, he maintains, he can orient his intentionality toward it. This involves an experience of *efficacy,* where the person makes or produces something. Scheler ignores the reality that the "most evident feature in an act of will is the efficacy of the personal self. This efficacy is immediately given: it is reflected in the awareness of the acting person in an act of will" (Wojtyla 1993, 8). Our ethical experience includes *both* an intentional relation to values *and* the experience of efficacy through acting. For example, I not only acknowledge the human rights of people living thousands of miles away from me, but I also will to respect them. There can be no doubt that "the will itself contributes a dynamic element to human psychic life, an element that appears in a tendency determined by the very self" (ibid., 10). In neglecting efficacy, John Paul II argues, Scheler mistakenly locates ethical value in emotion rather than in the will, and we are "standing here in the presence of the phenomenologist's fatal mistake" (ibid., 38). The emotions accompanying an act are important, but secondary to the will of the person acting. Scheler reverses this order, ignoring how the "central structural element of ethical experience is the element of willing" (ibid.).

Many of John Paul II's criticisms of Scheler include complex discussions of the will, all of which I will not rehearse. What is most important about them is his idea of self-determination. Using the Thomistic concept of potentiality, he analyzes the will as the potentiality to achieve self-determination, contained in the rational nature of a person. Subordinated to the person, it never determines or governs him, but to it the person "owes his specifically human form of dynamism, the dynamism of self-determination" (Wojtyla 1979, 122).[41] As Kupczak puts it, the person reveals a "certain potentiality in relation to different goods," which is actualized through "acts of will" (Kupczak 2000, 41). By defining the will in terms of self-determination, John Paul II accentuates its ethical value, making it the foundation of his well-known philosophy of action. Often, he begins with the traditional Thomist distinction between "human acts" and "acts of the human." Thomas distinguishes between human acts, which we do with knowledge and free will, and acts of the human, which lack these characteristics. On the one hand, we do things "freely and deliberately," and on the other hand, "things simply happen to us" (Schmitz 1993, 78).[42] John Paul II subtly revises the Thomistic theory of action to reflect modern philosophy's turn toward the subject. He suggests that we replace the term *actus humanus* with *actus personae* (Wojtyla 1993, 226–27). This alternative term captures both the freedom and knowledge in human acts and the person's efficacy, the strict connection between the person's act and self that "has a causal and efficient character" (ibid., 228). I cannot divorce my act from myself by attributing it to another. In contrast, when something happens to me, I experience no efficacy. For example, if I have an epileptic seizure, I lack any awareness of how I affect my environment. This "happening," therefore, cannot be a human act.

A person may experience his efficacy in different ways. His act may be *transitive* (taking an object), altering his environment. Or it may be *intransitive,* altering not only the environment but his character as well. Many beings shape their environment through transitive action, but it neither returns to them nor reveals self-governance. A beaver, for example, may alter the course of a river by building a dam, but his action is not reflexive. In contrast, by turning to the self, a person shapes not only his biological and psychological constitution but also his *value,* because an *actus personae* relates the person to good and evil. He has the *property* of self-determination, realized through acts of will, directing himself toward an object, and "going out" beyond himself toward a value (Wojtyla 1993, 191). "Going out" exceeds the intentionality of thought and act, because the person becomes a certain kind of being. By choosing a value, he defines himself as a value, gradually becoming more of a "somebody," an object to which other subjects respond (ibid., 192). For John Paul II, this is the "drama of the will" so central to human life (Wojtyla 1974, 275). In willing, "the subject is never passively directed to an object," and his intentional relation to a value never absorbs his person completely (Wojtyla 1979, 127). Ultimately, he retains an independence from presented objects, and must often *choose* among objects to which he is intentionally related.[43]

To summarize how John Paul II departs from Scheler, he accepts but carefully modifies his understanding of intentionality and value. Emphasizing its cognitive dimensions, he rejects Scheler's idea that feelings by themselves represent a reliable way of knowing. Furthermore, he maintains that without acknowledging the will's movement, we ignore a central element of our lived experience. We experience our efficacy, a movement from potency to actuality. In willing to move toward a particular value, we also shape our personhood, revealing that self-determination is a central aspect of our humanity.

Love as the Ground of Human Dignity

Self-determination alone, however, cannot account for the person's value. I can shape my character perversely, abusing my freedom for horrific ends. Self-determination is not, therefore, a sufficient condition for actualizing what is good. John Paul II is fully aware of this and insists that our capacity to love constitutes the deepest ground of human dignity. Andrew Woznicki correctly notes that for him, love "becomes the fundamental characteristic of human dignity through which each and every individual [person] can fulfill his/her own individual existing being" (Woznicki 1980, 61).[44] From his early plays to his papal encyclicals on the family, John Paul II grounds his rigorous defense of human dignity in an extraordinary account of love. For him, the revelation of divine love "pervades the whole earth to its very core, the revelation of the Fatherhood which gives creation its meaning" (Wojtyla 1979b, 22). Very soon after ascending to the papacy, he indicated how important love is for him. For example, in "Redemptoris Hominis," he declares, "a human being cannot live without love" (RH, 10). In "Dives in Misericordia," he warns that justice can "even lead to destruction of self, if that deeper power, which is love, is not allowed to shape human life" (DM, 12).[45] In "Dominum et Vivificantem," he expresses the hope that God's gift of love will "enable people to understand themselves in a new way" (DV, 59).

In emphasizing love in these ways, John Paul II shares one of Scheler's primary concerns. Scheler focuses heavily on love, repeatedly maintaining that the human being is primarily an *ens amans,* a being that loves.[46] Before we are knowing or willing creatures, we are loving beings. Scheler repudiates purely biological and psychological understandings of love, arguing that they fail to understand its essence. For him, Freud and other psychologists ignore love's spiritual character. Such an emphasis on spiritual love is hardly a hallmark of twentieth-century philosophy, and as John H. Nota aptly notes, Scheler is "one of the few philosophers to have written an extensive philosophy of love" (Nota 1983, 195).

This understanding of love is extraordinary, and here I consider only three elements of it: love as movement, love and the will, and love and cognition.[47] In reading Scheler, one gets a sense of the *movement* of the person toward values. For example, he opens his wonderful essay "Ordo Amoris" by saying, "I find myself in an immeasurably vast world of sensible and spiritual objects which set my heart and passions in constant motion" (Scheler 1973b, 98). Elsewhere, he rejects the idea that love is a passive feeling, insisting instead that it is "an *act* and a movement" (Scheler 1970, 141). In another place, he describes love as "dynamic becoming, a growing, a welling up of things" (Scheler 1973b, 109). Through love, the "nobler stoops to the vulgar, the healthy to the sick, the rich to the poor, the handsome to the ugly, the good and saintly to the bad and common, the Messiah to the sinners and publicans" (Scheler 1961, 86). In all of these passages, we get a picture of constant activity.

Nevertheless, Scheler also argues that love moves toward values without exertion. At one point, he says, "there is no sense of effort in love, as such, even through it does have the character of a movement, which we also find in effort" (Scheler 1957, 141). He illustrates this point with a rhetorical question, asking, "What does a mother's love seek to 'realize' when she gazes lovingly at her bonny child asleep?" (ibid.). Undoubtedly, love *gives rise* to efforts in relation to a loved object, but "these are no part of it" (ibid.). Scheler goes so far as to argue that in love there is an *"opposite law to that of effort"* where effort may exhaust itself and come to rest, whereas love either remains the same or increases" (ibid.). Any hint of effort destroys love's essence and beauty (ibid., 158). Nevertheless, love is never blind, but is directed toward *values*. It differs from value-feelings because feelings are *states* of being intentionally related to values, whereas love is an *act*. Its central characteristic, Scheler insists, is a *"movement of intention* whereby, from a given value A in an object, its higher value is visualized" (ibid., 153). Love seeks out the higher values not as its objective or goal, but instead "brings about the continuous *emergence* of ever-higher value in the object" (ibid., 157). It is directed toward the object as it is, yet simultaneously moves toward an ideal implicit in it.

Scheler believes that his analysis of love avoids the pitfalls of pedagogy, complacency, or subjectivism. Love is pedagogical if we grant it only on the condition that a person becomes better. A father who loves his son only if he does well in school cannot be said to truly love him. Yet love that remains complacently satisfied with a person's imperfection lacks creativity. Someone who ignores a friend's self-destructive addiction loves her imperfectly. For Scheler, we never grant love contingently, but at the same time we move toward the ideal in the other (Scheler 1957, 157). Similarly, although in some sense love creates new values because it leads the subject toward them, in reality, it discovers these values. Repeatedly, Scheler rejects the subjectivist's claim that we fabricate value by thinking or social construction. Instead, through love, we discover values that exist independently of our valuation.

Love discovers values, as Scheler famously maintains, because it is a form of *knowing* that differs from cognitive process. I have already noted that Scheler sees feelings as a mode of knowing, but for him, love is an even more important source of knowledge. Eloquently, he rejects the idea that it follows the intellect, quoting Pascal's phrase *"Le coeur a ses raisons."*[48] He maintains that it is philosophically arbitrary to see in love a "chaos of blind feeling-states" (Scheler 1973b, 116).[49] This misguided view originates in the "general slovenliness in matters of feeling," propagated by the "fetishists of modern science" who ignore the order in our loves (ibid., 118–19). Scheler repeatedly urges modern people to pay more attention to the order in their hearts. So much of his work contains indictments of modernity's excessive rationalism, and clarion calls to recover a richer relationship to values. Twentieth-century philosophers come under particular attack, with Scheler noting how they link intentionality and consciousness but arbitrarily refuse to relate intentionality to feeling. In a memorable phrase, he calls this an "act of unequaled arbitrariness" (ibid., 122). In his more radical statements about the heart's reasons,

Scheler insists that it knows things "of which the understanding knows nothing and can never know anything" (ibid., 117). Often, it yields "contents and connections that are *simply not present* for an attitude of pure thought" (ibid., 122). If we were able to love only those things we knew through the intellect, our lives would be impoverished. Fortunately, Scheler maintains, love reveals higher values with a lawfulness "that operates with precision and exactness," uncovering a sphere of facts unknown to the intellect (ibid., 118). The dynamic element of love thus enables persons to move beyond restrictive values of a particular social group or family.

My brief summary of Scheler's thoughts on love cannot do them justice, but it does display what he thinks are love's central elements. Love is a movement from lower to higher values. It is an act, but one that does not involve effort. Finally, it is a source of knowledge that differs from intellectual processes but is essential for developing the person. Without it, we would remain trapped by our limited cognitive capacities, a limitation Scheler refuses to accept.

John Paul II and Love: The Will to Love

When writing about love, John Paul II finds much to appreciate in Scheler's work, while simultaneously departing from it. *Love and Responsibility,* I think, best illustrates this nuanced treatment of Scheler's thought. In it, we get the same sense of motion found in Scheler's work. John Paul II emphasizes love's intentional movement toward values through a rich analysis of kinds of love, including love as attraction, desire, goodwill, friendship, and self-gift. Like Scheler, he refuses to reduce love to biological processes, insisting that it is never "merely a biological or even a psychophysiological crystallization of the sexual urge, but is something fundamentally different from it" (Wojtyla 1960, 49).[50] Purely biological understandings of love degrade us, because they ignore our spiritual nature. In all its forms, love relates the person to values, because it is a "mutual relationship among persons," characterized by attitudes toward the good (ibid., 73). This movement toward the good appears particularly in love as attraction and love as desire. Love as attraction forms the basis for other kinds of love and is a *movement* of a person toward another that includes complex emotional and cognitive components. Like Scheler, John Paul II maintains that we are attracted to someone because of "various values" (ibid., 77). Love as desire arises out of creaturely limitations but "aims at finding a good it lacks" (ibid., 81). For example, love between a man and a woman emerges from the need the sexes have for each other. Love as desire, however, differs from simple desire. Desire includes an "unpleasant sensation that can be eliminated by means of some good" (ibid.). In contrast, love as desire includes both this sensation and a longing for a *good* for its own sake. In this form of love, I long for another person because she is good for me. In both love as desire and as attraction, we see that like Scheler, John Paul II accentuates love's movement toward values.

However, unlike Scheler, John Paul II is suspicious of the heart's capacity to establish order among values. Throughout many of his writings, he repeatedly states that by itself, emotion is an unreliable source of knowledge.[51] For example, discussing attraction, he warns that it may lead us astray and cannot be the sole criterion for ascertaining an object's value. Objects attract us for complex reasons involving particularities of our personalities. Some people, for example, are prone to respond to sensual values in a person. Because of this instability of the emotions, reason must discern the *proper* order of values. The sentiments, John Paul II argues, have "no cognitive power, but they have the power to guide and orient cognitive acts" (Wojtyla 1960, 77). He explicitly mentions Pascal and Scheler, only to reject Scheler's idea of feelings as ordered, arguing that they are "blind" (ibid.). Feelings alone are disassociated from the "truth about their object," because truth originates in the intellect rather than in feeling (ibid.). Moreover, emotions "often tend to distort or falsify attractions: through their prism values which are not really present at all may be discerned in a person" (ibid., 78). For example, I may find a person's body attractive, a value that is unimportant to her personhood. Making this value-feeling the basis of my love would be a grave error. Transient and unreliable, it lacks an anchor to truth and will surely lead me astray. In fact, if I think it will lead to genuine love, I will be deeply disappointed and may even turn against the person once my attraction to her body dissipates (ibid.). This is why it is vitally important to integrate our intentional relation to values with the truth about the person.

This integration requires the very effort Scheler thinks should be absent from true love. At about the same time he wrote *Love and Responsibility,* John Paul II also wrote a play called *The Jeweler's Shop,* which illustrates this idea in dramatic form. This play focuses on the marriage between two characters, Andrew and Teresa. At one point, Andrew describes how love resists sensations and emotions, saying, "I don't think I even know what 'love at first sight' means. After a time I realized she [Teresa] had come into the focus of my attention—I mean I *had* to be interested in her, and at the same time I *accepted* the fact that I had to" (Wojtyla 1987, 280). Andrew senses that Teresa *pursues* him, because he cannot avoid thinking about her. He could not account for the "strange persistence of Teresa in [him], the cause of her presence, the assurance of her place in [his] ego, and what creates around her that strange resonance, that feeling "you ought to" (ibid., 281). Often, in love, there is a sense that one person ought to belong to another, and a need to accept or resist it. It is one of the processes in the universe that "unite what was divided, broaden and enrich what was limited and narrow" (ibid.). Without this effort, love degenerates into transient feelings, providing no basis for an enduring relationship between persons.[52]

The Gift of Self: The Highest Form of Love

For John Paul II, this effort is particularly important for developing the reciprocal love that creates a community of persons. People must make love a "force that joins and unites, of its very nature inimical to division and isolation" (Wojtyla 1960, 85). They must create and sustain it by cultivating *reciprocity,* a mutual desire that another become a cocreator of love. This reciprocity can culminate in self-giving love, the "most uncompromising form of love," which "consists precisely in self-giving, in making one's inalienable and non-transferable 'I' the property of another" (ibid., 97).[53] Originating neither by accident nor through mere sentiment, it constitutes a "special crystallization of the whole human 'I,' determined because of its love to dispose of itself in this particular way" (ibid., 98). Unless the person giving the gift orients his will effectively, love degenerates into egotistical attraction or desire, often clothed in the language of love. As Kupczak notes, this love "cannot be based solely on the sensual attraction and emotions, but it must originate in the subject's intellect and will" (Kupczak 2000, 46).

The capacity to become a gift enables persons to develop a unique form of community in which love becomes an "authentic commitment of the free will of one person (the subject), resulting from the truth about another person (the object)" (Wojtyla 1960, 123). Self-giving love "forcibly detaches the person, so to speak," from his "natural inviolability and inalienability" (ibid., 125). Paradoxically, it makes him want to surrender himself to another, and by doing so, he enlarges rather than diminishes his being. By becoming available to another, he comes to understand that he is "someone willed by the Creator for his or her own sake. The person is unique and unrepeatable, someone chosen by eternal love" (Wojtyla, 1980, 65).[54] The result is a *communio personarum,* a community characterized by the *interior* act on the part of two or more persons toward self-donation, "the acceptance of the other as a gift" (ibid., 71).[55] Through it, John Paul II maintains, persons discover the true center of their humanity. By giving and accepting another, they determine their personhood.[56] God creates us with a natural urge to move beyond ourselves, but we retain the capacity to alter our orientation toward higher values. Moreover, unless we will to move toward them, we can never develop the highest forms of love. Love reaches culmination only when we will to give ourselves fully to another. This capacity to enter into a communion of persons constitutes for John Paul II the true mark of human dignity and value.[57] Moreover, as I will show in chapter 4, it shapes his understanding of international politics.

To summarize how John Paul II differs from Scheler on love, he agrees that love moves us toward objects but argues that we must accept or reject this movement through acts of will. For him, this effort is *essential* to love, whereas for Scheler it is inimical to it.

The Hierarchy of Value

John Paul II uses the capacity for self-giving love to establish a hierarchy of value, and in doing so, I think, he again shows close affinities with Scheler. Scheler makes a hierarchy of values central to his ethic, arguing for an *ordo amoris,* or an order of our loves. Descriptively, it is the means whereby we can discover, behind the initially confusing facts of man's morally relevant actions, behind his expression, his wishes, customs, needs, and spiritual achievements, the simplest structure of the most fundamental goals of the goal-directed core of the person, the basic ethical formula, so to speak, by which he exists and lives morally. Thus, everything we recognize as morally important to man (or to a group) must be reduced, however many steps it [may] take, to the particular structure of his acts of loving and hating and his capacities for love and hate; it must be reduced, in other words, to the *ordo amoris* which governs these acts and expresses all of man's stirrings and emotions. (Scheler 1973b, 99–100)

In this intriguing passage, Scheler offers a way of analyzing persons that focuses on the direction of love. In the period in which he wrote this essay, he was deeply influenced by St. Augustine, and some have suggested that he is a philosophical Augustinian. Thus, he maintains, "*Whoever has the* ordo amoris *of a man has the man himself* (Scheler 1973b, 100). He uses imagery of space to describe how a person is "encased" in a "shell," a ranking of values and value-qualities, which he carries "along with him wherever he goes and cannot escape from [. . .] no matter how quickly he runs" (ibid.). An *ordo amoris* limits the possibilities for action, because it focuses our interest on particular objects. Thus, Scheler maintains, "even prior to the unity of perception, a value-signal experienced as coming from things, not from us, announces, with a trumpet flourish, that 'Something is up!'" (ibid., 101). An *ordo amoris* is fairly fixed within a person, closely linked with what Scheler calls her fate. He defines fate as "the way a man's actual *ordo amoris* is formed—in accordance with definite rules for gradual functionalization of primary love—objects in early childhood—that govern the unfolding of the content of his fate" (ibid., 103). Thus, in surveying a person's life, we can discern an *ordo amoris* that develops throughout it, shaping and limiting choices.[58]

Scheler distinguishes between contingent and essential value orderings, focusing most of his attention on the latter. Contingent elements of an *ordo amoris* depend on the value-bearer's nature (Scheler 1973a, 583–95). For example, I am deeply attracted to philosophy, but this attraction is peculiar to my *ordo amoris*. Others may find philosophy boring. However, Scheler also insists that we can arrive at essential value orderings by separating values from their "contingent, actual bearers" (Scheler 1973b, 123). Employing a helpful image, he notes that "in the region of the heart and its goods, we can, as it were, see through the accidental movements of the heart and through our familiar contingently real realms of goods, to an eternal architecture and scaffolding which encompasses all possible spirits and all possible worlds of goods; an architecture which is reflected only here and there in our world" (ibid.). This is an ambitious task, requiring us to discern eternality within the world of contingent values, but Scheler devotes considerable effort to it, identifying value-modalities, or ways values exist (Scheler 1973a, 104–10). He describes four of these modalities. They include, first, values involving the agreeable and disagreeable, relating to sensible feelings. For example, a taste for a particular kind of food is a sensible value. Next, Scheler discusses the modality of vital values. What he has in mind are values related to the noble and the vulgar, and those of strength and weakness. Ernst Troeltsch once called Scheler the "Catholic Nietzsche," [59] and Nietzsche's influence is clear when Scheler discusses vital values. Third, Scheler describes the modality of spiritual values. For Scheler, values related to beauty and truth form a distinct set, irreducible to agreeable or vital values. Finally, Scheler identifies a modality that includes the values of the *holy* and *unholy,* which are given in intention as *absolute.* For example, in a difficult moment, I may feel God's love, realizing that it is the most important thing in the world.

Scheler identifies rankings between and within these four modalities. Within each, we find orderings of the pleasant over the unpleasant, the strong over the weak, the good over the bad, and the holy over the unholy.[60] Moreover, among the four modalities of value, we find a distinct ranking, moving from the agreeable as the lowest modality to the holy as the highest modality. Values related to the useful are lower in the scale of values than spiritual values.

Moral values differ from those in the four modalities, and are irreducible to them. Moral values have a special status because they "arise by themselves. They are not objects to be realized in any act correlated to the values of the five value-ranks" (Frings 1997, 40). Vociferously, Scheler objects to the idea that we should aim at producing goodness, labeling the person with this intention a "Pharisee." The Pharisee debases morality by using it instrumentally. Moral values differ from the other value modalities because they do not appear in things and are consequently "purely personal" (ibid., 41). Things can be useful, pleasant, beautiful, and even holy, but they can never be moral. In this context, Scheler again denies the importance of the will. The person is the locus of moral good and evil, realizing it through her actions. Yet she actualizes her value as a person through a series of acts, and "one specific act, such as the act of will, is not the seat for the occurrence of good and evil" (ibid., 44). In an odd phrase, Scheler notes that moral values "ride on the back" (*auf dem Rücken*) of acts aimed at one of the four value modalities.[61] Frings illustrates this concept with a good example. Suppose a child gives up playing and spontaneously picks a daisy, bringing it to his mother. Frings notes "the root of the good in this example lies in spontaneously realizing the value of love of the mother over preferring the play with toys. By no means is it a case of a good deliberately realized for any specific purpose; nor is the good willed before the spontaneous picking of the daisy" (ibid., 45). A moral value emerges because the child prefers a higher to a lower value. The will of the child is unnecessary for realizing it because the good attaches itself to the act without the need for it.[62]

Some scholars maintain that Scheler's argument is utterly arbitrary, a product of his subjective judgment rather than any objective order. Others argue that even if Scheler gives reasons for his ordering, they are historically contingent, and he is guilty of cultural relativism. Both charges are deeply mistaken. Central to Scheler's philosophical project is his conviction that reason must often simply uncover what the mind presupposes. This involves a "showing" of what an argument or experience implies. In fact, Scheler explicitly rebels against the modern demand for epistemological criteria.[63] Nevertheless, when he presents a normative *ordo amoris*, Scheler departs from this general approach, offering explicit criteria for ranking values. These criteria include characteristics of values like their *endurance* and *extension* and *divisibility*. Higher values are those that endure longest and partake less of extension and divisibility. Endurance differs from mere existence over time. Objects can be very valuable, Scheler notes, even if they endure for only a short time. A value is enduring "through its quality of having the phenomenon of being 'able' to exist through time, no matter how long its thing-bearer may exist" (Scheler 1973a, 91). It belongs to the *essence* of some values to have endurance. For example, if a person says, "I love you, but only for now," we know that this is not an instance of genuine love. However, a bond of interest between two persons may lack the quality of endurance in its essence. There is nothing strange about a person saying, "Our business partnership is over because it no longer makes money." The essence of such a partnership includes *transience,* a coming in and out of being. Scheler applies this idea of endurance and transience to his five value modalities, establishing that those values that are higher have endurance, while lower values are transient. For example, values of sensibility are fleeting and transient, whereas those of the holy have endurance. Therefore, we can conclude that in a hierarchy of value, the latter are higher than the former.

Scheler suggests, in addition to endurance and transience, *divisibility* as a way of classifying values as higher or lower. Values can be divided to a lesser or greater extent, and those least susceptible to division are the highest. For example, we can distribute material values only by dividing them into pieces, and therefore, they rank low on a hierarchy of value (Scheler 1973a, 93). In contrast, spiritual values, such as those connected to art, are valuable precisely because we *cannot* divide them. It makes little sense to say that we enhance the value of a painting by cutting it to pieces (ibid.). Consequently, aesthetic and spiritual values are located higher in a hierarchy than material ones. Scheler suggests not only that it belongs to the essence of lower values to be divisible, but also that divisibility produces divisiveness. People want as much of material values as possible, leading to conflicts with those who feel likewise. In contrast, spiritual values need not be divided in order for many to enjoy them. It lies in their essence to be "*communicable* without *limit* and without any division and diminution" (ibid., 94). In fact, Scheler insists that it lies in the "*essence* of the *intention toward the holy* to *unite and join together* (ibid.). People with a common object of worship are united in a way that few other people are.

Given humanity's history of religious warfare, the idea that religious values unite people may seem odd. Terrorism in the early twenty-first century has provoked renewed debates about religion and violence, with some people arguing that both Christianity and Islam encourage intolerance and violence.[64] However, Scheler's argument does not rest on historical claims. How people have treated or treat others of different religions is irrelevant to his argument. To apply such arguments is to

misunderstand phenomenology, which focuses not on inductive historical or social-scientific arguments. We do not survey history and then
inductively argue that values have divisibility or endurance. Instead, we
grasp the essence of a value through intuition.[65]

Because I do not intend to consider all of Scheler's complex axiology,
I pass over other criteria he proposes for ranking values.[66] What I have
done is to outline two criteria he uses to establish a normative *ordo amoris*. After detailing the value modalities characterizing our intentional
relation to value, he maintains that love continually guides and shapes
them. Although the *ordo amoris* is an important descriptive tool, Scheler
also defends it as a normative idea. He uses the criteria of endurance and
divisibility to rank values, developing an *ordo amoris* ranking values of
the holy as the highest values.

John Paul II and the Hierarchy of Value

In turning to John Paul II's treatment of ethical hierarchies, we find
that he agrees with Scheler on key points.[67] Early in his career, he began
developing an ethical hierarchy. For example, while still a student after the
Second World War, he wrote an intriguing play called *Our God's Brother.*
This work is based on the life of Adam Chmielowski, a nineteenth-century
artist and founder of the Albertine Brothers.[68] Chmielowski struggles to
understand his moral responsibilities toward the poor, ultimately deciding to reject revolutionary violence as a means to end poverty. Through
dialogues with artists and a "Stranger" who espouses revolutionary violence, he comes to understand the complex interaction between material
and spiritual goods.[69] The Stranger tries to recruit Adam for the cause of
violent revolution. Scathingly, he condemns charity as an ineffective and
immoral means for achieving justice and celebrates anger as an indispensable tool for social change. In powerful words, he insists that alleviating
material want is more important than spiritual development. Despite this
arresting presentation, Adam refuses to embrace violent revolution. He
is sympathetic to the goals of this revolution, maintaining that the anger
and violence of the oppressed is understandable. However, in a dramatic
confrontation with the Stranger, he insists that "man's poverty is deeper
than the resources of all goods" (Wojtyla 1987, 242). A revolution that

elevates the material over the spiritual may temporarily relieve material want, but in the long term yields only further destruction. True solutions to human suffering must consider *both* material and spiritual goods but must subordinate the material to the spiritual.

Years after writing this wonderful drama, John Paul II repeated its themes before an international audience. Speaking before the United Nations General Assembly for the first time in 1979, he develops a conception of human rights and peace that became critical for his papacy.[70] After noting the common aims of the Holy See and the United Nations, John Paul II explores peace and human rights. Analytically, he maintains, we may distinguish between material and spiritual values but must keep in mind that within the human person, they are inseparable, because human beings never relate solely to the material or the spiritual (1979UN, 14). Nevertheless, John Paul II makes the startling claim that there exists a "constant rule of the history of mankind" that spiritual values are preeminent over material values (ibid.). This preeminence defines the proper use of material values, and it is indispensable for achieving true peace. Moreover, it ensures that scientific and technological developments serve the person. Too often, scientists ignore the priority of the spiritual, developing and employing dehumanizing technologies. Understanding this priority enables people to have full access to "truth, moral development, and to the complete possibility of enjoying the goods of culture which [they have] inherited, and of increasing them by [their] own creativity" (ibid.). John Paul II also suggests that material goods lack the unlimited capacity to satisfy human needs and often produce dissension and conflict. Spiritual goods lack these characteristics, because they are "open to unlimited enjoyment by many at the same time, without diminution of the goods themselves" (ibid.). In fact, the more people who share in them, the more they are enjoyed. Spiritual goods are preeminent over material goods because of their plenitude, possessing longevity and the capacity to respond to deep human needs.

In this speech, the echoes of Scheler's work are remarkable. Naturally, John Paul II does not include footnotes in his speeches, and so we can only speculate about how much Scheler influenced him. Nevertheless, what he seems to take from Scheler is a *justification* for ranking some values over others. Like Scheler, he maintains that we should rank spiritual values over material values. Like Scheler, he argues that material values give rise to tensions and dissension, while spiritual values foster unity. The criterion of divisibility thus becomes central for John Paul II at the United Nations, and Scheler is clearly a presence in this remarkable speech.

John Paul II also focuses attention on a hierarchy of value in his writings on culture.[71] In one important essay, "The Problem of the Constitution of Culture through Practice," he explicitly engages Scheler as he develops a hierarchy of values.[72] Focusing on the category of *praxis,* he recognizes that economic and social circumstances undoubtedly shape who we are. *Praxis* is a technical term, often used by Marxists, that emphasizes putting ideas into practice or action. John Paul II links it carefully to his philosophy of action. Recall that for him, action is both transitive and intransitive, and its intransitive character enables the person to determine herself. Work creates not a human product, but a human self that "radiates out to the world of products" (Wojtyla 1993, 265). Therefore, John Paul II argues, "the essence of praxis consists in realizing ourselves and, at the same time, in making the nonhuman reality outside ourselves more human" (ibid., 267).[73] He takes the concept of praxis out of the economic realm and locates it within the development of the person, thus reversing a common materialistic approach to it.

This definition of praxis allows John Paul II to argue that values related to the person are higher than those related to material goods. Without hesitation, he speaks of the person as being more "perfect" than other things because "that which conditions the value of human beings and comprises the essentially human quality of their activity is more important than that which is objectified in some product" (Wojtyla 1993, 268). He warns that we must "very precisely distinguish that which is merely a condition for a truly human life from that which is decisive for such a life" (ibid.). Like Scheler, John Paul II acknowledges the importance of the material conditions necessary for life, without falling into the trap of elevating them to a supreme value. In fact, he cites Scheler in defense of the value of contemplative activity. Contemplating the holy is not a means to an end but is valuable in itself, because it can awaken "within the full richness of human praxis its deep relation to truth, goodness, and beauty, a relation that has a disinterested—pure and non-utilitarian—character" (ibid., 270). The proper order of values recognizes these values as more important than those of the useful.

With Scheler, John Paul II also insists that spiritual values are higher than material ones because they endure over other values. Like people, products die and often "bear the mark of something to be used up, something to be consumed, and cannot rise above this level in the *hierarchy of values*" (Wojtyla 1993, 272, emphasis mine). However, by relating us to spiritual values, praxis "contains the power to transcend that which is merely *utile* (useful), and which, in being used up, is destined to die" (ibid.). These values lack the divisibility characteristic of material values. Action produces changes in the person that are remembered for generations and continue to relate to the eternal values of truth, goodness, and beauty. Here, again, although John Paul II draws on Thomistic sources, Scheler's influence is quite apparent.

In preparing for the 2000 Jubilee, John Paul II repeatedly discussed higher values, focusing particularly on values related to holiness. In an apostolic letter at the close of the Jubilee year, he insisted that before "making practical plans, we need *to promote a spirituality of communion,* making it the guiding principle of education wherever individuals and Christians are formed, wherever ministers of the altar, consecrated persons, and pastoral workers are trained, wherever families and communities are being built up" (NMI, sec. 43). A spirituality of communion does not focus on immediate effectiveness, a key political virtue, but instead "indicates above all the heart's contemplation of the mystery of the Trinity dwelling in us, and whose light we must also be able to see shining on the face of the brothers and sisters around us" (ibid.). Repeatedly in his speeches during the Jubilee, John Paul II accentuated a range of values and practices aimed at developing holiness.

Critics often warn that by emphasizing values related to holiness, we may disregard social justice. Those pursuing holiness, they allege, retreat into a private life of prayer that ignores the pressing needs of the poor. This is an important caveat against a spiritualism that denigrates material values, but John Paul II is fully aware of it. In emphasizing spiritual values, he never abandons his concerns with justice, always insisting on a close relationship between spiritual values and political and social justice. For example, forcefully, he notes that "we must reject the temptation to offer a privatized and individualistic spirituality which ill accords with the demands of charity, to say nothing of the implications of the Incarnation and, in the last analysis, of Christianity's eschatological tension" (NMI, sec. 52). Elsewhere, he maintains that "moral integrity is a necessary condition for the health of society. It is therefore necessary to work simultaneously for the conversion of hearts and for the improvement of structures" (1986Liberation, 75). Ranking spiritual values over material ones provides no warrant for disregarding the material needs of persons. Explicitly, John Paul II declares, "it does not follow from the fact that the value of the person is superior to the value of all goods other than moral goods that the norms which bid us realize those lesser goods admit of exceptions" (ibid.). Within the person, we find an intimate relationship between spiritual and material goods. John Paul II's subtle depiction of the relationship between the spiritual and material should render moot charges that he ignores material goods, retreats into spirituality, or justifies depriving persons of material goods in order to promote spiritual goods.

Despite his agreement with Scheler that a hierarchy of value is important, John Paul II criticizes him for neglecting moral norms, charging that his hierarchy of value is primarily descriptive rather than normative. For example, in his habilitation thesis, he maintains that Scheler's resistance to norms makes his ethic incompatible with Christian ethics. Repeatedly, he attributes Scheler's rejection of norms to his rebellion against a Kantian ethics (Wojtyla 1993, 84).[74] Scheler establishes regularity between contact with a value and emotions of "good" and "bad," but it "has a primarily descriptive character, not a normative one" (ibid., 85). He also provides some directives for ethics by establishing positions of values in a hierarchy, but they are only *remote* directives, offering little practical guidance (ibid.). Illustrating this point, he cites prayer, which involves values that are undoubtedly superior to sensual ones. Yet this gradation cannot "provide [him] with a more proximate and adequate basis for saying that this concrete prayer is a morally good act" (ibid.). An intentional relation to a particular value tells us little about what to do in a concrete situation. Similarly, because praying involves religious values, it is a more perfect action than eating. However, when we cannot both eat and pray, what should we do? John Paul II maintains that a "host of other examples could be advanced to show that the mere feeling of a hierarchy of value does not provide us with a sufficient basis for the immediate positing of norms, even though it cannot be denied that values have a certain remote influence on this process" (ibid.). Without such norms, we cannot make difficult decisions and risk denigrating lower values in favor of higher ones. Notice that John Paul II accepts Scheler's *descriptive* account of how we develop hierarchies of values. Moreover, he recognizes that our intentional relation to values offers some general direction for choice. The order of our feelings and loves, Scheler's *ordo amoris,* is important for ethics. For John Paul II, however, norms are also indispensable for the moral life. Scheler's hierarchy of value is illuminating but remains primarily an insightful descriptive account of the human as a creature who values.

As a way of concluding this discussion of a hierarchy of value, let me offer a few examples of how John Paul II uses it. Discussing work, he demonstrates how labor has greater value than capital because it develops persons. Thus, "Laborem Exercens" begins with a very general definition of labor, yet, by the end of the encyclical, we come to see it as part of the *imago dei.* This idea shapes John Paul II's discussion of corporations, unions, and wages. Similarly, in defending the "culture of life" in "Evangelium Vitae," he insists that life is a value of the highest order. It is a necessary and indispensable condition for the development of persons, and we must "show reverence and love for every person and the life of every person" (EV, 41). Nevertheless, life in its earthly state is not an "absolute good and we might even be asked to give it up for a greater good" (ibid., 47). We must reject the idolatry of life that values it more than our relationship to God. Health is a final example worth considering. Undoubtedly, it is a good, and John Paul II often praises health professionals and researchers.[75] Nevertheless, he subordinates its value to the development of personhood. In his meditation on suffering, "Salvifici Doloris," he considers redemptive suffering. Some in Western industrialized nations, he maintains, view physical and mental suffering as an enemy that they must eliminate at all costs. Yet, this impoverished understanding of value ignores how suffering may reveal the deepest dimensions of our personhood, affording the opportunity to exercise our capacity for self-giving love (SD, 13). Through this analysis, John Paul II combats the idea that suffering is always an evil. We should pursue the values related to bodily health, but they are penultimate values, subordinate to the person's development.

This all-too-brief survey of some of John Paul II's words on work, life, and health illustrates how the value of personhood orders his ethics. I will consider other examples and some contemporary objections to his hierarchy of value in a later chapter. What is important here is that although he makes few references to him, Scheler influences his thinking considerably. John Paul II usually presents a hierarchy of values that is more general than what Scheler offers, simply distinguishing between material and spiritual values. Moreover, he often draws explicitly on the Thomistic transcendentals of goodness, truth, and beauty. Nevertheless, for both John Paul II and Scheler, ethical hierarchies are essential, and for both men, the spiritual is more important than the material.

Love, Will, and Cognition: Concluding Reflections

John Paul II has a critical, creative, and engaging mind that builds on philosophical and theological traditions but weaves them into new patterns. In this chapter, I have demonstrated how he engages Scheler, a central influence on his thought. What this engagement yields is a conceptual framework that has great import for his political thought. With Scheler, he affirms that we are intentionally related to values. We find ourselves related to them, rather than creating or constructing them. Moreover, the direction of our love shapes a hierarchy of value. Finally, John Paul II insists that we adopt a hierarchy that gives priority to spiritual over material values without denigrating the material. This idea of an ethical hierarchy provides John Paul II with a conceptual framework he uses to analyze how persons and communities relate to values.

However, ultimately, he thinks that Scheler offers primarily a descriptive hierarchy of value and argues that we need a normative one. Therefore, he departs from Scheler by emphasizing our capacity to shape our personhood through willing. This capacity enables us to give ourselves to others, embodying the highest form of love, and it becomes the ground for affirming human dignity. Carefully developing this idea, John Paul II uses it to establish a normative hierarchy of value. It is not an arbitrary or subjective ranking, but one that reflects what is most important in human life: the development of the person.

Unfortunately, too many contemporary scholars accentuate the differences between John Paul II and Scheler, ignoring their commonalities. Both men reject skepticism as a legitimate starting point for ethical reflection. Skepticism reflects distortions in the modern turn toward the subject, threatening to undermine its positive elements. In contrast, epistemologically, Scheler and John Paul II begin with our intentional relation to values, arguing that the experience of values is a legitimate starting point. They also make love the center of their ethical analysis, maintaining that it is the source of human dignity and value. Finally, both Scheler and John Paul II defend hierarchies of value, arguing that spiritual values are more important than material values. Their shared philosophical idiom marks them as radically different from many in contemporary ethics. Their criticisms of contemporary thought, therefore, challenge dominant ethical frameworks, calling for a deep appreciation of the value of the person. As I will argue in the rest of the book, this emphasis has much to teach us.

2

John Paul II and Political Disorder

What is lacking among all of these moralists, whether religious or rational, is an understanding of the brutal character and the behavior of all human collectivities, and the power of self-interest and collective egoism in all inter-group relations.

Reinhold Niebuhr[1]

"For many years I have lived like a man exiled from my deeper personality yet condemned to probe it."

Adam, in John Paul II's *Radiation of Fatherhood*[2]

In his influential primer on international relations, *Politics among Nations,* Hans Morgenthau famously argues that the essence of politics is a struggle for power. Maintaining that "whatever the ultimate aims of international politics, power is always the immediate aim," he defines power as "man's control over the minds and actions of other men" (Morgenthau 1985, 30–31). For several decades in the twentieth century, Morgenthau, Reinhold Niebuhr, George F. Kennan, E. H. Carr, Henry Kissinger, and other political realists emphasized that politics involves an intense struggle for power. They condemned "moralists" and "idealists" for ignoring power and accused them of applying abstract moral principles to politics without considering their consequences. Describing the anarchical character of international relations, they argued that no power exists strong enough to impose order and peace among nations. In such circumstances, nations ruthlessly pursue their own interests, creating continual conflict and disorder.

During the height of the great realist debates of the last century, political realists argued that Roman Catholic thinkers embraced a naïve understanding of sin and politics. For example, in a well-known article on St. Augustine's realism, Reinhold Niebuhr criticized natural law ethics, saying that it was the "basis of so much lack of realism in both the classical and medieval period" and still persists "long after the Aristotelian idea of fixed form for historical events has been overcome" (Niebuhr 1953, 133). Repeatedly, Niebuhr condemned Roman Catholic thinkers for underestimating the depth of human corruption. Similarly, Paul Ramsey accused *Pacem in Terris* of having "natural law optimism," because it refers only in passing to "the disordering of God's design by sinfulness" (Ramsey 1983, 71). He praised the Second Vatican Council for its extraordinary achievements but also maintained that it embraced a dangerous naïveté about human nature.

More recently, Roman Catholic thinkers have leveled similar charges against John Paul II. For example, Dennis McCann accuses him of holding an "unconstrained vision" of economic life that amounts to utopianism (McCann 1991, 139). John Langan comments that after reading "On Social Concern," he suspects that the "underlying tendency of this Pope's social thought is a utopian and ahistorical moralism" (Langan 1991, 285). Finally, David Hollenbach charges that John Paul II's theology of work is incomplete because it neglects the "problematic and even sinful dimensions of human agency and action" (Hollenbach 1983, 66).[3]

When discussing John Paul II and realism, Hollenbach, McCann, Langan, and others level several charges without distinguishing them adequately. Someone may be utopian because he fails to understand what his position implies. For example, when the United States Catholic Bishops issued their 1986 "Economic Justice for All" document, they endorsed a number of economic goals and policies, including full employment and increases in the minimum wage. Some critics charged that they failed to recognize the inevitable trade-offs in public policy, such as how raising the minimum wage may increase unemployment. In this sense, the bishops were unrealistic, because they failed to consider the consequences of their proposed policies. In another sense, a person may be utopian because she embraces an overly optimistic view of human nature. For example, she might propose that we dismantle our prison system, maintaining that vicious criminals will refrain from criminal activity if we choose dialogue over incarceration. Or she might argue that the al-Qaeda terrorist network will cease its violent activities when confronted with acts of charity.

Later in this book, I will argue that criticisms of the first kind do apply to John Paul II, particularly when he proposes that the United Nations promote a "civilization of love." However, charges that he overestimates human goodness have little merit and demonstrate considerable ignorance of his philosophical project. To rebut them, in this chapter I explore the darker sides of John Paul II's philosophical anthropology, showing how his engagement with Scheler enables him to carefully analyze the human fault. First, I discuss his account of how we use others merely as tools for our projects. Second, after presenting his "personalistic norm," which prohibits using persons merely as a means to an end, I show how we violate it by orienting our intentionality toward using others. I trace this perversion to its deepest root, our alienation from God. Third, I discuss "structures of sin," a deeply controversial concept during John Paul II's papacy. Using both self-determination and a hierarchy of value, John Paul II rejects the idea that structures can be sinful in anything more than an analogical sense. Fourth, I consider structures of sin in international relations, focusing on economics and nationalism. In the economic arena, John Paul II sharply criticizes philosophical materialism in market economies. Marked by a greedy drive for power, this perversion overturns the proper order of values by elevating the material over the spiritual. Among nations, sin creates an idolatrous identification with political communities, leading to war and atrocities. I show how John Paul II astutely analyzed nationalism after the Cold War's end by emphasizing its moral dimensions. I conclude by noting how his vision of sin is as compelling as that of any of the great political realists.

The Personalistic Norm

When analyzing sin, John Paul II focuses heavily on the idea of using persons. As I noted in the last chapter, he criticizes Scheler for neglecting moral norms, arguing that they are part of lived experience and indispensable for practical reasoning. In *Love and Responsibility,* he corrects this perceived deficiency by presenting what he calls the "personalistic norm," which states that "whenever a person is the object of your activity, remember that you may not treat that person as only the means to an end, as an instrument, but must allow for the fact that he or she, too, has, or at least should have, distinct personal ends" (Wojtyla 1960, 28). Negatively, it establishes that the person is the kind of good that we should never use merely as a means, and anyone who "treats a person as the means to an end does violence to the very essence of the other, to what constitutes its natural right" (ibid., 27). Positively, the personalistic norm confirms that "the person is a good towards which the only proper and adequate attitude is love" (ibid., 41). John Paul II carefully distinguishes between different notions of using. In its first sense, *to use* means to "employ some object of action as a means to an end" (ibid., 24). Subjects act with ends in view, employing objects to achieve them. They subordinate some objects (means) to others (ends). Using persons as means, John Paul II emphasizes, is inevitable in complex social relations. What he rejects is using someone *merely* as a means (Wojtyla 1960, 26).[4] This act degrades the person, denying that she has an inner life and ends of her own. John Paul II's examples in this context are illustrative (ibid., 29–30). Employers often use employees merely as instruments for economic gain, military officers use enlisted personnel merely as a means to victory, and men use women merely as tools for sexual pleasure. In the first two examples, inequality encourages a superior to abuse an inferior. In the last example, a relationship between equals becomes instrumental. Each example illustrates how a social relationship degenerates into a situation in which persons use others merely as means.

In these relationships, the experience of pleasure may contribute to use. Here, John Paul II introduces a second meaning of the verb *to use,* focusing on the emotional overtones accompanying action (Wojtyla 1960, 32). In this analysis, Scheler's influence is quite apparent. With Scheler, John Paul II describes how an emotion "may precede the activity, co-incide with it, or emerge into consciousness when the action is already complete" (ibid.). Emotions throw an act "into relief," highlighting its importance. We call a positive overtone "pleasure," and a negative one "pain." In this context, *to use* means to experience pleasure through an activity or the object sought in an activity. Human beings can identify and isolate pleasures, and then pursue them as ends. They can also try to shape their actions solely by pursuing pleasure and avoiding pain. John Paul II insists that there is nothing wrong with experiencing pleasure from relationships with others.[5] However, often, we perversely make persons merely instrumental for maximizing pleasure.

Intentionality and the Inversion of the Order of Values

If we consider use and the personalistic norm by themselves, the etiology of sin seems puzzling. Why do we continually use others? If the values associated with persons are central, why do so many people turn away from them? John Paul II's engagement with Scheler helps illuminate this pervasive tendency to use others. A distortion in our intentional relation to values characterizes sin, a movement from acknowledging the value of persons to using them merely as objects. John Paul II offers a rich account of this process in his audience on the theology of the body, in which he makes extensive use of phenomenology.[6] Sin, he argues, involves rejecting communion with others, and denying the gift of self that characterizes love. For example, discussing lust, he emphasizes that psychological interpretations of it identify an intense inclination toward an object. Although including such an idea, the biblical conception of lust accentuates the idea that "a value is being impaired."[7] The value impaired is the "communion by means of mutual giving," and this impairment indicates a change in our intentional relation to values. Lust reverses the proper "intentionality of thought and heart" that "constitutes one of main streams of universal human culture." John Paul II remarks that what he has in mind is an "intentional reduction, almost a restriction or closing down of the horizon of mind and heart." This is an *axiological reduction,* a reduction in value, through which a person restricts her intentional relation to values. When he lusts, a man reduces all the "rich storehouse of values" in a woman to one, the "gratification of sexuality itself." By virtue of "axiological intentionality itself," lust "aims at an exclusive end—to satisfy only the sexual need of the body, as its precise object." Potentially, a relationship to a woman frees in a man "a gamut of spiritual-corporeal" desires of an especially personal and "sharing" nature" to which "a proportionate pyramid of values corresponds." Unfortunately, lust diminishes this gamut, "obscuring the pyramid of values that marks the perennial attraction of male and female."

In this analysis, John Paul II repeatedly refers to the "heart" and seems to endorse Scheler's idea of the disorders of the heart. However, he again differs with Scheler on cognition and will. For example, he notes that lust's "intentional and axiological reduction can take place in the sphere of the look," emphasizing that looking is a *cognitive* act. Taking as its object the person as source for sexual gratification, it represents a form of "lustful knowledge." We must also *will* to change our orientation toward value. Cognitive intentionality "itself does not yet mean enslavement of the heart," which occurs only when the "intentional reduction, illustrated previously, sweeps the will along into its narrow horizon." The person decides to relate to another person "according to the specific scale of values of lust." Thus, our *ordo amoris* changes in fundamental ways when we will to alter it. Through the will, the "very way of existing with regard to another person is established," and instead of willing to love her as a gift, we will to reduce her to a mere object.

This change in intentionality also alters the user's "very intentionality of existence" (Wojtyla 1980, 151). Others exist as a call to enter into communion, but by willing to use them as a mere means, we allow lust to dominate our subjectivity, fundamentally changing our personhood. Thus, even something that appears to be a private and inner act actualizes "a change (subjectively unilateral) of the very intentionality of existence" (ibid.). Adultery in the heart, for example, shapes a person, even if he never acts on it.[8] This change also alters his freedom. Through an axiological reduction, he thinks he can expand his freedom but, in reality, diminishes it. Severing his relationship to the extraordinary values present in the person, he traps himself in a self-imposed attachment to limited values. An important dimension of freedom, John Paul II often argues, is the capacity to direct intentionality toward the rich world of values. Freedom in this sense is the "acting person's intentional flexibility and partial independence with respect to possible objects of volition" (Wojtyla 1979, 138). One is truly free when "which of the various objects of desire one makes one's own is not determined either by the objects themselves or by the way they present themselves" (ibid.).[9] The lustful person lacks freedom because he cannot control his intentional relation to values.

In contrast, an orientation toward higher values requires us to become "aware of the internal impulses" of the heart so as "to be able distinguish them and qualify them maturely" (Wojtyla 1980, 172). John Paul II uses the language of "mastery," insisting that the person pay careful attention to the workings of his heart. This knowledge of the heart "cannot be learned only from books," and Christ calls on us to "acquire a mature and complete evaluation" of its movements (ibid.). What he calls for is discerning and evaluating our relation to values. Depicting a complex interplay between reason and the heart, he urges the person to learn to "read" his relation to values. For example, a "noble gratification" is "one thing, while sexual desire is another," and through reflection and action a person learns to differentiate between these two values (ibid. 173). Gradually, through inner discipline, he develops spontaneity in relation to the rich world of values. The lustful man, in contrast, lacks this spontaneity, because he embraces an inadequate hierarchy of values.

"The Ways of Denial"

This phenomenology of using others, however, is incomplete because it ignores our alienation from God. Sin is never simply using others because of a perverted hierarchy of value. Instead, in its essence, it is "a negation of God as Creator in his relationship to man, and of what God wills for man, from the beginning and for ever" (DM, 9). In his 1975 Lenten lectures, *A Sign of Contradiction,* John Paul II describes this negation as modernity's "ways of denial," which include indifference, forgetfulness, and radical repudiation of God. Citing Henri de Lubac's work, he notes that the "tragedy of atheist humanism" is that it "strips man of his transcendental character, destroying his ultimate significance as a person" (Wojtyla 1979b, 16).[10]

This tragedy originates in a perverse drive for independence from God, which John Paul II sometimes illustrates by analyzing the parable of the prodigal son. The prodigal son is

> every human being: bewitched by the temptation to separate himself from his Father in order to lead his own independent existence; disappointed by the mirage which had fascinated him; alone, dishonored, exploited when he tries to build a world all for himself; sorely tried, even in the depths of his own misery, by the desire to return to communion with the Father. (RP, 5)

Both the Prodigal Son and his elder brother, who resents his father for welcoming his brother home, illustrate the futile attempt to gain independence from God. The elder brother displays jealousy and irritation at his father's love, and his selfishness "blinds him and shuts him off from other people and God" (RP, 6). Both brothers and their father portray "the situation of the human family, divided by forms of selfishness" and vainly attempting to assert itself against God (ibid.).

Repeatedly, John Paul II emphasizes that humanity's "history of sin began the moment it wished to be independent and to determine what is good and what is evil" (VS, 102). In his play *Radiation of Fatherhood,* for example, he details how human beings strive to evict God from their lives. The narrator of the play, Adam, says:

> I have decided to throw the word "mine" out of my vocabulary. How can I use it when I know that everything is Yours? Although You yourself do not give birth with every human birth, still he who does give birth is Yours. And I myself am more Yours than mine. I have learned that I must not call what is Yours mine, must not say, think, feel it to be mine. I must free, divest myself of it; I must not have or want anything of my own ("mine" means "own"). (Wojtyla 1987, 337)

In this arresting passage, we sense the depth of humanity's rebellion. Instead of embracing God's presence within him, the person tries to excise it, disowning much of his personality in the process. Rather than facing God, he turns away from him, engaging in a radical form of inner surgery. Here, we have a dramatic form of rebellion similar to what we find in Dostoevsky's great works.

In depicting this rebellion, John Paul II uses strong causal language to emphasize how the rupture between humanity and God produces disorder. For example, in "Reconciliation and Penance," he uses the Tower of Babel story to illustrate how attempting to achieve independence from God has disastrous consequences for the social order.[11] In this story, "the exclusion of God is presented not so much under the aspect of opposition to him as of forgetfulness and indifference toward him."[12] Those building the tower see God as irrelevant to their project, and their forgetfulness leads to the "exclusion of God, rupture with God, disobedience to God," all of which represent historic forms of sin.[13] This causality explains the intimate relationship between using others, intentionality, and rebellion against God. A creature explicitly or implicitly rejects "the very one from whom he came and who sustains him in life." This "suicidal act" destroys his internal balance, creating conflicts and contradictions within him. In turn, these internal conflicts lead him to invert the proper order of values, creating an intentional relation to others and his environment characterized by use and domination. This causal chain, John Paul II maintains, is an "objective law and an objective reality, verified in so many ways in the human psyche and in the spiritual life, as well as in society, where it is easy to see the signs and effects of this internal disorder."[14]

Despite these consequences, human beings continue to seek independence from God, and this futile aspiration "rebounds" and enslaves them (Wojtyla 1979b, 34). In a compelling section of "Evangelium Vitae," we see how the eclipse of God produces disregard for the value of human life. Without relating to God, we are reduced to "being a 'thing' no longer able to grasp our 'transcendent' character" (EV, 22). We become a "complex of organs, functions, and energies to be used for pleasure and efficiency" (ibid.). Once we embrace materialism, the natural world becomes mere matter "subject to every kind of manipulation," and spiritual values disappear, replaced by "economic efficiency, inordinate consumerism, physical beauty and pleasure" (ibid., 23). In this context, using others merely as instruments seems no different than using inanimate objects. We experience a sense of meaninglessness, and

> the loss of the sense of God has coincided with the progress of a nihilistic culture that impoverishes the sense of human existence and, in the

ethical field, relativizes even the fundamental values of the family and
respect for life. All this is carried out not in a flashy way but, rather,
with the subtle method of indifference that makes all forms of behavior
appear as normal, so that moral problems will no longer stand out.
(1999Love, sec. 2)

Thus, people may not even notice the most destructive ways in which
they deny God's existence and love. Even when it is not self-conscious,
the eclipse of God often leads to relativism or nihilism, with destructive
consequences for the social order.

Sometimes, however, people appear to self-consciously reject God's
goodness. For example, terrorists who deliberately murder the innocent
in the name of religious beliefs use others merely as a means, alienating
themselves from God. A few months after the 2001 terrorist attacks
against the United States, John Paul II made this point unequivocally.
Terrorism in the service of religion, he proclaimed, *"exploits not just people,
it exploits God:* it ends by making him an idol to be used for one's own
purposes" (2002Celebration, 6). By intentionally relating themselves
toward others in hatred, terrorists generate "isolation, mistrust and closure," rupturing their relationship with God" (ibid., 4). Terrorism in
the name of God is so horrible because those committing it may think
that such a crime enhances their relationship with God, when in reality,
it leads only to alienation from God.

Moral Responsibility and Structures of Sin

By linking our relationship to God, our internal life, and social relations, John Paul II inevitably raises questions about structures of sin. Are
terrorists trapped in structures of sin that inevitably lead them to kill the
innocent? Are there sinful conditions that we can change only by using
violence? Responding to liberation theology in the 1980s, John Paul II
became deeply interested in the concept of structures of sin. Marxist analyses, interdependence theory, a global arms race, and other developments
led many people in the latter half of the twentieth century to see sin as
something structural. The language of structures thus entered theological,
political, and ethical discourse, and John Paul II analyzes it carefully. In

"Sollicitudo Rei Socialis," he argues that development has failed in many parts of the globe because of a world "structured in sin," and "divided by blocs, in which instead of solidarity imperialism and exploitation hold sway."[15] The proximate causes of these divisions, he notes, are "selfishness, shortsightedness, mistaken political decisions, and imprudent economic decisions." However, sin is their ultimate cause, including "sins committed by individual persons, who introduced these structures and reinforced them again and again," rejecting God's will and plan for humanity. These structures of sins, John Paul II emphasizes, will remain strong as long as we retain our perverse orientation toward others.

Clearly, in this document, John Paul II focuses on *individual* causes and responses to sin, stating that "we have to change our spiritual relationship with self, with neighbor, with even the remotest human communities, and with nature itself, in view of the common good of the whole individual and of all people" (SR, 38).[16] Critics of "Sollicitudo Rei Socialis" charge that by emphasizing individual conversion, he ignores institutions and social sins. For example, Leslie Griffin maintains that he "downplays the capacities of political and social institutions to resolve the problems confronting persons in the late twentieth century" (Griffin 1991, 249). John Howard Yoder praises "Sollicitudo Rei Socialis" for addressing social sins but asserts that it "sweeps those promising possibilities aside by a rapid argument which explicitly reduces all 'evil structures' to nothing but the evil decisions and actions of individuals" (Yoder 1991, 270). These and other thinkers maintain that John Paul II ignores the institutional complexities of the modern world, retreating instead to a naïve faith in individual conversion.

These critics express genuine concerns about an overly individualistic approach to social analysis but neglect important elements of John Paul II's personalism. If we restrict ourselves to "Sollicitudo Rei Socialis," Yoder is correct in saying that John Paul II provides only a "rapid argument," but it is not the only document in which the pope considers social sins. In "Reconciliation and Penance," he explores several meanings of the term "social sin." In its first sense, it refers to how sin affects others in a "mysterious and intangible" way.[17] By directing our intentionality toward using them, we connect to a perverse communion of sinful persons. John Paul II insists that "there is no sin, not even the most intimate and secret one, the most strictly individual one, that exclusively concerns the person committing it." In any sin, the sinner participates in a "law of descent," a perverse mirror image of the law of ascent characterizing the communion of saints. Lowering ourselves through sin, we drag others down with us, and thus "every sin can undoubtedly be considered social sin."

What John Paul II's critics miss is how this idea of social sin resembles Scheler's writings on the same topic. John F. Crosby is one of the few contemporary scholars to draw attention to the similarities between the two thinkers (Crosby 1997). Scheler emphasizes the same sense of movement toward lower values and also rejects the idea of a purely individual sin. He insists that the principle of solidarity

> is for us an eternal component and a *fundamental article of the cosmos of finite persons.* The *total* moral world—no matter how far its sphere may extend in space and time, here on earth or on discovered and undiscovered planets or even beyond these—becomes *one encompassing whole* through the validity of this principle. This whole *rises and falls as a whole* whenever this principle suffers the slightest change. (Scheler 1973a, 534–5)

Sin is never merely an individual matter, and for Scheler, "the idea of moral solidarity, which has become almost incomprehensible to modern man, presupposes, as it were, an *inner capitalization* of moral values in the "kingdom of God" in whose result *all* individuals share and can share again and again" (Scheler 1961, 142). Scheler, in fact, develops a complex account of common guilt in which human beings contribute social evils through action and inaction.[18] Crosby details how it extends responsibility beyond the interpersonal realm, while retaining individual responsibility (Crosby 1997). John Paul II aspires to the same goal with his idea of a mysterious and sinful law of descent.

Social sin also has two other meanings for John Paul II. The first involves any direct attack "against love of neighbor," including "every sin against justice in interpersonal relationships, committed either by the individual against the community or by the community against the individual," such as denying rights and refusing to serve the common good. It also covers both commission and omission. Additionally, social sin refers to departures from God's plan for "justice in the world, and freedom and peace between individuals, groups, and peoples." Under this rubric, we find class struggle, the Cold War conflict between the United States and the Soviet Union, and disputes between groups within nations. In discussing social sin, John Paul II is thus clearly aware of its institutional elements, and through the concept of solidarity in sin, offers a metaphysical ground for affirming sin's social character.

Given this complex notion, why do Griffin, Yoder, and others accuse John Paul II of ignoring the institutional dimensions of sin? Are they simply unaware of his larger philosophical project, or is there something philosophically at stake in their criticisms? I believe that there is an important philosophical issue concerning sin and subjectivity. Those working in business ethics are aware of the long-standing debate about whether we can ascribe moral responsibility to corporations.[19] This is precisely the issue John Paul II considers, saying that with social sin, "one may ask whether moral responsibility for these evils, and therefore sin, can be attributed to any person in particular" (1986Liberation, sec. 74). Social structures, "being necessary in themselves," often "tend to become fixed and fossilized as mechanisms relatively independent of the human will, thereby paralyzing or distorting social development and causing injustice. However, they always depend on the responsibility of man, who can alter them, and not upon an alleged determinism of history" (ibid.). In these circumstances, we use the term "sin" analogically, employing it to remind individuals of their moral responsibility to "change those disastrous and intolerable conditions" (ibid.).

In this analysis, John Paul II emphasizes that the *person,* rather than the collective, is the locus of sin. Attributing sin to collectives dilutes responsibility, leading "more or less unconsciously to the watering down and almost the abolition of personal sin." Whether the analyst intends it or not, once he endorses the idea of collective sin, he diminishes the person's relation to value. In contrast, John Paul II insists that social sins result from the accumulation and concentration of personal sins. Many fail to act against this gradual accumulation out of laziness, fear, indifference, or a tendency to "take refuge in the supposed impossibility of changing the world," ignoring necessary sacrifices by producing "specious reasons of a higher order." Too often, moral agents retreat from responsibility by blaming systems or structures for their sinful behavior.

Saying that institutions are sinful, moreover, creates ontological puzzles, because an institution, structure, or society "is not itself the subject of moral acts. Hence, a situation cannot in itself be good or bad" (RP, 16). Like Scheler, John Paul II insists that we attach moral value to persons. Scheler puts this well, stating that "only persons can (originally) be morally good or evil; everything else can be good or evil only *by reference to persons* no matter how indirect this reference may be" (Scheler 1973a, 85).[20] For both him and John Paul II, the relationship between structures and persons may be remote, but it must exist if we are to identify moral value. Those who attribute sin to structures are confused about the locus of moral value, and John Paul II challenges them to explain how an institution lacking personality can contain moral value. Naturally, we may talk about it having value, but this is not the moral value associated with the person, and therefore, we cannot say that an institution sins. For personalists like John Paul II and Scheler, ascribing moral value to something impersonal ignores the person as the necessary locus of moral value.

Gregory Baum suggests one response to this argument when he urges us to see social sins as the "unconscious" and "non-voluntary" sins appearing in cultural symbols and people's self-understandings (Baum 1989). I think emphasizing non-voluntary and automatic processes illuminates social and political life. However, if Baum wants to use the word *sin* in anything more than an analogical sense, he will confront conceptual difficulties. How precisely does an institution commit a sin in an unconscious and non-voluntary way? Ascribing unconscious sin to an institution is no more enlightening than saying that it acts consciously. A collective entity lacks an unconscious just as much as it lacks consciousness. The central mistake Baum makes is to ascribe moral value to something other than persons.

By severing sin from the person, we also run the risk of achieving only superficial social and political change. Discussing spiritual communion, John Paul II states: "Let us have no illusions: unless we follow this spiritual path, external structures of communion will serve very little purpose. They would become mere mechanisms, rather than means of expression and growth" (NMI, section 43) Without attending to persons, changing institutions will be ineffective in the long run. Legal and structural changes will prove to be "incomplete, of short duration, and ultimately vain and ineffective—not to say counterproductive if the people directly or indirectly responsible for that situation are not converted" (RP, 16). Without inner change, people become disillusioned and give up trying to effect positive transformation. Those excessively concerned with institutional change should carefully heed this warning.

To summarize what John Paul II says about structures of sin, he objects to ascribing sin to collectives because he has deep misgivings about removing responsibility from persons. Like Scheler, he develops a philosophical argument that nonpersonal things lack moral value. Fundamentally, he seeks to reestablish human dignity, which disappears when people become part of an anonymous collectivity.

International Politics and Distortions in Value

By emphasizing the person and social sin, John Paul II insightfully analyzes disorder in international politics, focusing particularly on the idea of a perverted hierarchy of value. In his 1979 United Nations speech, in which he distinguishes between spiritual and material values, he offers a clear statement about this axiological disorder. Modernity, he argues, has often subordinated the spiritual to the material, reversing the proper *ordo amoris*. Consequently, it has reduced the meaning of human life "chiefly to the many different material and economic factors" such as the market and consumption (1979UN, 19). This development inevitably produces a struggle for material goods and divisions among peoples. We need to reduce this conflict "systematically and radically" by emphasizing the spiritual values that unite people, doing so "before everyone's eyes, in the sight of every society" (ibid.).

For many years after this speech, John Paul II applied this analysis of value distortions to the economic order, provoking considerable debate about the morality of the market and socialism. I will not enter this complex dispute in detail, but let me briefly comment about his moral assessment of the market. In his early economic works, he adopts prophetic language that seems to be antimarket. Some used these works to support democratic socialism, while others insisted that John Paul II supported the free market. Nevertheless, in 1991, in "Centesimus Annus," he clearly stated that "the free market appears to be the most efficient tool for utilizing resources and responding to needs" (CA, 34). He also extolled market-related values such as "organizational skills, planning, timing, and management" and "discipline, creativity, initiative and entrepreneurial ability" (ibid., 32). Commentators note how strong this support of the market is, occasionally contrasting it to what other twentieth-century papal documents say about the market.[21]

However, this support for the market is *conditional* on whether it promotes a just society. State and society, working in tandem, must actively promote justice and help the poor.[22] For example, John Paul II says "society and state need to afford protection against the nightmare of unemployment through economic policies that ensure balanced growth and full employment or through unemployment insurance and retraining programs" (CA, 15). He argues that many people simply cannot participate in a market economy because they lack the education, skills, or income to do so. The free market is the most efficient economic arrangement we know of, but "this is true only if you are able to buy and sell" (ibid., 34). Until all persons have access to a market, "justice and truth demand that basic human needs should be met, and that none should be left to perish" (ibid.). For John Paul II, both state and society must promote participation in the market and meet the basic needs of those unable to participate in it.

I want to keep this conditional support in mind as I consider John Paul II's understanding of sin and the economic order, because his analysis may leave the impression that he thoughtlessly rejects a market economy. When he turns to the market, he emphasizes how work can value the person. For example, in "Laborem Exercens," one of his earliest writings on economics, he develops his well-known personalist account of work.[23] Drawing heavily on the book of Genesis, he maintains that work reflects divine creation and possesses both objective and subjective dimensions. Objectively, it includes "what a human being does when dominating the earth" (LE, 5). Subjectively, it leads to the "self-realization of the person," and its value "does not depend on the type of work done, but on the person who is doing the work" (ibid., 6). Work promotes the values of the useful and enjoyable, but at its heart, it also "expresses and increases the worker's dignity" (ibid., 9). By distinguishing between subjective and objective elements of works, John Paul II shows how the economic order shapes the person.

Despite this positive treatment of work, John Paul II also criticizes economic approaches that elevate values of the useful over spiritual values. He attacks "economism," which emphasizes the priority of capital over labor. In it, "capital and tools become two opposed impersonal forces" that take on "greater importance than the spiritual and human" (LE, 13). Consequently, the worker becomes a "cog" in a "huge machine moved from above" (ibid., 15). The Church opposes this vision, affirming that "work concerns not only the economy, but also, and mainly, personal values" (ibid.). It seeks to reverse perversions in our relation to values, changing the way "we are thinking and doing, so that the worker is put first and labor above capital" (ibid., 13). Economism embodies an intentionality of use, because it views work as "merchandise" that the worker sells to her employer (ibid., 7). Work loses its connection to the person, becoming a "threat to the right order of values" (ibid.). Often, this development occurs thoughtlessly, merely reflecting a practical orientation toward the useful. People become so busy that they forget why they are working. However, occasionally, individuals and societies adopt it as a philosophical position that explicitly rejects spiritual values. In either case, we have an "axiological reduction" of values as dramatic as what we find in sexual relations. It also illustrates the entrenched forms of idolatry characterizing the international economic order. They take the form of "greed and the thirst for power," making everything "a commodity to be bought" (SR, 37).[24] John Paul II insists that state and society must resist "an idolatry of the market," which "cannot do all that should be done" (CA, 40). For him, commodification betrays a profound ignorance about the nature of values. Moral and spiritual values are qualitatively different from other values and cannot become commodities.

With some justification, critics charge that John Paul II sometimes adopts a moralistic tone, a "prophetic" stance that overlooks the complexities of economic policy. However, his discussion of idolatry has more depth than initially meets the eye. Idolatry orients the self toward a restricted order of values. Greed and the drive for power distort our *ordo amoris* by directing love toward finite and impersonal goods unworthy of such attention. As a person becomes increasingly attached to an idol of class or market, the "deeper human hopes remain unsatisfied and even stifled," diminishing the person's being (SR, 28). Thus, "having more things only helps us when it contributes to a more complete "being" (ibid.).[25] Ignoring spiritual and moral values, however, "makes the person a prisoner of economic planning and selfish profit," and technological and material progress "will prove unsatisfactory and even debasing" (ibid.,

33). We do not merely find ourselves in this condition, but *will* to move away from the rich values of the person, and toward lower values.[26]

This effort will never be successful unless we relate properly to God. In "Sollicitudo Rei Socialis," John Paul II maintains that economic injustice originates not solely in failed political will, negligence, or mistakes, but in our drive for independence from God. Structures of sin arise when "God's will, God's plan for humanity, God's mercy and justice—expressed in the Ten Commandments—are not respected" (SR, 36). Similarly, in "Laborem Exercens" John Paul II argues that economism originates when we abandon "God's original intention for us" (LE, 9). Workers, he tells us, should have no doubt that a personalist approach to work is "God's intention" (ibid., 25). The disease of economism is, therefore, ultimately linked to the refusal to acknowledge divine goodness. When considering value distortions, we must always consider them in light of humanity's "ways of denial."

The Perils of Globalization

In tone, "Centesimus Annus" is less "prophetic" than John Paul II's earlier discussions of sin in the economic order and perhaps reflects the optimism accompanying the end of the Cold War. However, the 1990s saw significant changes in international economics, requiring a different kind of analysis. As Robert Gilpin notes, the term *globalization* captures these trends, referring to "the increasing linkage of national economies through trade, financial flows, and foreign direct investment (FDI) by multinational firms" (Gilpin 2000, 299). New markets in the former Soviet Union and Eastern Europe, rapid movement of capital, the growth in the power of international economic institutions, and the 1997 Asian financial crisis led many to think hard about markets and morality.

John Paul II frequently entered debates about these developments, and I see no evidence that he abandoned his conditional support of the market. Nevertheless, he became deeply worried about globalization's dangers. He focuses his criticisms on the idea of value-free economics, axiological distortions in the global economy, and cultural homogenization. When considering economics and other social sciences, he notes that far from being foreign to economics and business, they [values] help to make them a fully "human" science and activity. An economy which takes no account of the ethical dimension and does not seek to serve the good of the person—of every person and the whole person—cannot really call itself an "economy" understood in the sense of a rational and constructive use of material wealth. (2000Peace, sec. 16)

All too frequently, John Paul II argues, we have seen post–Cold War economic policies that ignore spiritual values, emphasizing economics as a technical discipline concerned only with material advancement. Addressing American bishops in Mexico City in 1999, he noted:

More and more, in many countries of America, a system known as "neo-liberalism" prevails; based on a purely economic conception of man, this system considers profit and the law of the market as its only parameters, to the detriment of the dignity of and the respect due to individuals and peoples. At times this system has become the ideological justification for certain attitudes and behavior in the social and political spheres leading to the neglect of the weaker members of society. Indeed, the poor are becoming ever more numerous, victims of specific policies and structures which are often unjust. (1999America, sec. 56)

In this speech, what obviously disturbs him is how economic policy focuses solely on material values. This distortion eliminates from policy consideration what is most important in human life. I agree with Michael Therrien, who argues that this speech gives little warrant for a whole-sale condemnation of the free market. Instead, it criticizes economic reductionism, "a worldview held by certain free-market economists who believe man's social existence should be understood primarily in terms of economic considerations. This system of belief has led many to ap-proach the market as though moral norms have no bearing upon market activity" (Therrien 2000, sec. 4). Alarmed by such reductionism, John Paul II condemns it.

John Paul II expresses similar concerns about international environ-mental policy. Too often, nations see environmental problems as technical issues, focusing their energies on the minutiae of scientific and economic data. Although indispensable, we should never isolate this knowledge from the values of the person. John Paul II insists that "the protection of the environment is not only a *technical* question; it is also and above all an *ethical* issue. All have a moral duty to care for the environment, not only for their own good but also for the good of future generations" (1999Asia, sec. 41). Unfortunately, debates about limiting greenhouse gases or other issues in international environmental policy often focus narrowly on economic growth or other indexes of economic health.

As a social science, John Paul II maintains, economics cannot divorce itself from moral values. Throughout his papacy, he has carefully engaged various sciences, affirming their insights but rejecting how some people use them in a reductionistic and amoral fashion.[27] For example, he repeatedly speaks about genetic technology, arguing that it cannot disregard the value of the person. He rejects a value-free approach to scientific advances, and his criticisms of economics are part of this larger critique. Speaking before the Pontifical Academy of Social Sciences in 2000, he warned that social doctrines must "not ignore the spiritual nature of human beings, their deep longing for happiness and their supernatural destiny which transcends the merely biological and material aspects of life" (2000Science, sec. 15). Ethical principles must guide economic policy, and we should challenge the concept of "prosperity itself," in order to "prevent it from being enclosed in a narrow utilitarian perspective which leaves very little space for values such as solidarity and altruism" (2000Peace, sec. 15).

Unfortunately, with disastrous consequences, international economic policy sometimes ignores these principles, and John Paul II traces globalization's negative elements directly to a diminished relation to values. For example, in his travels during the late 1990s, he cited a litany of social and economic problems, including the drug trade, corruption, terrorism, regional arms races, racial and ethnic discrimination, religious intolerance, and income inequality. Keenly aware of their complexity, he returns again and again to the idea that we cannot address them without altering our hierarchy of value. For example, speaking to American bishops in 1999, he insisted that social sins "are the sign of a deep crisis caused by the loss of a sense of God and the absence of those moral principles which should guide the life of every person. In the absence of moral points of reference, an unbridled greed for wealth and power takes over, obscuring any Gospel-based vision of social reality" (1999America, sec. 59). During the Jubilee celebrations, he held a Jubilee for workers, noting that globalization's distortions are an invitation to address the economic and social imbalances in the world of work by re-establishing the right hierarchy of values, giving priority to the dignity of working men and women and to their freedom, responsibility and participation. It also spurs us to redress situations of injustice by safeguarding each people's culture and different models of development. (2000Workers, sec. 3)

Globalization has brought tremendous changes in the workplace, particularly in the areas of finance and information technology. These require rediscovering the personalist nature of work, and unless this occurs, workers will again become tools to be used by others. In a radically new workplace, we must consider how work arrangements shape our relations to values. Despite the development of the Internet and the new workplace symbolized by Silicon Valley, workers and employers must still recognize the ever-present danger of the love of use.

Axiological distortions may also marginalize segments of the population. Repeatedly, John Paul II notes how some countries lack the resources to benefit from the massive changes in the international economic system. Eloquently, he warns that "Our world is entering the new millennium burdened by the contradictions of an economic, cultural and technological progress which offers immense possibilities to a fortunate few, while leaving millions of others not only on the margins of progress but in living conditions far below the minimum demanded by human dignity" (NMI, section 50). Eight years after issuing "Centesimus Annus," he again voiced concerns about equal access to the markets stating:

Within the framework of a liberalism without adequate controls, the gap between the "emerging" and the "losing" countries is widening. The former have capital and technologies that allow them to enjoy the world's resources at will, a possibility that they do not always use with a spirit of solidarity and sharing. The latter, instead, do not have easy access to the resources needed for adequate human development, and sometimes even lack the means of subsistence; crushed by debt and torn by internal divisions, they often end up wasting their meager wealth on war. (1999Migration, sec. 3)

The market allocates goods and services efficiently, but only for those who have access to it. An untrammeled world market may raise some living standards but cannot address economic inequalities without considering spiritual and moral values.

In addition to these concerns about inequality, John Paul II joins those who see in globalization a force for cultural homogenization. Speaking to Asian bishops in 1999, he noted that

> there is also the aspect of a *cultural* globalization, made possible by the modern communications media, which is quickly drawing Asian societies into a global consumer culture that is both secularist and materialistic. The result is an eroding of traditional family and social values which until now had sustained peoples and societies. All of this makes it clear that *the ethical and moral aspects of globalization* need to be more directly addressed by the leaders of nations and by organizations concerned with human promotion. (1999Asia, sec. 39)

International economic policy often implicitly endorses philosophical materialism, thereby denigrating the cultural heritages of the countries it affects. In fact, "everywhere the media impose new scales of values which are often arbitrary and basically materialistic, in the face of which it is difficult to maintain a lively commitment to the values of the Gospel" (1999America, sec. 20). John Paul II emphasizes this theme when speaking to American audiences, identifying it as a particular difficulty in industrialized nations like the United States.

At first glance, these criticisms of globalization seem like pretty standard fare in globalization debates. Globalization's critics attribute a litany of ills to it, often bemoaning the commercialism that undermines cultural diversity. In the last decade, some activists have condemned globalization thoughtlessly, offering a series of clichés about cultural diversity and economic growth that have little analytic power. These critiques demonstrate extraordinary ignorance of international economics and have little ethical or theological substance. Moreover, since the September 11 terrorist attacks on the United States, they risk legitimizing nihilistic violence designed to destroy international financial institutions. No one has ever identified John Paul II with the radical fringes of the antiglobalization movements, but some scholars argue that he embraces a simplistic view of global economics. For example, Gilpin charges that he is among the "communitarian" critics of globalization who "argue that international trade and activities of multinational corporations are leading to increased international inequality" (Gilpin 2000, 300). He sharply criticizes communitarians, arguing that they exaggerate the extent of globalization, overlook how important the state is in the economic order, and ignore significant empirical data indicating that globalization has contributed little to global inequality. Whatever the merits of Gilpin's criticisms, they point to a risk in John Paul II's discussions of globalization. Repeatedly, he warns that the Church should avoid endorsing particular economic models. However, he often uses controversial economic ideas like dependency theory and neoliberalism, making empirical claims that some consider to be unsophisticated and ill-informed. Consequently, he risks alienating those with expertise in international economics, jeopardizing his stature as a moral leader.

Nevertheless, a closer look at John Paul II's critique of globalization reveals that it is more than just another antiglobalization diatribe. Like Scheler, who decried modernity's leveling effect on culture, he is concerned about how cultural homogeneity diminishes our relation to value. Often, globalization aggressively displaces attachments to nationality and local culture, all in the name of a uniform global culture. John Paul II sees this as a dangerous development because it overlooks how persons develop within a particular *ordo amoris*. People are, he notes, "marked by the culture whose very air they breathe through the family and the social groups around them, through education and the most varied influences of their environment, through the very relationship which they have with the place in which they live" (2000Peace, sec. 5). They bear a unique culture, and without having it as the "structuring element" of their personalities, they are vulnerable to "an excess of conflicting stimuli which could impair their serene and balanced development" (ibid., sec. 6). Globalization often threatens to undermine cultures that protect persons from such forces.

Globalization may also diminish the person because it conforms her to a culture that neglects our relationship to God. Humanity's rejection of God is one of John Paul II's deepest concerns about globalization. He accuses Western nations of promoting a materialism that undermines a commitment to God and persons. For example, he charges that "Western cultural models are enticing and alluring because of their remarkable scientific and technical cast, but regrettably there is growing evidence of their deepening human, spiritual and moral impoverishment. The culture which produces such models is marked by the fatal attempt to secure the good of humanity by eliminating God, the Supreme Good" (ibid., sec. 9). Looking forward into the twenty-first century, he warns that if globalization continues to produce this effect, we are likely to relive the "tragic events of the twentieth century" or propagate the "the nihilism present in some prominent circles in the Western world" (ibid.).

Thus, John Paul II grounds his criticisms of globalization in his axiology and conception of the person. His speeches and writings in the 1990s illustrate that for him, globalization's negative effects are not an inevitable consequence of impersonal forces. Too often, rapid global changes seem utterly impersonal and anonymous, and no one seems responsible for them. For example, in 1997, many in Thailand and Indonesia suddenly confronted a major recession, brought about by the rapid movement of capital out of their countries. Partly a product of changes in information technology and corruption within Southeast Asia, this sudden change baffled many of its victims. They struggled to explain it, targeting the International Monetary Fund for responsibility for the crisis.[28] In analyzing such developments, John Paul II warns that the Church lacks a program providing easy solutions. What he contributes to debates about globalization is his resistance to depersonalizing the international economic system. Undoubtedly, technological developments, bloated bureaucracies, and corruption create economic chaos. However, human choice also plays a significant role, and John Paul II always returns to our will and internal life. Critics may see this as unsophisticated and condemn him for failing to understand collective action. Nevertheless, for him, the person and his choices should always be the primary focus of analysis. Anything else is a dehumanizing distortion of the proper order of values.

The Dangers of Nationalism

We see this same concern for the person and values when John Paul II discusses nationalism. Scholars note how globalization creates both economic integration and dangerous nationalism. For example, Canadian journalist Michael Ignatieff describes two narratives about international politics, noting that the "story of globalization tells us that the world is becoming one," while the narrative of fragmentation is "chaos" (Ignatieff 1997, 97). Stanley Hoffmann notes that the post–Cold War international system shows signs of both increasing interdependence and increasing fragmentation. Nationalism is a driving force of fragmentation, leading to ethnic and political conflict.[29] Finally, Robert McNamara and James Blight argue that despite interdependence, ethnic and political groups clamor for self-determination, creating a dangerous situation that international leaders must approach carefully (McNamara and Blight 2001). For many people, the September 11 terrorist attacks on the United States perfectly illustrated the forces of fragmentation. The al-Qaeda terrorists possessed a dark vision of the world, embracing disorder as a *modus operandi*. They deliberately targeted the World Trade Center because it is a symbol of tremendous economic success in the 1990s. Such destructive acts are likely to remain part of international politics for many years.

John Paul II has shown remarkable awareness of these developments, focusing particularly on nationalism's destructive potential. He began expressing concerns about it shortly after the Cold War ended, and he has eloquently warned of its dangers for many years. As early as 1991, in "Centesimus Annus," he warned that "when a culture becomes inward-looking, and tries to perpetuate obsolete ways of living rejecting any dialogue, it is heading for its end" (CA, 50). In 1994, he stated that

> after 1989 however there arose *new dangers and threats.* In the countries of the former Eastern bloc, after the fall of Communism, there appeared the serious threat of exaggerated nationalism, as is evident from events in the Balkans and other neighboring areas. This obliges the European nations to make a serious *examination of conscience,* and to acknowledge faults and errors, both economic and political, resulting from imperialist policies carried out in the previous and present centuries vis-à-vis nations whose rights have been systematically violated. (TMA, sec. 27)

When discussing nationalism, however, he confronts a conceptual and political difficulty. Prima facie, his criticisms of globalization as a ho-mogenizing and leveling force seem to support it. Nationalists often frame their commitment to statehood in spiritual and moral terms, arguing that globalization diminishes cultural diversity. For example, those fighting the war in the former Yugoslavia in the 1990s appealed to cultural and religious values to support their causes. Symbols of the nation and calls to retrieve the glories of the past played an important role in galvanizing populations to support war. In such cases, John Paul II cannot legitimately criticize nationalists for subordinating the spiritual to the material, for they often agree with him about the debasing character of globalization. Moreover, post–Cold War politics has brought many oppressed minority groups freedom, and nationalism appears to expand our relation to values by allowing neglected cultures to express themselves. Therefore, how can John Paul II legitimately criticize nationalism as a distortion of values?

In the early 1990s, he began addressing this difficult problem, and in his 1995 speech to the United Nations General Assembly, he suggests one way of approaching it. He describes the changes in international politics as a sign of "an extraordinary global acceleration of that quest for freedom which is one of the great dynamics of human history" (1995UN, 2). He emphasizes that international politics must affirm a universal conception of human nature, warning that without it, we cannot reduce conflict and foster economic justice. Human rights, he argues, make no sense if people around the world are essentially different and cannot communicate with one another. In a world of incommensurable cultures, we have no reason to affirm that persons far away from us have value and dignity.

Within this framework of a universal human nature, John Paul II discusses nationalism. During the Cold War, he notes, the Soviet Union artificially and unjustly violated the rights of nations. The Baltic States and "extensive territories in Ukraine and Belarus were absorbed into the Soviet Union, as had already happened to Armenia, Azerbaijan, and Georgia in the Caucasus" (1995UN, 5).[30] The end of the Cold War high-lighted this injustice for many people in the world. Taking his audience back to fifteenth century, John Paul II reminds it of that period's debate about sovereignty and the rights of nations. Reiterating key elements of globalization, he notes that

we see the powerful re-emergence of a certain ethnic and cultural consciousness, as it were an explosive need for identity and survival, a sort of
counterweight to the tendency toward uniformity. This is a phenomenon
which must not be underestimated or regarded as a simple left-over of

the past. It demands serious interpretation, and a closer examination on the levels of anthropology, ethics and law. (1995UN, 7)

Some thinkers recognize this tension between the universal and the particular in contemporary politics. However, unlike many of them, John Paul II immediately turns to the person. Globalization highlights a tension between the universal and the particular that "can be considered immanent in human beings" (ibid.). We share a universal human nature, but a particular historical and social location conditions it. This conditioning binds us in an intense way to particular communities, yet we are also aware of what we share with people beyond them. Consequently, the "human condition thus finds itself between these two poles—universality and particularity—with a vital tension between them; an inevitable tension, but singularly fruitful if they are lived in a calm and balanced way" (ibid.).

Unfortunately, many nationalistic movements around the globe fail to achieve anywhere near this balance. Nationalism is particularly dangerous, because it restricts spiritual and moral values to one nation or ethnic group. As both John Paul II and Scheler repeatedly emphasize, spiritual values are preeminent over other values because they endure and can be shared with others. Consequently, when a nationalist maintains that he is promoting spiritual values while excluding and oppressing others, he undermines what is distinctive about them. This axiological distortion, John Paul II argues, is too often a product of fear.[31] Mentioning the wars in the Balkans and Central Africa, he suggests:

> The fact of "difference," and the reality of "the other," can sometimes be felt as a burden, or even as a threat. Amplified by historic grievances and exacerbated by the manipulations of the unscrupulous, the fear of "difference" can lead to a denial of the very humanity of "the other" with the result that people fall into a cycle of violence in which no one is spared, not even the children.[32]

Although he does not explicitly mention it, the 1994 genocide in Rwanda exemplifies this fear of difference. In that terrible event, Hutus massacred hundreds of thousands of Tutsi, including thousands of children. Leading up to this massacre, Hutu leaders labeled the Tutsi "cockroaches," and this vicious rhetoric fueled a grassroots genocide in which people hacked each other to death with machetes and crude weapons. This horror occurred not long before the United Nations speech, and could not have been far from John Paul II's mind.

In an illuminating essay entitled "The Narcissism of Minor Differences," Ignatieff notes that a virulent nationalist takes

> the neutral facts about a person—their language, habitat, culture, tradition, and history—and turns these facts into a narrative whose purpose is to illuminate the self-consciousness of a group, to enable them to think of themselves as a nation with a claim to self-determination. A nationalist, in other words, takes "minor differences"—indifferent in themselves—and transforms them into major differences. (Ignatieff 1997, 51)

Ignatieff notes how the "systematic overvaluation of the self results in systematic devaluation of strangers and outsiders" (ibid.). Narcissism, he maintains, takes the form of anxiety and an extreme self-absorption, leading to an "investment in intolerance" that makes nationalism "so uniquely unresponsive to rational argument" (ibid., 53). Drawing on his experience in the former Yugoslavia, Ignatieff describes in disturbing detail how this process moves from nonviolent expressions to genocidal fury, creating a cycle of violence and retaliation.

John Paul II helps us understand these dynamics by emphasizing how virulent nationalism turns the intentionality of the will onto itself and the group. It perverts the movement of our love, directing it toward objects undeserving of such focus. As Ignatieff notes, with extreme nationalism, "traditions are invented, a glorious past is gilded and refurbished for public consumption, and a people who might not have thought of themselves as a people at all suddenly begin to dream of themselves as a nation" (Ignatieff 1997, 51). Superficially, to desperate people, this may seem like an expansion of values, an opening to communal values unavailable to solitary individuals or families. However, this is precisely nationalism's false promise, for it limits our relationship to value by severing us from other groups or cultures.

Such distortion also alienates us from God. For John Paul II, culture is an attempt to "ponder the mystery of the world and in particular of the human person; it is a way of giving expression to the transcendent dimension of human life. The heart of every culture is its approach to the greatest of all mysteries; the mystery of God" (1995UN, 9). Diverse attempts to probe it demand our respect, even when we disagree with them. Culture reflects the internal life of persons, taking "shape from an impulse by which human individuality seeks to rise above its limitations in an interior drive to communicate and share" (1999Culture, section 2). Thus, international political arrangements must acknowledge cultural differences. In fact, to "cut oneself off from the reality of difference—or, worse, to attempt to stamp out that difference—is to cut oneself off from the possibility of sounding the depths of the mystery of human life" (1995UN, 10).[33] In such sentences, John Paul II condemns narrow forms of nationalism by appealing to a vision of human persons who transcend themselves through culture. In interpreting culture theistically, he enables us to see virulent nationalism as a refusal to acknowledge God's richness. It falsely assumes that because the nation is the highest value, other nations or communities lack value. Although modernity has seen many nations claim that God is entirely on their side, John Paul II undermines such claims by celebrating cultural diversity as a reflection of the divine.

Thus, John Paul II considers the problem of nationalism in light of the intentionality of the will, love, and alienation from God. Undoubtedly, political arrangements, long-standing grievances suppressed by Cold War politics, and economic globalization all foment nationalism. However, John Paul II also emphasizes how nationalism reflects and distorts the values of the person. It starkly reveals our distorted *ordo amoris* with its perverse desire to be independent from God.

Conclusion

In 1944, Reinhold Niebuhr attacked "foolish children of light" who underestimated "the power of self-interest, both individual and collective, in modern society" (Niebuhr 1944, 11). These people embrace a "superficial and facile view of man" that consistently underestimates the "problem of anarchy and chaos on both the national and international level of community" (ibid.). Niebuhr blamed the children of light for misjudging the "children of darkness," who pursue naked self-interest undisciplined by any commitment to a higher good. For him, their mistakes contributed to the horrors of the Second World War.

In this chapter, I have argued that we cannot credibly view John Paul II as one of the "foolish children of light." I have painted a somewhat one-sided picture of his philosophical anthropology, ignoring his discussions of grace, repentance, and redemption. However, I have done so deliberately, in order to counter the charge that he is naïve about human nature, a claim that contemporary thinkers sometimes level against him. He is immune to this charge precisely because he uses his philosophical project to analyze sin. Sin involves willingness to use others merely as a means to our ends, and it reflects a distortion in our intentional relation to values. Rather than ranking the moral and spiritual values highest, we use persons merely as a means for pursuing lower values. Ultimately, this axiological reduction originates in our attempt to be independent from God. Despite the complex social, political, and economic forces conditioning this distortion, John Paul II insists that we apply the term *sin* to social structures only analogically. Otherwise, we succumb to the conceptual confusion of applying a personal concept to impersonal structures and risk embracing one of the many forms of determinism so prominent in twentieth-century thought.

Analyzing the international economic system, John Paul II denounces the greed and drive for power that produce vast inequities of wealth and resources. Exploring the problem of increased nationalism after the Cold War, he condemns nationalists who elevate the nation to the highest value, committing horrific crimes in its name. In considering both topics, John Paul II displays his knowledge of international and economic affairs and clearly keeps abreast of changes in thinking about them. However, what most characterizes his analysis is its axiological dimension. Time and again, he returns to the distortions in our intentional relation to values, urging us to reorient our persons toward the proper order of values. This focus on values, more than anything else, allows him to develop a conception of the human fault that matches anything the political realist tradition has to offer.

Niebuhr and other realists are very successful in showing how hidden positive assumptions about human nature enter into the idealist's arguments. By including these assumptions, the idealist is able to avoid the dilemmas of political realism. However, what happens if a thinker accepts the realist assumptions about the distorted character of human nature? Machiavelli, Weber, Morgenthau, and many other realists maintain that if one understands human depravity, one must either allow evil to prevail or accept an ethic of consequences. This is the force of Weber's famous distinction between an "ethic of responsibility" and an "ethic of ultimate concerns." Although ideal-types, these concepts point to a choice that anyone entering politics must make. She must decide whether to calculate the consequences of her actions or adhere to moral rules and submit to evil forces. For Weber and many other realists, there really is no other choice for the politician. Someone who refuses to accept responsibility for the consequences of political action belongs outside of politics.

In the next chapter, I will suggest that although this picture is deeply compelling, John Paul II articulates another option. Because he cannot be credibly accused of underestimating human evil, it would seem that he must either endorse consequentialism or retreat into a politically in-effective ethic of rules. Yet, I will argue that his sophisticated axiology challenges the coherence of consequentialism and offers a political ethics differing fundamentally from that of the political realists.

3

An Ethic of Responsibility Is neither Responsible nor Feasible

John Paul II and Consequentialism

A distinction must be drawn between the moral and social behavior of individuals and of social groups, national, racial and economic . . . this distinction justifies and necessitates political policies which a purely individualistic ethic must always find embarrassing.

Reinhold Niebuhr[1]

Utilitarianism often has devastating political consequences, because it inspires an aggressive nationalism on the basis of which the subjugation, for example, of a smaller or weaker nation is claimed to be a good thing solely because it corresponds to the national interest.

Pope John Paul II[2]

In 1973, Michael Walzer wrote a well-known article on the ethics of torture. He asked his readers to imagine a scenario in which a politician captures a rebel with information about a ticking time bomb. Should he torture him in order to extract this information? Carefully analyzing this case under the rubric of the "problem of dirty hands," Walzer maintained that the politician would be morally justified in using torture. Nevertheless, he would also be guilty of a moral crime that would leave his hands sullied. In political and moral thought, Walzer's article created a rich dialogue about moral guilt and consequentialism. This discussion, however, remained largely an academic one, conducted by moral philosophers, theologians, and political theorists.

In the aftermath of the September 11 terrorist attacks on the United States, circumstances have changed, and the ethics of torture has now become a matter of public discussion. Soon after the attacks, noted legal scholar and public figure Alan Dershowitz urged the U.S. government to issue "torture warrants" that would institutionalize the torture of suspected al-Qaeda terrorists (Dershowitz 2002). These documents would specify precisely how and when torture could be used. This way, Dershowitz argued, we could closely monitor law enforcement officials, ensuring that they torture only within established bounds. Bruce Hoffmann wrote sympathetically about soldiers in Algeria and Sri Lanka who tortured suspects (Hoffmann 2002). Michael J. Glennon reported that 45 percent of Americans surveyed believed it would be justifiable to torture Taliban and al-Qaeda prisoners if they had information about future terrorist attacks (Glennon 2002). For some people, the potential consequences of saving lives appeared to outweigh the moral indecencies of torture.

Such sentiments would come as no surprise to political realists like Machiavelli and Weber. In disorderly times, human beings are likely to embrace an ethic of consequences in order to preserve their security. However, political realists go further, arguing not only that chaos often breeds such an ethics but also that it *ought* to do so. For example, writing about political ethics, Morgenthau advises statesmen to exercise prudence and avoid appealing to universal moral principles. Powerfully depicting the pursuit of political power, he declares that "realism, then, considers prudence—the weighing of the consequences of alternative political actions—to be the supreme virtue in politics" (Morgenthau 1985, 13). Individuals may evaluate their actions using moral laws, but politicians should always weigh the consequences of their acts. Morgenthau wielded consequentialism like a club, making him a formidable presence in American public life during the Cold War. For example, he was an early critic of the Vietnam War, condemning it as a dangerous adventure that harmed the

U.S. national interest. American policy-makers, he maintained, pursued policies grounded in moral abstractions, with terrible consequences for Americans and people of other countries.[3] More recently, Robert Kaplan, a controversial American journalist, has presented political realism as a model for diplomacy. Describing anarchy in West Africa, he urges the United States and other powers to reduce their aspirations for democracy and to focus instead on enhancing order. Echoing Reinhold Niebuhr, he writes that the defining characteristic of realism is the idea that "international relations are governed by moral principles different than domestic politics" (Kaplan 2002, 103). Like Morgenthau, he believes that foreign policy must adopt a consequentialist ethic. U.S. foreign policy in the 1990s, Kaplan argues, ignored consequences, moralistically trumpeting its support for democracy and free markets, while harming large numbers of people. Like their ancestors, realists like Kaplan claim that the pursuit of power *requires* the statesman to weigh the consequences of his actions. Power-seeking political actors rarely respond to moral suasion, they argue, and responsible statesmen should never count on rare recognitions of the moral law. Instead, they must embody prudence, carefully navigating their way around a disordered world. Unless they embrace an ethic of consequences, they cannot successfully battle evil, and will invariably perish at the hands of those who have no moral scruples.

Among Roman Catholic thinkers, debates about political consequentialism have focused heavily on "moral absolutes." Basic goods theorists and others maintain that regardless of circumstances, there are some things people should never do. To put this in technical language, there are "intrinsically evil acts" that are "certain kinds of behavior that are always wrong to choose, because choosing them involves a disorder of the will, that is, a moral evil" (VS, 78). Proportionalists either deny that such acts exist or insist that we can identify them only by using proportionate reasoning, weighing good and evil acts in order to arrive at a proportionately just act. In recent years, the debate about this topic has been complex and heated, with charge and countercharge. Much of it focuses correctly on action theory, with the structure of the human act as a key question in the dispute. For example, should we define acts primarily by their object, or do circumstances play some role in defining them? Among others, Germain Grisez, John Finnis, Jean Porter, and Richard A. McCormick, S.J., have all made important contributions to this discussion.

This debate is seminal for political realism because if intrinsically evil acts exist, then the realist's counsel to govern politics by an ethic of consequences is obviously flawed. Nevertheless, the contours of the debate about action theory are well defined, and I will not rehearse them.[4] Instead, I will focus on value theory, a crucial part of consequentialism. As the utilitarian Russell Hardin put it more than a decade ago, the greatest difficulties for utilitarianism are in its value theory, which has "come to seem increasingly problematic as it has been increasingly investigated and understood" (Hardin 1988, xvii).

John Paul II exploits this weakness in consequentialism, and I now turn to his theory of value. First, I consider his arguments that consequentialism cannot calculate the consequences of action and harms the weak. I suggest that without further elaboration, they do little to undermine consequentialist reasoning. Second, I discuss John Paul II's claim that consequentialism embraces a distorted value-theory and violates the personalist norm. This compelling thesis undercuts forms of consequentialism based on pleasure or preference, but consistent consequentialists can resist it. Third, I consider John Paul II's claim that consequentialism inadequately grounds moral norms, because it cannot quantify indivisible spiritual values. This argument differs from basic goods theory because it presupposes a hierarchy of value. Fourth, I defend this argument against four objections often appearing in contemporary Roman Catholic moral thought. Some thinkers claim both that we cannot establish an objective hierarchy of value and that hierarchies of values tell us little about how to act. Others argue that we need an "ethical currency" in order to sustain a hierarchy of value, or cite the common practice of weighing values as evidence that we can measure them. I maintain that all these criticisms ignore how John Paul II develops his hierarchy of value. Using both a Thomistic conception of being and lived experience, he maintains that we *apprehend* the fundamental distinction between spiritual and material values. Unfortunately, contemporary basic goods theorists and proportionalists embrace a defective understanding of value and obligation and therefore completely misunderstand how John Paul II radically challenges their positions. Finally, focusing on Robert Kaplan's political realism and George Weigel's moderate Christian realism, I demonstrate how John Paul II undermines a realist ethic of consequences.

Utilitarianism: Impractical and Dangerous?

For much of his career, John Paul II has been deeply concerned about utilitarianism. He discusses it in his early plays, Lublin lectures, writings on sexual ethics, and economic writings. Despite this long-standing interest, however, he often uses the term *utilitarianism* imprecisely, assuming his readers understand what he means. Additionally, he rarely distinguishes between its types. For example, he ignores differences between rule and act utilitarianism, fails to distinguish between utilitarianism and consequentialism, says little about modern welfare economics, and never carefully discusses preference utilitarianism. Despite this imprecision, we can identify two arguments John Paul II often makes against utilitarianism. The first focuses on its incapacity to calculate consequences. In a highly controversial section of "Veritatis Splendor," John Paul II identifies "certain 'teleological' theories" that "draw their norms to evaluate the rightness of an action from the weighing of the goods to be gained and the consequent values to be respected" (VS, 74). These theories, he acknowledges, are helpful in rationally ordering societies, but as a basis of an ethic, they are "false solutions" that undermine moral norms. Almost casually, he notes that consequentialism fails because "everyone recognizes the difficulty or impossibility of evaluating all the good and evil consequences of one's own acts" (ibid., 77). Contemplating acting, we can never have satisfactory knowledge of the consequences of our actions and therefore cannot know which will yield the greatest good. Epistemologically, our knowledge and powers of prediction are too limited to perform this task.

More commonly, John Paul II argues that consequentialism harms the weak and defenseless. For example, in his 1995 speech to the United Nations, he characterizes utilitarianism as the doctrine that "defines morality not in terms of what is good but of what is advantageous" (1995UN, 13). He charges that it enables large nations to subjugate smaller ones in the name of national interest. Similarly, in "Evangelium Vitae," John Paul II argues that utilitarianism leads some to devalue the lives of others. The modern state often "arrogates to itself the right to dispose of the life of the weakest and most defenseless members, from the unborn child to the elderly, in the name of a public interest that is nothing but interest of one part" (EV, 20). Carefully linking materialism and utilitarianism, he repeatedly maintains that both undercut the value of human life. Finally, in "Centesimus Annus," John Paul II condemns forms of political consequentialism that subordinate the person to the collective. When political leaders "think that, possessing the secret of a perfect social organization, they can make evil impossible, they also think they can use any means, even violence and deceit, to realize it" (CA, 25). Utopianism combined with ethical consequentialism has disastrous consequences, destroying the person in the name of slogans or abstractions.

Many utilitarians find such arguments unconvincing. Since the days of Jeremy Bentham and John Stuart Mill, critics have charged that consequentialism has negative effects and is impractical. To the first charge, utilitarians often respond by denying that they require calculating the utility of every act. For example, Mill recognizes the impossibility of such calculations, and appeals to human experience as a stable source for judgments about the utility of acts. We have, he suggests, "intermediate generalizations" that guide our action, and have no need to reinvent the wheel every time we act (Mill 1979, ch. 2). Many utilitarians follow Mill, defending what is known as rule utilitarianism, the idea that people should employ rules that have utilitarian benefits. They grant that moral agents can never know everything about the consequences of their acts, and concede that demanding such a calculation would paralyze them. They argue, however, that people should employ "rules of thumb" that have long-term beneficial consequences.[5] Following these rules, they can avoid assessing consequences each time they act. For example, a soldier going to war need not calculate whether he should adhere to the principle of noncombatant immunity but can follow it, knowing that it does more good than harm.

Many utilitarians, in fact, emphasize the limits of reason, arguing that utilitarianism has the conceptual resources to respond to them. For example, game-theorist Hardin maintains that reason's limits make utilitarianism attractive. Legal rights and other institutional devices enable agents to adjust to poor information, and promote long-range utility. In fact, Hardin maintains, "one of the first lessons of any serious attention to the problem of rationality is that a complete account of everything involved in one's significant decisions is not possible" (Hardin 1988, 1). Limited information, diverse actors, and rapid social changes all make predicting consequences very difficult. Nevertheless, Hardin maintains, utilitarianism responds well to these difficulties, because it devises institutions taking them into account. He and other utilitarians see the appeal to poor information as a red herring that does little to challenge their position.

Similarly, utilitarians strenuously object to the charge that their position harms the weak. First, they maintain that critics of utilitarianism focus excessively on situations of extremity, ignoring utilitarianism's import for everyday decisions. For example, Philip Pettit acknowledges that in horrendous circumstances, a utilitarian may have to act in morally repugnant ways. However, he insists that such circumstances are rare, and once we realize this, the claim that utilitarianism can be harmful "ceases to be clearly damaging" (Pettit 1991, 234). All ethics, Pettit maintains, have to condone some evil, and on this score, utilitarianism is no worse off than any other position. Second, consequentialists often argue that consequentialism, in fact, protects the weak. "Situation ethicist" Joseph Fletcher famously condemned legalism, arguing that excessive adherence to ethical rules damages human persons. Recognizing that some principles are necessary to guide us, he nevertheless rejected rules in favor of utilitarianism (Fletcher 1966). A host of philosophical ethicists in the last few decades have agreed with him, devising examples of extreme circumstances in which adhering to moral rules causes deep harm. For example, I have mentioned "trolley problems" that place moral agents in circumstances in which they must steer a trolley toward one person, killing her, or veer off the track, killing many others.[6] In these circumstances, utilitarians argue, adhering to a moral rule embodies a self-indulgent concern for one's own moral integrity. Or, perhaps worse, it represents a rule-worship that values rules over persons. In either case, the utilitarian maintains that her approach to ethics does more good in the long run than any adherence to rules. Those who reject it are themselves guilty of harming the weak in the name of abstractions.

These utilitarian rejoinders are inadequate, but John Paul II seems unaware of disputes about them, and his argument is therefore incomplete.[7] His charges that utilitarianism is impractical and fails to protect the weak require a much longer argument than he provides. Too often, he states a correct conclusion but offers little in the way of argument, leaving utilitarianism unscathed. Such a well-developed tradition of moral reasoning will not collapse under the weight of a few general arguments.

Consequentialism: A Perversion of Value
and the Antithesis of Love

In addition to these superficial criticisms, John Paul II also offers a
more precise critique of consequentialism, appearing primarily in *Love and
Responsibility*. There, he acknowledges that "utilitarianism has undergone
a complicated evolution since the days of its founders"(Wojtyla 1960,
292 n. 13). He then criticizes hedonistic utilitarianism and all forms of
utilitarianism to the "extent that they represent an instrumentalist and
reductionist view of the human person" (ibid.). Hedonistic utilitarianism
evaluates actions by how much pleasure they produce, arguing that the
best action is the one that generates the most pleasure. In his critique,
John Paul II focuses carefully on the goal of maximizing pleasure. Acknowledging its attractiveness, he agrees that few people willingly forgo
pleasure and seek pain. Yet he maintains that on a closer look, the maxim
of increasing pleasure is superficial because pleasure is "essentially incidental, contingent, something which may occur in the course of action"
(ibid., 36). Hedonistic utilitarians mistakenly take pleasure as the *end*
of human activity, whereas it is *incidental* to it. They also fail to distinguish between pursuing pleasure and pursuing something producing a
pleasurable effect. I may run a marathon because I value a sound body,
and as a side effect, I experience pleasure (once the race is over!). In this
case, I produce pleasure without it motivating my actions.

In this discussion of hedonistic utilitarianism, Scheler's influence on
John Paul II is very strong. Repeatedly, Scheler attacks utilitarianism
because it directs us toward ephemeral lower values. Utilitarianism, he
observes, reduces all value modalities to the sensible or useful. Purporting to provide an understanding of morality, it instead offers only a
theory of social praise and blame within a particular society.[8] Additionally, Scheler maintains that because the sensible values are founded on
higher values, it is absurd to make them the goal of our action. Pleasure,
he maintains, is founded on vital values because it can be experienced
only by a mind that "acts through some specific form and organization
of *life* which, taken as a *whole*, represents a certain vital *value*" (Scheler
1961, 150). Scheler also applies his well-known account of *ressentiment* to
utilitarianism, arguing that modernity embraces utilitarianism because

it perversely elevates values of sensibility and utility over higher values.[9] *Ressentiment* arises when those incapable of achieving higher values turn against them, creating a debasing countersystem of values. With utilitarianism, those incapable of developing higher values reduce all value to lower values, basely denying that higher values exist.

Freely adopting Scheler's position, John Paul II also draws on Kant's work, arguing that utilitarianism violates the personalistic norm. If we act primarily for pleasure, he argues, persons inevitably become mere means to an end. When I accept pleasure as the highest goal, "I must see myself as a subject desirous of as many experiences with a positive affective charge as possible, and at the same time as an object which may be called upon to provide such experiences for others" (Wojtyla 1960, 37). Others become merely a means for achieving my pleasure, while I become similarly objectified for them. In other words, we find ourselves violating the personalistic norm. In such a world, concern for the inner life of the person disappears, and human interaction produces short-term relationships that link persons together only for as long as they remain useful to each other. Pleasure is ephemeral, highly individual, and rarely transsubjective. Once it subsides, pleasure-maximizing creatures abandon painful relationships to seek pleasure elsewhere. They maintain fidelity to others only by adopting "a fiction, a semblance of altruism" (Wojtyla 1960, 38). They decide to value someone else's pleasure as long as it gives them pleasure. However, once others interfere with their pleasure, their obligation to further the well-being of others disappears.

Without any objective conception of pleasure, we confront unstable social relations that undermine trust and other social virtues. A utilitarian may respond by proposing that we harmonize egoisms, but John Paul II argues that this proposal is incompatible with self-giving love. For example, we might create a social order in which persons *agree* to enter into long-term pleasure-producing relationships. We might even adopt an explicit contract codifying such social arrangements. Yet harmonizing egos remains egoism nevertheless, and on the utilitarian account, love can only be "a union of egoism, which can hold together" only on condition that people "confront each other with nothing unpleasant, nothing to conflict with their mutual pleasure" (Wojtyla 1960, 39). A paradoxical situation obtains; each person seeks her own gratification, but consents to serve another's egoism. Such mutual egoism clashes with the gift of self so essential to love, because the person approaches another only to turn back to the self.[10] Instead of moving from lower to higher values, she moves from higher to lower, reducing all values to the ego's pleasure. She sees others not as unique and unrepeatable, but as objects for mutual satisfaction. She never gives her "I" to another but remains possessive of it. The interior act of giving and accepting the other as a gift is completely missing, making the *communio personarum* impossible. Thus, in John Paul II's view, hedonistic utilitarianism is entirely incompatible with the highest form of love. By relating ourselves intentionally to lower values, using other people, and moving primarily toward the self, we sever our relationship to higher values. The result is a sadly diminished person.

By focusing on the hierarchy of value, the personalist norm, and love, John Paul II presents a convincing case against hedonistic utilitarianism. I also think that it is telling against some contemporary versions of preference utilitarianism. Preference utilitarianism proposes that we maximize the preferences of people within a community. Generally, its theorists avoid morally evaluating the *kinds* of preferences people have. I may prefer classical music, while you prefer heavy metal, but I cannot claim that my preference is superior to yours. As Hardin puts it, theorists often "stipulate simply that the satisfaction of what people want is, with corrections for misunderstandings and akratic tendencies that run against their interests, good" (Hardin 1988, 202). Methodologically, this amounts to subjectivism about values. In fact, Hardin boldly states that "we commonly assert with Hume, and rightly so, that values are not objective" (ibid, 169). Although not characterizing all forms of preference utilitarianism, this axiology is common among preference utilitarians.

Like its hedonistic cousin, preference utilitarianism allows us to use and debase persons. In the social order it devises, persons can devote themselves to the lowest values, utterly ignoring higher values like beauty or truth. They may freely use each other for "preference-satisfaction," disregarding the personalistic norm. We *may* find among a person's preferences an appreciation of a person's value, but this remains an optional preference, not required by the preference utilitarian position. Moreover, if we make no judgments about the direction or object of our love, we countenance a *modus vivendi* that may do little to promote human dignity. Someone pursuing preference satisfaction may disregard self-giving love, refusing to see others as gifts. Those making policy may embrace the lowest common denominator that ignores what is most important in humanity, our capacity to give ourselves fully to others.

In sum, to my knowledge, John Paul II never focuses explicitly on preference utilitarianism. Nevertheless, his critique of hedonistic utilitarianism clearly applies to it. Prima facie, preference utilitarianism represents "an instrumentalist and reductionist view of the human person" that violates the personalist norm and undermines the highest forms of love.

A Compelling but Incomplete Critique

Although compelling, this critique remains an external one that some utilitarians are unlikely to find persuasive. First, they may reject the personalistic norm as an antiquated remainder from religious ethics. For example, J. C. Smart ends his debate with Bernard Williams by acknowledging that circumstances may arise in which a consistent utilitarian "ought to be unjust" (Smart and Williams 1973, 71). Acknowledging that they are rare and tragic, he nevertheless accepts the possibility that one may use others merely as a means to an end. To take a more recent example, Peter Singer insists that the "traditional ethic of the sanctity of human life" has collapsed (Singer 1994). Dismissing the idea that each person has intrinsic value, he calls for radical changes in how we treat infants and animals, notoriously maintaining that infanticide may be morally justifiable. To thinkers like Singer and Smart, John Paul II's appeal to the personalistic norm carries little weight and does nothing to challenge utilitarianism.

Second, utilitarians like Hardin simply deny that values are objective, and therefore reject the idea that we can objectively judge some to be higher than others. Some simply define value in terms of what people are willing to pay. For example, in a seminal text that shaped the modern Law and Economics movement, Richard Posner develops an economic analysis of justice. Law and Economics, a movement developed at the University of Chicago in the last half of the twentieth century, uses economics to analyze the law. Posner, one of its chief architects, is critical of some variants of utilitarianism, but he focuses his analysis on preference satisfaction. Deftly analyzing issues as varied as child-rearing and pollution, he uses wealth as a key conceptual tool. For him, "the wealth of a society is the aggregate satisfaction of those preferences" that are "backed up by money, that is, that are registered in the market" (Posner 1981, 61). This kind of analysis not only ignores the personalistic norm, but also denies the objectivity of values. It allows people to debase themselves by pursuing lower values but accepts this implication.

John Paul II and the Indivisibility of Spiritual Values

Responding to such challenges, John Paul II presents another argument against consequentialism based on his distinction between spiritual and material values. Both critics and proponents of consequentialism recognize that it uses some "currency" or common yardstick to evaluate whether an act promotes the good. Otherwise, how could we say that one state of affairs produces greater good than another? Historically, thinkers like Bentham and Mill used pleasure, differing over its precise nature. Other utilitarians have proffered preference, proposing sophisticated ways to measure it. This history clearly demonstrates that "what is proposed is a computation" (Finnis 1983, 87). A consequentialist must find some way of measuring various values along a scale.

Both Scheler and John Paul II maintain that this project is problematic, because it ignores the fundamental difference between spiritual and material values. Recall that for both thinkers, spiritual values differ from material ones because they are indivisible. I cannot divide beauty into distinct parts that I can distribute. Moreover, material values are divisible and have a limited capacity to satisfy our needs, often producing conflicts. In contrast, spiritual values are indivisible, and their capacity to satisfy is unlimited and undiminished by increasing the number of persons enjoying them. The indivisibility of spiritual values makes it difficult to calculate them in any precise manner. How can I include beauty and holiness in a calculus if I cannot divide them? Without such a division, it is difficult to see how the consequentialist project can ever succeed. John Paul II notes that it should not surprise us that historically, utilitarianism first focused on pleasure, something we can supposedly measure. However, a calculus of value is "all the more difficult to apply in practice when the highest good which is the measure of all particular goods is understood in any but a straightforwardly sensual way" (Wojtyla 1960, 293 n. 13). Utilitarianism is attractive precisely because it pretends to be able to calculate. Moreover, it involves a danger "that 'calculable' goods will be preferred to those whose realization sometimes takes a long time and considerable dedication, and which are themselves not measurable" (ibid., 300 n. 38). Values related to love are particularly difficult to measure. For example, how we give ourselves to others does not admit of precise quantification. Consequently, in a technocratic and scientistic culture, people will often abandon self-giving love in favor of measurable values.

The value of the person is particularly difficult to measure. Crosby notes that persons are not subject to the "laws of numerical quantity" (Crosby 1996, 50). Undoubtedly, we can, and in many situations, should, consider persons in terms of their physical natures. Crosby cites population estimates as a proper arena for such calculations. However, as a person, "no person becomes small in the presence" of many others, and "no one comes to represent an inconsiderable quantity in the realm of personal being, and to be overwhelmed by the many other persons" (ibid.).[11] Consequently, calculations involving spiritual values make little sense. John Paul II never affirms a strict incommensurability thesis, but he does argue that calculating spiritual goods makes little sense. Proposals to ground an ethic in computations of value often simply ignore spiritual values, focusing solely on material ones. Or they include spiritual goods in their calculus but, when confronted with their indivisibility, rely on ad hoc or subjectivist intuitions to commensurate values. Either way, consequentialism is a shaky foundation for ethics.

Let me illustrate John Paul II's thesis with a few examples. Earlier, I mentioned the Law and Economics movement. It embraces a reductionistic ethic, measuring value according to "what people are willing to pay for" (Posner 1981, 60). It assumes we can measure what people are willing to pay for, and then quantify the wealth of a society. However, how can we quantify spiritual values linked to love? Perhaps a Law and Economics scholar might say that all she is doing is measuring how much a person prefers these values, leaving measurement problems to the individual. In fact, Law and Economics scholars often adopt this view, scoffing at the common intuition that some things cannot be bought or sold. However, this response only shifts the measurement problem to individuals. How can they measure spiritual values and ascertain how much they are willing to pay for them in a marketplace? John Paul II's analysis suggests that they cannot do so, because they cannot divide them into measurable units or commensurate their spiritual and material values. Consequently, the Law and Economics scholar provides no guidance for moral choice.

Similarly, if we cannot divide and measure spiritual values, consequentialist analyses of noncombatant immunity falter. For example, Richard Brandt once offered a utilitarian defense of rules in warfare. Rational, impartial people in appropriate contractual circumstances, he argued, would endorse rules of war like noncombatant immunity because they "maximize expectable utility generally" better than alternative arrangements (Brandt 1974, 32). If John Paul II is right about spiritual values, however, Brandt's rule utilitarianism cannot, in principle, measure the overall utility of the rules of war. If we restrict our calculation to material values, we may be able to ascertain that rules of war promote overall utility. However, if we expand it to include spiritual values, it is difficult to see how we can make judgments about future utility. How do we measure how violating rules of war affects our capacity to love? How do we calculate the aesthetic values we gain or lose by adhering to rules of war? These are only some of the questions rule utilitarians rarely address.

Rules are essential in political life, and nothing in John Paul II's position requires that we jettison them, plunging us into political and social chaos. We can make tentative calculations involving material values or only one spiritual value. We can also argue that a rule protects a specific value. However, we cannot go further and argue that rules involving multiple values of different kinds promote overall goodness. More importantly, John Paul II demonstrates why calculating consequences cannot support the core of our moral life. As he maintains in "Veritatis Splendor," one can never come to "an absolute obligation" based on "debatable" calculations" (VS, 77). A calculation about consequences can only have a tentative character that cannot sustain a sound ethic.

Basic Goods Theorists and the Incommensurability of Basic Goods

The charge that we cannot calculate values should be familiar to those who have followed debates about proportionalism over the last several decades. Contemporary basic goods theorists propose a strict incommensurability thesis that has provoked considerable controversy. Germain Grisez, John Finnis, and Robert P. George all argue that consequentialism cannot, in principle, calculate consequences. Proportionalists like Richard A. McCormick, S.J., Edward Vacek, S.J., and Garth Hallett, S.J., respond by proposing ways to commensurate goods. The result has been a lively and important debate about theories of value.

Despite surface similarities to basic goods theory, however, John Paul II's argument differs from it because he presupposes a different theory of value. To illustrate this difference, let me consider Finnis's well-known version of the incommensurability thesis. Finnis relies on the controversial idea of a "basic good"; a basic good is a good that is not instrumental to actualizing another good but provides a terminus of explanation for why a person acts. We come to understand that a good is basic through an act of noninferential insight, which is not based on deductive or inductive arguments (Finnis 1980, 63–69). Finnis puts it this way:

> My method has been the method of practical understanding and reasoning itself. That involves attention both to one's own inclinations and to the whole range of possibilities open to one. By an insight which is not an "intuition" (because it is not made in the absence of data, nor by any "noticeable" intellectual act) and not a deduction or inference from one *proposition* to another, one understands some of those inclinations as inclinations towards *desirable* objects, and some of those possibilities as opportunities rather than dead-ends. (Finnis 1983, 51)

Using this insight, Finnis distinguishes between purely instrumental and basic goods, making basic goods a key element of his theory of value. He develops a list of basic goods that includes life, knowledge, play, aesthetic experience, sociability, practical reasonableness, and religion (Finnis 1980, 85–90). He emphasizes that this list is not exhaustive, acknowledging that other theorists have developed alternative inventories.

Finnis insists that basic goods are all equally fundamental, using this idea to attack consequentialism. For him, there is "no objective hierarchy" among basic goods (Finnis 1980, 92). For example, when we focus on knowledge, it seems more important than anything else. However, if we shift our attention to life, it also appears to be the most fundamental good. Individuals may and often do establish hierarchies, but only on the basis of subjective reasons indexed to their personalities. As Finnis notes, these reasons "properly relate to one's temperament, upbring- ing, capacities and opportunities, not to differences of rank of intrinsic value between the basic values" (ibid., 94). In other words, basic goods are incommensurable; there is no way we can rank them or weigh one against the other. Consequentialism assumes, Finnis argues, that we can compute basic goods and maximize the good, but if basic goods are incommensurable, this calculus is clearly impossible. The only way to maximize the good would be to assume that one basic good is more important than others, viewing all others in terms of it. However, this is untenable, and therefore Finnis dismisses consequentialism as a valid way of structuring the moral life.

Along with Grisez and George, Finnis has rehearsed and refined this critique of consequentialism in many places. Whatever its merits, how- ever, exegetically, I do not believe we can identify basic goods theory with John Paul II's theory of value. Basic goods theorists consistently ignore his many discussions of a hierarchy of values. There is little or no trace in his work of the idea that basic values are fundamentally equal. In fact, John Paul II draws on two ethical traditions that explicitly reject the equality of values. We have already seen how he critically retrieves Scheler's hierarchy of value, which on the face it of directly contradicts the claims of basic goods theorists. Similarly, in his writings on Thomas Aquinas, John Paul II repeatedly argues for a hierarchy of value. For ex- ample, he writes that Thomas "places supernatural goods above natural goods, goods of the soul above goods of the body, and internal goods (of the human being) above external goods (things)" (Wojtyla 1993, 90).[12] This hierarchy of goods "contains a general directive for every choice made by the human will," representing one of Aquinas's important contributions to ethics (ibid.). Whether or not John Paul II interprets Thomas correctly is certainly open to debate, but we cannot legitimately read him as a supporter of the equality of goods.

Additionally, I think reading John Paul II as a basic goods theorist makes nonsense of his compelling discussion of martyrdom. For example, in "Veritatis Splendor," he insists that "martyrdom confirms in an elo- quent way that moral norms are valid without exception" (VS, 90). Prima facie, this appeal to martyrdom is an odd way to support moral absolutes.

What precisely can it tell us about a controversial question in ethics? In contemporary ethics, martyrdom rarely appears as a topic, except in discussions about defining suicide and distinguishing between intentional and unintentional killing. However, John Paul II's interest lies elsewhere. For him, martyrdom illustrates the possibility of fidelity to God's law in extreme circumstances, dramatically refuting the claim that adhering to moral norms is impossible. It "rejects as false and illusionary whatever 'human meaning' one might claim to attribute even in 'exceptional' circumstances to an act that is morally evil in itself" (ibid., 92). It represents the "high point of the witness all Christians must daily be ready to give," one that may require "heroic commitment" (ibid., 93).

For John Paul II, life is neither the highest good nor equal to other basic goods. In fact, through her heroic sacrifice, the martyr demonstrates the preeminence of spiritual values. Her martyrdom reawakens a commitment to these values even in the darkest times, exalting the best in a person. Throughout his papacy, John Paul II has repeatedly made this point, leaving no doubt that spiritual values are more important than material or vital ones. For example, in eloquent testimony honoring Bernhard Lichtenberg and Karl Leisner, two Germans martyred during the Second World War, he notes:

> History put them both to a difficult test, but they were not afraid of "those who kill the body." The frightful totalitarian systems condemned to death, on an unparalleled scale, those who did not submit to the system. In this manner they sought to dominate souls. Our blesseds, however, drew from Christ's words the certainty that they "cannot kill the soul." This is how their victory is to be understood. They achieved this victory because they acknowledged Christ before others: "every one who acknowledges me before men, I also will acknowledge before my Father who is in heaven" (Mt 10:32). (1996Lichtenberg and Leisner, sec. 1)

These martyrs demonstrate that spiritual values are far more important than vital values such as life or the political values of the nation-state. We cannot reconcile such affirmations of the importance of martyrdom with basic goods theory. For John Paul II, spiritual values connected to the person are architectonic, ordering other values. There is not and cannot be an equality among values.

The Inequality between Spiritual
and Material Values

Thus, exegetically, John Paul II is clearly no basic goods theorist.
However, philosophically, what should we make of his differences with
basic goods theorists? Are they merely a matter of emphasis, or do they
signify something important?[13] To address this question, let me consider
why basic goods theorists refuse to rank values. Responding to Russell
Hittenger's criticisms, Robert P. George repeatedly maintains that we
cannot establish an "objective" hierarchy of values or goods, reducing
basic goods to each other or to some common feature constitutive of
their value (George 1999, 271). Like Finnis, George believes we can
take differing perspectives from within the viewpoint of values. From
a particular perspective, one basic good appears preeminent, but this is
an epistemological reality, implying nothing ontologically. If we change
viewpoints, another basic good will appear preeminent.

Unfortunately, in this discussion, George ignores John Paul II's sophisticated use of both Thomism and phenomenology. To establish a hierarchy
of value, the pope utilizes a "cosmological" and a "personalist" approach
to the person.[14] A cosmological approach, as Crosby notes, studies human
beings in terms of "substance, potentiality, rationality, and the like," while
the personalist approach considers human beings in terms of "self-presence,
inwardness, self-donation" (Crosby 1996, 82). We cannot derive the personalist approach from the cosmological one, but it is not "the antinomy
of the cosmological type, but its complement" (ibid., 213).

I think this distinction illustrates John Paul II's philosophical project
very clearly, and it is vitally important for understanding his ethic.
Thinking cosmologically, he uses the Thomistic categories of being and
perfection to establish the person's preeminent value. For example, in
the opening pages of *Love and Responsibility,* he distinguishes between
persons and things, asserting that there is a "great gulf which separates
the world of persons from the world of things" (Wojtyla 1960, 21). A
person possesses greater perfection than things because he has an inner
life organized around truth and goodness. He differs from a thing in
"structure and degree of perfection," and "possesses spiritual perfect-
ibility, and is by way of being an (embodied) spirit, not merely a 'body'

magnificently endowed with life. Between the psyche of an animal and the spirituality of a man there is an enormous distance, an uncrossable gulf" (ibid.). The ontological structure of the person reveals how he differs in value from material things.

John Paul II uses this Thomistic framework dramatically in his writings on evolutionary theories. For example, in his pivotal 1996 letter on evolution, he affirms scientific theories of evolution. However, he warns Catholics to selectively embrace them and reject those that presuppose philosophical materialism. There is, he writes, an "ontological leap" in the history of evolution, through which humanity emerges (1996Truth, sec. 6). Unlike with any other creature, God directly creates each person with a spiritual soul. Drawing on Aquinas, John Paul II identifies both the soul's intellectual capacities and its power to form relationships as signs of its spiritual nature. His remarks are worth quoting at length:

> With his intellect and his will, he [man] is capable of forming a relationship of communion, solidarity and self-giving with his peers. St. Thomas observes that man's likeness to God resides especially in his speculative intellect, for his relationship with the object of his knowledge resembles God's relationship with what he has created (*Summa Theologica* I–II:3–5, ad. 1). But even more, man is called to enter into a relationship of knowledge and love with God himself, a relationship which will find its complete fulfillment beyond time, in eternity. (1996Truth, section 5)

This important statement illustrates perfectly how John Paul II uses Thomism to develop his hierarchy of value. Ontologically, persons have spiritual souls that give them a greater value than material objects or other animals.[15] They can enter into relationships of love with other persons and with God. Christians must, therefore, firmly reject any scientific theory that denies the ontological difference between persons and other animals. There should be no question, therefore, that the person's value is grounded in being itself. Those who fail to see how persons and things differ suffer from deep philosophical ignorance.

When he adopts the personalist approach, John Paul II defends induction and reduction as ways we experience the difference between persons and things. Induction is not a form of argument, as it is for many modern philosophers. Instead, it is the transition from "the multiplicity and complexity of 'factual' data to the grasping of its essential sameness" (Wojtyla 1979, 14). The mind grasps meaning out of multiplicity, without repudiating the diversity of experience. For example, out of the multiplicity of what we perceive, we come to distinguish between things and persons. John Paul II closely links induction to reduction, the attempt to "convert to suitable arguments and items of evidence or, in other words, to reason, explain, and interpret" (ibid., 17). Through induction, we grasp the person in her acts, and then through reduction, reason about this experience, revealing the deeper elements of her personhood. Gradually, we arrive at "an intentional image of the object, an image that is adequate and coincident with the object itself" (ibid.).

Kupczak helps us understand this process by noting that in *The Acting Person,* John Paul II describes two forms of the "stabilization of the object of experience" (Kupczak 2000, 70–71). The first, which both humans and other animals perform, occurs when the mind uses individuals to capture how "particular sets of sense qualities converge" (Wojtyla 1979, 6). The second, peculiar to human experience, occurs when the mind stabilizes experience using "mental discrimination and classification" (ibid.). It yields the knowledge of the human person so essential to anthropology and ethics.[16] For example, it enables us to recognize persons in other countries who are entitled to human rights. Kupczak notes that this method of induction has deep roots in Aristotelian and Thomistic traditions but is also compatible with modern phenomenology.[17]

I agree with Kupczak's analysis but want to describe the movement toward knowledge of the person in more depth in order to highlight how John Paul II uses phenomenology. *Induction* is an Aristotelian term, and John Paul II often uses it interchangeably with phenomenological terms like "categorial knowledge" and "eidetic intuition." Josef Seifert suggests that perhaps "this concept of 'induction' is too broad, and may not precisely capture various forms of intuition" (Seifert 1981, 9).[18] I agree, and I propose to restrict the concept of induction to categorial intuition of value, rather than eidetic insight.[19] Categorial intuition is "the kind of intending that articulates states of affairs and propositions, the kind that functions when we predicate, relate, collect, and introduce logical operations into what we experience" (Sokolowski 2000, 88). Initially, we passively perceive an object, zero in on one of its aspects, and then interrupt the flow of perception, grasping a whole. The last stage of this process is *categorial intuition,* because "the categorial object, the thing [. . .] in its articulation, is made actually present to us" (ibid., 90). Sokolowski summarizes categorial intuition by saying that we move "from sensibility to intellection, from mere experiencing to an initial understanding" (ibid.).[20] The second term, *eidetic intuition,* a central concept in Husserlian phenomenology, involves the "grasp of an eidos or form. We can intuit, or make present to ourselves, not only individuals with their features, but also the essence things have" (ibid., 177).[21] Eidetic intuition is essential for deepening our knowledge of what we encounter in the world.

In writing about the person's value, John Paul II describes a categorial intuition of both a person's existence and value. Initially, when we relate to another human being, we apprehend him as a member of species, yielding knowledge of the "human being" (Wojtyla 1993, 200).[22] We apprehend a person-action relation that unifies various acts. Categorial knowledge of species membership also includes awareness of a person's features and value, which may be only implicit. For example, I may be fixated on a person's body but am "simultaneously aware" of the value of her personhood (Wojtyla 1960, 122). I know that I am encountering a 'someone' rather than a thing," an awareness that is "ever present in consciousness" (ibid.). I do not have the same experience of a domestic animal or my computer. John Paul II sometimes uses the word "sense" to describe it (Kupczak 2000, 74). Confronting the person and his acts, we have a sense that he has "an existence that is real and objectively independent of the cognizing subject and the subject's cognitive act" (Wojtyla 1993, 115).[23] We grasp that he differs in value from a thing, even if this apprehension is muted or even distorted by sin.

Is this apprehension of the person some irrational process that mysteriously produces knowledge? Too often, those working in Anglo-American ethics view it as such, associating the language of intuition with the British intuitionism of the mid-twentieth century. However, John Paul II is working from a completely different philosophical tradition that uses terms like *intuition* and *perception* carefully.[24] Here, I think Dietrich von Hildebrand can help us understand the perception of value we find in John Paul II.[25] Von Hildebrand details the elements of value-perception, understanding perception much more broadly than do most Anglo-American philosophers. Value-perception is a cognitive act, involving a direct contact with a value, in this case, the value of the person. His value *presents* itself to me; I neither invent it nor construct it from sense data or my cultural heritage (von Hildebrand 1953, 229). This presentation requires no deduction or induction, in the modern sense of the term. I encounter the person directly, and he bestows a new knowledge on my mind, in von Hildebrand's phrase, "fecundating" it.[26] Finally, in value-perception, the person's value unfolds itself to me intuitively. I learn more about it not by positing it or representing it, but through immediate and direct contact with it. Von Hildebrand illustrates how we grasp the value of the person, even inchoately, through a direct contact with values. For John Paul II, this encounter makes us aware of the fundamental axiological difference between persons and things. We come to know that the person is "not to be compared with anything in the world outside the world of persons" (Wojtyla 1960, 290 n. 4).

Although indispensable, this knowledge only opens the way to knowing the person. (Wojtyla 1960, 201). It is a necessary but not sufficient condition for further understanding him. Von Hildebrand puts this nicely by saying that the disclosure of species and genus is "decidedly not equivalent to a philosophical *prise de conscience* of it and still less to a complete knowledge of it" (von Hildebrand 1960, 113). A philosophical *prise de conscience* is an "acute and fully conscious awareness of facts which are presupposed and thus in some way known in our lived contact with being" (ibid., 136). The perception of the person's value produces only a very general awareness, but can it "do justice to *man as a person?*" (Wojtyla 1993, 269). To understand the person in his particularity, we must consider his action, and this is why John Paul II develops his complex philosophy of action. Action, he thinks, "gives us the best insight into the inherent essence of the person and allows us to understand the person most fully" (Wojtyla 1979, 11). Perceiving species membership and its value "somehow provokes the mind to the effort of grasping and explaining as fully as possible the reality of person and action when it has been apprehended" (ibid., introd., sec. 3).[27] This is what John Paul II means by the term *reduction.* It differs from the various reductionist projects we find in the modern social sciences, which attempt to reduce the person to biological or psychological processes. Reduction gradually reveals a personality, a person's particularity, something we become aware of by experiencing his acts. I realize that he, like me, is a unique and unrepeatable being.

I will not rehearse the details of this reduction, the subject of *The Acting Person*. What I want to emphasize instead is that it gradually leads to an "eidetic insight" of the person. The person's action "allows us at the same time to 'get an insight' into the very dynamic reality of the person, allows, and even more demands it, for *the act is the fullest manifestation of man-person in the dynamism proper only to him*" (Wojtyla 1976, 278). We never grasp the entire person and, at some point, arrive at a moment that "defies reduction," a moment that merely reveals and discloses the "person's essence" (Wojtyla 1993, 213). At this point, we must "pause at the irreducible," recognizing that "everything in the human being that is invisible and wholly internal and whereby each human being, myself included, is an 'eyewitness' of his or her own self—of his or her own humanity and person" (ibid., 214).[28] What is revealed stubbornly resists attempts to reduce it to philosophical categories, calling instead for awe and respect.

In analyzing our knowledge of the person, John Paul II masterfully brings together phenomenological and Thomistic elements of his thought. Cosmologically, the person is a spiritual soul, created by God, and capable of knowing and loving God. Metaphysically, we must articulate what all human beings share; otherwise, we cannot begin to understand the personhood of others. However, John Paul II also suggests that a strictly metaphysical analysis fails to capture an individual's uniqueness. It is only through a personalist examination that we come to know the person's irreducible elements. On my reading, John Paul II moves us from an initial categorial knowledge of species membership and value to an eidetic insight into a person's particularity.[29] Through either the personalistic or the cosmological approach, we can clearly distinguish between the value of the person and other values. Both methods, therefore, enable us to develop a hierarchy of values.

Given this compelling argument, it is hard to understand why Finnis, George, and others believe it impossible to establish an "objective" hierarchy of value. Do they reject the preeminent value of the person? Do they think we cannot know his value? Do they maintain that we cannot apprehend the difference in value between persons and things? I can only speculate about why basic goods theorists ignore John Paul II's careful arguments. I think that intuitionism has cast such a spell on them that they retreat from any ideas about apprehending values. They may see John Paul II's personalist approach as nothing more than old-style intuitionism, which disappeared with W. D. Ross and his ilk. For example, Finnis admirably rejects the argument that intentions, meanings, and truth are "queer" entities having no place in our everyday or scientific discourse (Finnis 1984, 57–60). He also refutes various forms of subjectivism, showing how they are self-defeating. Nevertheless, he shows little awareness of the phenomenological apprehension of value developed by John Paul II and others in the twentieth century. Repeatedly, he rejects the charge that he is intuiting value from metaphysics or an account of human nature.[30] He views with suspicion any appeal to moral intuitions, arguing that they are often a product of cultural conditioning or emotion (Finnis 1983, 125–26).

Like many contemporary thinkers, Finnis pays little attention to phenomenology. In his lifetime, Scheler confronted charges that he was a "subjectivist" or "cultural relativist" who reduced ethics to the ethos of a particular era. He responded carefully to them, critically engaging the social sciences. Making use of Husserl's brilliant attack on nominalism, he refuted relativism.[31] In my mind, his compelling arguments should disabuse any reader of the idea that Scheler is an intuititionist in the way Finnis uses the term. Similarly, we cannot reasonably classify John Paul II's method of induction and reduction as intuitionism. Instead, it involves rigorous reflection on human experience, yielding knowledge of the person's value. This method, with its roots in both Thomistic and phenomenological traditions, enables us to ground our axiology in the value of the person.

The person is, undoubtedly, mysterious, and we must reveal rather than demonstrate her existence. In fact, John Paul II often refuses to demonstrate the realities we grasp through induction and reduction. Discussing the connection between morality and humanity, he states that "we do not prove and we do not feel the need to prove that this connection occurs" (Wojtyla 1993, 121). The demand that we provide such demonstrations ignores a key insight of both Thomism and phenomenology. Both traditions maintain, over against so much of modern philosophy, that we cannot know without using induction, insight, or some grasping of essences. Such a project, far from being antithetical to metaphysics, supports it. Unfortunately, influenced by previous generations' experience with intuitionism, contemporary thinkers falsely identify positions with it and arbitrarily declare them to be irrational.

Can a Hierarchy of Value Tell Us How to Act?
A Story of Strange Bedfellows

Although sophisticated, John Paul II's arguments may, nevertheless, seem impractical to some contemporary thinkers. In fact, strangely, basic goods theorists join forces with proportionalists to argue that even if a hierarchy of value exists, it has no import for action.[32] For example, focusing on hypothetical conflicts between religious obligations and other activities, George argues that we cannot resolve them by using a hierarchy of value. Do our religious obligations require us to attend religious services rather than go to work? Do we behave immorally if we listen to music rather than attend Mass? Appealing to the preeminence of spiritual values, George maintains, cannot answer such questions. Summarizing his conclusion about knowledge of spiritual values, he states that nothing in judgments about God's existence and nature "need alter one's grasp of foundational practical and moral principles, nor one's basic understanding of how to employ these principles in one's practical thinking" (George 1999, 72). Hallett echoes George's argument, systematically denying the practical import of a hierarchy of value. A hierarchy of value, he argues, makes no "connection with concrete action verdicts" (Hallett 1995, 148). Abstract value ordering cannot adjudicate between rival courses of action unless we know the probability, extent, and kind of values involved. Hallett also maintains that defending a hierarchy of value requires that we hold that "any higher value, no matter how slight or unsure," must take precedence "over any lower value, however massive and certain" (ibid.). However, this is utterly implausible, because many situations require us to choose lower over higher values. For example, if I am certain that walking will enhance my health but have little certainty about enjoying a concert, why not choose the vital over the spiritual value? Hallett sees no convincing reason to choose the higher value in such circumstances. He also maintains that vague concepts like "spiritual," "material," or "aesthetic" provide insufficient content with which to make decisions. We cannot, he says, compare "uniform essences with uniform essences," such as the essence of the "aesthetic" with the essence of the "religious" (ibid.). These labels yield no clear ideas and, therefore, tell us little about how to act.

Significantly, Hallett also charges that we cannot have a hierarchy of value without some "ethical currency" with which to compare values. How can we know, he asks, that one value is preeminent over another if we cannot measure values? Either we have some way of commensurating values, or we refuse to declare one value superior to another. For example, Hallett notes that when Jesus says persons are worth more than sparrows (Matt. 10:31), he presupposes some way of comparing the value of persons and sparrows. Here is what he says on this matter:

> The standard objections to transcategory comparisons—the lack of any "principle" or "method," the absence of any "common scale" or "common denominator," the impossibility of "measuring" the reliance on mere "intuition"—would rule out this and similar gospel comparisons. Otherwise, he [Jesus] would be unable to make the claim he makes. (Hallett 1995, 25)

Those who believe that spiritual and material values are incommensurable, Hallett suggests, simply cannot make sense of Jesus' comparisons.

Thus, for all their differences, basic goods theorists and proportionalists agree that a hierarchy of value has little import for moral decision-making. They believe that ranking values tells us little about how to act when they conflict and produces bizarre preferences for higher values. Moreover, hierarchies of value rest on ill-defined language and presuppose an undefined ethical currency. In sum, even if a hierarchy of value exists, it is useless as a guide for moral action.

To respond to these challenges, let me note that John Paul II agrees that a hierarchy of value cannot answer all moral questions. This is why he argues carefully in his habilitation thesis and Lublin writings that Scheler's ethic is ultimately unsuitable for Christian ethics. In his mind, Scheler fails to recognize the experience of obligation, neglecting the importance of moral laws. By itself, John Paul II notes, a hierarchy of value provides only remote directives for choice, but ethics requires more proximate directives that only norms can provide.[33] In "Veritatis Splendor," John Paul II makes this point clearly, insisting that "human freedom finds its fulfillment precisely in the acceptance" of the law (VS, 35).[34] The Decalogue and the

Sermon on the Mount both confront us with the law in inescapable ways. Throughout John Paul II's corpus, we find many such affirmations of the necessity for norms and the law, and they should leave no doubt that for him, a hierarchy of value alone provides insufficient guidance for action.

Nevertheless, despite these arguments, John Paul II would never agree that a hierarchy of value has, as Hallett maintains, "no connection with concrete action-verdicts." On the contrary, he insists that ranking values is vitally important for moral action. Let me consider Hallett's example of Jesus and the sparrows. In this case, a hierarchy indicates clearly that we ought to choose a person's life over that of a sparrow. Someone who chooses the sparrow's life makes a perverted choice, because she ignores the fundamental differences between the value of persons and animals. The probability of actualizing the value in this choice is irrelevant. It is one thing to say that a hierarchy of value by itself provides insufficient ethical guidance, and another to say that it offers no guidance. These are two different claims that George, Hallett, and others uncritically conflate.

The Dreaded "Is-Ought" Problem

I think some contemporary thinkers disregard the importance of a hierarchy of value because they possess defective understandings of value and obligation. For example, Finnis, George, and others repeatedly refer to the "is-ought," problem, arguing that we cannot infer or deduce moral obligation from metaphysical or biological premises.[35] George notes that "logically, a valid conclusion cannot introduce something that is not in the premises" (George 1999, 88). Putting the matter precisely, he insists that "basic practical principles and the specific moral norms derived from them cannot be deduced, inferred, or, in any strict sense, derived from purely theoretical premises" (ibid., 91 n. 20). Similarly, Finnis often considers the "is-ought" problem," taking great pains to deny he is deriving moral norms from claims about human nature.[36] Because the "is-ought" problem is so central to how basic goods theorists formulate their position, it should be obvious that a hierarchy of value by itself can have little import for them. Claims about hierarchies of value are "is" claims that cannot yield a moral "ought." Consequently, basic goods theorists spend little time considering them.

In operating within this "is-ought" framework, basic goods theorists again depart from John Paul II, who rejects it in several places in his corpus. For example, in *Love and Responsibility,* he argues that the "is-ought" fallacy applies only to forms of ethics that artificially separate natural realities from value. In particular, in debates about sexual ethics, critics often raise the specter of "biologism," the illicit practice of deriving an ought from biological data. John Paul II maintains that this charge illegitimately assumes "in advance that the sexual urge in man has only a biological sense, that it is a purely natural fact" (Wojtyla 1960, 294–95 n. 20). However, this assumption strips the natural world of its axiological dimension, representing an untenable form of biological reductionism. Strongly, John Paul II charges that those invoking the "is-ought" deny the importance of the cognition of value. In *The Acting Person,* John Paul II returns to the "is-ought" question, explicitly arguing that it has little philosophical merit (Wojtyla 1979, 162).[37] Through conscience, he maintains, we confront the truth so essential to our action. Once we apprehend it, it is then "the normative function of the evaluated and recognized truth to condition not only the performance of an action by the person but also his fulfillment of himself in action" (ibid., 161). Carefully, John Paul II describes the transition from "is" to "ought." The recognition of value, he notes, yields the assertion, "X is good." The conscience is then activated, and "thus sets off what is like an inner obligation or command to perform the action that leads to the realization of X" (ibid., 163). The experience of obligation, the "ought" is thus "intimately united with the experience of truthfulness" (ibid., 164). It emerges not from a claim about a valueless state of affairs, but from one that already possesses value. A norm simply objectifies this value, requiring us to refrain from harming a value.

This analysis suggests just how impoverished the "is-ought" problematic really is. Logically, we cannot derive an "ought" from premises that do not contain it, but this obvious point begs a host of questions. In particular, it ignores the way in which states of affairs are ordered in ways that move us to acknowledge their goodness. Von Hildebrand makes this point very well, maintaining that "every good possessing a value imposes on us, as it were, an obligation to give to it an adequate response" (von Hildebrand 1953, 38). This obligation may or not be moral, but it is obligation nevertheless. Describing his well-known concept of a "value response," von Hildebrand argues that here we are thinking of the awareness which we have as soon as we are confronted with something intrinsically important, for instance, with beauty in nature or in art, with the majesty of a great truth, with the splendor of moral values. In all these cases we are clearly aware that the object calls for an adequate response. We grasp that it is not left to our arbitrary decision or to our accidental mood whether we respond or not, and how we respond. (von Hildebrand 1953, 38)

Echoing von Hildebrand, Crosby notes that through "affirming that which we understand to be objectively good we conform to an objective oughtness and strive to give things their due" (Crosby 1996, 189). Values call us to respond to them properly, creating a powerful "ought."

John Paul II affirms this insight in "Veritatis Splendor" when he describes how we are moved by "the splendor of truth." The encyclical opens by affirming that answers to questions about obligations are "made possible thanks to the splendor of truth that shines forth deep within the human spirit" (VS, 2). It then discusses Jesus and the rich young men, emphasizing the import of God and Jesus as exemplars of moral action (ibid., 10). Jesus reveals truths that are "felt to all human beings" in an inescapable way (ibid., 50). Nowhere in "Veritatis Splendor" does John Paul II maintain that we can deduce or infer an "ought" from an "is." However, focusing on this philosophical dispute simply misses the point about the splendor of truth. When the young man confronts Jesus, he is drawn to his person, apprehending an invitation to embrace a life that "involves holding fast to the very person of Christ, sharing his loving obedience to the will of the Father. To imitate the Son means to imitate the Father" (ibid., 19). We cannot legitimately dismiss this call merely as a natural "fact" or "metaphysical" concept without normative implications. On the contrary, Jesus embodies values that call us to moral action. Naturally, we are not logically compelled to embrace them, and may even reject them. In fact, this is precisely what the young man does when he refuses to follow Jesus. However, he exercises this freedom in opposition to a world of values that powerfully moves him.

To summarize, the "is-ought" problematic presupposes a radical dichotomy between the natural world and our experience of value. John Paul II rejects this division, maintaining that the natural world is suffused with values. We directly experience them, and it is absurd to maintain this experience has no implications for our action. Both basic goods theorists and proportionalists dismiss the import of a hierarchy of value because they ignore our intentional relation to values. In this way, they embrace a feature of modernity that both Scheler and John Paul II condemn. Here, we witness a dramatic difference between John Paul II and many contemporary writers. With his emphasis on the power of values to move us, I cannot imagine him ever acceding to the idea that value hierarchies have no practical import. *Contra* George, encountering Jesus does indeed alter "one's basic understanding of how to employ" moral principles in "one's practical thinking." *Contra* Hallett, confronting the values present in Jesus does indeed have some "connection with concrete action verdicts." To think otherwise is to ignore the powerful tug of spiritual values, illustrated most concretely and dramatically in Jesus' life and death.[38]

Can We Defend a Hierarchy of Value without Using an Ethical Currency?

Given the practical import of a hierarchy of value, does it require us, nevertheless, to adopt some ethical currency or yardstick with which to rank values? Hallett and other proportionalists claim that it is incoherent to defend a hierarchy of values while resisting attempts to commensurate them. A hierarchy of value, they insist, presupposes an ethical currency with which to rank values. In leveling this charge, they betray a serious ignorance of modern phenomenology. Both John Paul II and Scheler reason not by computing with a common currency, such as pleasure, happiness, preference, or value. Instead, they focus on how lived experience enables us to apprehend a hierarchy of value. Scheler develops his a priori essential value relations without ever computing values. Instead, drawing on Franz Brentano's work, he defends axioms about value. He presents the axiom "the existence of a positive value is itself a positive value," never suggesting that we understand it by calculating values (Scheler 1973a, 81–82).[39] Similarly, Scheler argues for a priori interconnections between values and persons that require no empirical grounding. For example, he maintains that "only persons can (originally) be morally good or evil; everything else can be good or evil only *by reference to persons*, no matter how indirect this "reference" may be" (ibid., 85). When turning to a hierarchy of value, Scheler argues, we apprehend it through the act of preferring. By its essence, the height of a value is "given" to the person in a "value-cognition." Preferring encompasses whole complexes of goods, and a value's "height" in the hierarchy of values is given through it (ibid., 88).[40] Similarly, Scheler thinks love leads persons from lower to higher values, without requiring them to compute values. In fact, calculating values undermines love's essence, which is devoid of striving. Hallett suggests that we intentionally seek to maximize value, but as Scheler puts it, in love "there is no attempting to fix an objective, no deliberate shaping of purpose, aimed at higher value and its realization" (Scheler 1957, 157).[41] Thus, we can safely say that computing values with a common currency is antithetical to Scheler's ethic.

Despite his difference with Scheler, I think I have already shown that John Paul II also develops his hierarchy of value without computing values. Metaphysical analysis of the spiritual nature of persons and categorial intuition both enable us to apprehend value without any calculation. Hallet simply ignores this possibility when he discusses the example of Jesus and the sparrows ("you are worth more than many sparrows" [Matt. 10:31]). He is undoubtedly correct in saying that Jesus uses an ethical currency if that is the only way of arriving at a hierarchy of value. However, this is shortsighted, because we can make value comparisons through categorial intuition. Perhaps Jesus simply grasps the distinction between persons and animals. For John Paul II, this experience differs from deduction, or contemporary kinds of induction or abduction, but this is no reason to deny its importance. Hallett and others arbitrarily insist on one form of moral reasoning, ignoring how we grasp wholes or essences.

The Indivisibility of Values: Impractical and Unrealistic?

Proportionalists make a final and important criticism against those who doubt we can measure values. McCormick, Hallett, and others argue that people measure them all the time in their day-to-day lives. Edward Vacek is particularly articulate on this question, so let me consider his voice. We are, he argues, "sure that loving a friend is in itself more valuable than tasting peaches, even if the former is fraught with pain and the latter consistently gives pleasure" (Vacek 1985, 304). Given this experience, it is "up to epistemologists to explain" how we make value comparisons, rather than to "declare that such judgments are impossible" (ibid.). Additionally, Vacek insists that "value" can serve as a common standard with which to make value comparisons. He acknowledges that it is not "strictly a quantifiable standard, but does nonetheless yield comparisons" (ibid.). Like "being," value is indefinable but still useful for comparisons. Vacek also emphasizes that people make value comparisons by relying on prior commitments. These commitments are indexed to personality and circumstances but are not necessarily subjective. In fact, they may involve objective values that enable people to commensurate values.

Vacek's arguments are insightful but exhibit some important errors. First, like Hallett, he confuses possessing a common denominator and apprehending a value hierarchy. A person can indeed be sure that loving her friend is more valuable than tasting peaches, but she need not use a common currency to arrive at this knowledge. For both Scheler and John Paul II, values of the person are preeminent over the sensible values involved in eating peaches. One choosing to eat peaches over loving her friend possesses a perverse *ordo amoris*, and we understand this without employing a common currency. Thus, Vacek correctly notes that we make value differentiations but equates emotional or cognitive apprehension of values with calculating them. Second, Vacek's concept of "value" is too ill-defined to do the work that he wants it to do. What exactly does he mean when he says that "value" is a common denominator for making decisions? Because the concept is so vague, proportionalists end up appealing to some standard other than value with which to make decisions. For example, McCormick maintains that "*somehow* or *other*, in fear and trembling, we commensurate. In a sense, we *adopt* a hierarchy" (McCormick 1978, 227). However, he tells us little about what this "somehow or other" really is. Moreover, the idea that we *adopt* a hierarchy of value clashes dramatically with the view I am presenting in this book. We have the freedom to shape our relationship to values and our personhood. Nevertheless, we choose *within* a hierarchy of value that we neither adopt nor create. Through our intentional relations and cognitive apprehension, we have an inescapable contact with values. Naturally, we can turn against them, but this power differs significantly from the capacity to adopt a hierarchy of values.

Is the problem here subjectivism, as basic goods theorists argue? Finnis and others charge that proportionalists compute "value" by appealing to subjective standards such as personal preference, prior commitments, or culturally relative mores. Vacek resists this allegation, insisting that using personal commitments to commensurate values does not imply subjectivism. Why, he asks, do we assume that a personal commitment is necessarily subjective? Vacek's point here is well taken. Proportionalists often fall prey to subjectivism with their vague talk about "value" as a means for making decisions. However, Vacek is right to say that using prior commitments to commensurate value does not *necessarily* entail subjectivism. We may embrace an objective value that enables us to commensurate values. In fact, Scheler's axiology leads us to be skeptical of the claim that too many people are subjectivists.

The problem is less with subjectivism than with *value-perversion*. Proportionalists do little to show why "adopting" a hierarchy of value according to "personal aims, vocations, life commitments, possibilities" protects us from embracing axiological distortions (McCormick 1978, 228). In conflict situations, we may use a personal aim to commensurate values but also embrace a perverted hierarchy of value. For example, Scheler describes how many moderns adopt utilitarianism out of *ressentiment*. Systematically, he examines modern virtues, dramatically stating that the *"most profound* perversion of a hierarchy of values is the *subordination of vital values to utility values* which gains force as modern morality develops" (Scheler 1961, 154–55). In this case, we have not subjectivism but axiological perversion. John Paul II often illustrates similar distortions. For example, in "Centesimus Annus," he observes that twentieth-century totalitarians subordinated all values to state power, believing that by "possessing the secret of a perfect social organization, they could make evil disappear" (CA, 25). This aspiration represents a profound axiological distortion that arbitrarily reduces spiritual to material values, confusing political society with the "kingdom of God" (ibid.). Similarly, in modern democracies, many people commensurate values by perverting human rights language. Using it to legitimate profoundly immoral acts like abortion and euthanasia, they adopt debased forms of individualism and hedonism (EV, 11). Finally, people often make complex economic decisions by subordinating all values to economic growth. In some visions of the international economic order, vital and sensible values engulf spiritual values, alienating human beings from God.

These and other examples demonstrate why we cannot uncritically accept how people normally commensurate values. Appealing to convention or ordinary experience robs us of the capacity to critically engage value perversions. In conflict situations, proportionalists tell us that we should resolve conflict by using "value" to maximize the good. When pressed to define what this means, they point to how people maximize values by using prior commitments. However, although not necessarily subjective, these commitments are often distorted, relating the person in a perverse way to values. I cannot see, therefore, how proportionalists can confidently support conclusions about moral action that may simply validate existing social and political prejudices.

Vacek correctly advises us to try to understand how people commensurate values, but John Paul II can explain this without calculating values. As Scheler famously said, "whoever has the *ordo amoris* of a man has the man himself" (Scheler 1973b, 100). All persons have an *ordo amoris* enabling them to make moral decisions. Often, it includes a preeminent value to which all other values are subordinated. Some people elevate vital or sensible values over higher values, revealing a perverted structure of loving. Others correctly apprehend the preeminence of spiritual values, willing to actualize them in their acts and persons. Both Scheler and John Paul II use the concept of an *ordo amoris* to good effect, analyzing social issues in terms of our orientation toward values. Richly developed, this analysis explains our choices without any need to consider an ethical currency.

Measurement Problems and Political Realism: A Decisive Critique

With the objections to John Paul II's position out of the way, I now want to argue that without an adequate ethical currency, political consequentialism confronts serious difficulties. I will do so by considering the work of two contemporary realists, Robert D. Kaplan and George Weigel. Kaplan represents a popular form of American political realism that emerged after the Cold War ended. He makes no pretenses about engaging texts in a scholarly fashion, presenting himself as a well-traveled journalist with a deep interest in political theory. He makes large historical generalizations and shows little understanding of Christian political thought. Nevertheless, his work is attractive because he writes well, avoids the jargon often found in academic writings, and draws on extensive knowledge of international affairs. He is best seen as a journalist who uses an engaging style to influence policy-makers.

Drawing heavily on Thucydides, Machiavelli, Hobbes, and Kissinger, Kaplan presents a classic realist vision of international politics. Approvingly, he states that Machiavelli teaches us that "primitive necessity and self-interest drive politics, and that this can be good in itself, because competing self-interests are the basis for compromise" (Kaplan 2002, 63). In the twenty-first century, Kaplan writes, there is "no global Leviathan monopolizing the use of force in order to punish the Unjust" (ibid. 105). Without such a power, nations operate in a self-help system and cannot rely on international institutions in order to survive. Like Morgenthau, Kaplan believes that fear and a lust for power drive human beings, and they can be moved to act only by these forces. Vividly, Kaplan describes the chaos that has plagued West Africa and other troubled parts of the world in recent years. Convincingly, he shows how violent nationalism, global disease epidemics like HIV/AIDS, overpopulation, terrorism, and economic depression plague many parts of the globe. Using numerous examples, he challenges the popular notion that exporting democracy necessarily leads to peace and justice. Countries that lack infrastructure and good institutions, he maintains, may adopt democracy, only to find themselves victimized by corruption and violence. Russia after the Cold War illustrates this danger perfectly. It embraced democracy and market measures but squandered opportunities through massive corruption and criminal activity. Kaplan also maintains that new information technologies are unequally distributed among nations and that diffusing them will not necessarily bring justice to the globe. Terrorists, rogue states, and organized criminals may use them to create disorder. Sadly, the September 11 terrorist attacks on New York City's twin towers illustrated his point, revealing how airline technology can become a deadly weapon. In sum, what Kaplan presents is a traditional form of political realism that emphasizes the pursuit of power, unpredictable group dynamics, and continual struggle. Updated with vivid examples from around the globe, it draws on past realists to illuminate our current situations.

There is much that is true in Kaplan's work, and John Paul II's discussion of human nature's darker elements supports some of his judgments. In the last decade, the pope has often expressed deep misgiving about nationalism, political corruption, and globalization. He has often identified profoundly sinful patterns of behavior, recognizing that the end of the Cold War has created enormous problems. Thus, Kaplan's descriptive realism is, in important ways, compatible with John Paul II's vision of the political order.

Unfortunately, we cannot say the same of Kaplan's normative claims. Kaplan endorses the Weberian distinction between an ethic of intention and an ethic of consequences, urging the statesperson to guide her actions by considering their consequences. For example, he says that Immanuel Kant "symbolizes the morality of intention rather than of consequences, a morality of abstract justice rather than of actual result" (Kaplan 2002, 113). This ethic may prevent political actors from descending into barbarism, Kaplan maintains, but most of the time, politics requires us to adopt an ethic of consequences. Writing about Machiavelli, he praises him for his conception of *virtu*. On Kaplan's reading, *virtu* includes the capacity to use violence effectively, marshal one's forces, consolidate power, and create political order. With a dazzling array of examples from Israel, Uganda, the Sudan, and Turkey, Kaplan dissects how political leaders employed or failed to employ *virtu*. *Virtu*, he writes, has "little to do with individual perfection and everything to do with political result. Thus, for Machiavelli, a policy is defined not by its excellence but by its outcome: if it isn't effective, it can't be virtuous" (ibid., 53).

In an intriguing essay on foreign aid, Kaplan develops this ethic of consequences (Kaplan 2000, ch. 6). Taking up the question of how to respond to "failed states," particularly in sub-Saharan Africa, he calls for a new, realistic approach to foreign aid. His proposals for foreign aid are

> inspired in some measure by the principle known as proportionalism, adopted by some Catholic theologians on certain vexing moral issues. Proportionalism provides a useful moral approach to the Third World. In theological terms proportionalism is about doing or accepting a certain amount of "evil" to make possible a proportionately greater amount of good; it underlies theories of a just war and also, for some Catholics, the

argument in favor of promoting the use of contraceptives as a means of reducing abortion. In everyday, non-theological terms it is about beating a retreat in order to preserve what is most important. Proportionalism is anathema to moral and ideological purists. It tempers implacable principle with common sense. (Ibid., 121–2)

Undoubtedly, Kaplan's understanding of proportionalism is simplistic and defective, but it illustrates his consequentialism. He advocates a foreign aid policy emphasizing targeted aid rather than large projects, early warning to prevent disasters, and rare but decisive intervention. In order to achieve long-term beneficial consequences, it also accepts evil consequences such as famines or massacres. The idea of seeking the "lesser evil" is central to Kaplan's vision of foreign policy. Moral rules offer little guidance to statespeople struggling to retain power in a chaotic world. We must, instead, recognize that in politics, Kaplan embraces a Weberian ethic of consequences, denying that moral motivation is important in politics (Kaplan 2002, ch. 5). Writing about how to battle terrorism, Kaplan advises the U.S. government to resurrect practices such as assassinations of foreign leaders. He maintains that the "war on terrorism will not be successful if every aspect of its execution must be disclosed and justified—in terms of universal principles—to the satisfaction of the world media and world public opinion" (Kaplan 2003, 77). Retaining the rigid rules of international law only strengthens the hand of vicious terrorists like Osama bin Laden. What we need instead is political prudence that accepts ugly practices if they produce beneficial consequences.

Kaplan severely underestimates the conceptual difficulties of consequentialism. First, like many twentieth-century realists, he completely ignores spiritual values. Self-consciously, he presents a "pagan ethics," arguing that a "Judeo-Christian" ethic is largely inapplicable to politics. However, he offers no argument for why a pagan ethic should ignore spiritual values. Aesthetic and moral values figure prominently in the works of many pagan thinkers. Unfortunately, this kind of omission is common among modern realists, and we should notice what role it plays in Kaplan's argument. If we ignore spiritual values, we can promise to calculate consequences in a straightforward way. We simply assume that statespeople will measure power using demographics, culture, and geography. Once we admit spiritual values into our calculus, however, Kaplan's ethic of consequences collapses into arbitrary judgments. For example, writing about Machiavelli, Kaplan praises Israeli general and later prime minister Yitzhak Rabin for his *virtu*. Referring to Palestinian protesters during the 1988 Palestinian intifada, Rabin reportedly told Israelis to "go in and break their bones" (Kaplan 2002, ch. 5). Rabin, Kaplan argues, understood that compromising with street anarchy undermines a nation, and by taking a hard line against it, he consolidated his power. This enabled him to eventually reach out to the Palestinians in a peace initiative. Like Machiavelli, he understood that good men must sometimes commit evil acts, sacrificing their individual virtue for the social order. Like the true man of *virtu,* Rabin knew how to use violence selectively, limiting his evil acts to achieve a good end. In a world marked by terrorism, he provides a model for how to use violence efficiently.

Empirically, Kaplan may be right that Rabin's actions enabled him to become a man of peace. He may also be right in saying that selective violence against those directly involved in the intifada was morally justified. However, he arrives at these judgments using a flawed ethic. Violently attacking protesters profoundly affects victims and attackers. Even those using violence to preserve the common good cannot ignore the deep spiritual effects of their action. Those attacked suffer physical and spiritual harms associated with being a victim of violence. These become part of their personhood, affecting those who are close to them. Often, violence undermines a person's capacity for giving and receiving love, making it difficult for her to trust others. Over a long period of time, this may cripple a community's capacity to develop a peaceful civil society and nation. The capacity to love, the dignity of the person, the moral health of a community—these are all spiritual values. For his ethic to succeed, Kaplan must indicate how they figure in an assessment of the policy of the "lesser evil." How can he calculate the loss of human dignity? How does he propose to measure the long-term harm a victim experiences after an act of violence? By what yardstick does he quantify how attacking another person stunts that person's capacity to love others? Kaplan's calculus cannot be anything but an arbitrary preference for material over spiritual values. Or it involves some mysterious process of commensurating values, guided by the statesman's *ordo amoris.* However, surely leaders or journalists like Kaplan owe us some explanations for their preferences, which strike many as deeply troubling. Appealing to prudence or political experience does little to help us in this matter.

Responding to this challenge, realists often scoff at appeals to love or character, dismissing them as intangibles that should play no role in political life. Confronting aggression by a vicious foe with little interest in moral niceties, it seems absurd to talk about spiritual values. Instead, we need to firmly and immediately stop aggression. As Machiavelli once wrote, "so let a prince win and maintain his state; the means will always be judged honorable, and will be praised by everyone" (Machiavelli 1964, 18). Like Machiavelli, Kaplan derides those concerned with what he considers to be moral niceties in extreme circumstances. Starving masses on the African continent, frightened Israelis under attack, and thousands of victims of violence in East Timor all may have little patience for questions of personhood and intentionality. Americans terrified by the threat of an anthrax attack may have difficulty respecting the personhood of captured al-Qaeda terrorists.

These circumstances illustrate how order is an essential value. People in Afghanistan, Sierra Leone, Liberia, and Iraq appreciate it in ways that few in developed countries do. Foolishly, some people overlook how it is often a prerequisite for developing other values. As Hobbes famously argues in his description of a state of nature, without order there is

> no place for Industry; because the fruit thereof is uncertain; and consequently, no Culture on Earth; no Navigation, nor use of the commodities that may be imported from Sea; no commodious Building; no Instruments in moving, and removing such things as require much force; no Knowledge of the face of the earth; no account of Time; no Arts; no Letters; no Society; and which is worst of all, continual feare, and danger of violent death; And the life of man, solitary, poore, brutish, and short. (Hobbes 1991, 89)

Few passages in political theory capture so vividly the value of political order.

However important this insight may be, it cannot lead us to ignore spiritual values and accept Kaplan's idea that "freedom becomes an issue only after order has been established" (Kaplan 2002, 83). In fact, John Paul II has rejected this argument for years, because it ignores central elements of our humanity. Kaplan's arguments are really no different from those of the Stranger in *Our God's Brother,* who argues that through righteous and destructive anger, the poor can possess all goods. Derisively, he dismisses Adam's appeal to spiritual goods, insisting that through revolution, the oppressed can have all goods. Adam accepts these arguments, acknowledging that the social order often systematically denies people their basic human rights. However, he maintains that proposals for revolutionary violence ignore the spiritual dimension of justice. Human poverty, he says, "is deeper than the resources of all goods" (Wojtyla 1987, 242). The Stranger derides this appeal to the intangible, but Adam asks him if he has ever "tried to feel the whole vastness of the values to which man is called," urging him to regard "not one section of the truth, but the whole truth" (ibid., 243). Confronting calls for political "responsibility" or appeals to "real world" action, these words provide guidance and inspiration.

More than fifty years after writing this play, John Paul II returned to its themes while responding to the September 11 terrorist attacks on the United States. Speaking a few months after the event, he acknowledged that "the recruitment of terrorists in fact is easier in situations where rights are trampled upon and injustices tolerated over a long period of time" (2002Celebration, 5). Systematic injustices often lead people to embrace terrorism, and like his character Adam, John Paul II understands these dynamics. However, he writes that "it must be firmly stated that the injustices existing in the world can never be used to excuse acts of terrorism" (ibid.). Those committing terrorist acts may gain in the short term, but by committing heinous crimes, they denigrate human dignity, pervert their persons, and lose in the long term. This is because "terrorism springs from hatred, and it generates isolation, mistrust and closure. Violence is added to violence in a tragic sequence that exasperates successive generations, each one inheriting the hatred which divided those that went before. *Terrorism is built on contempt for human life*" (ibid., 4). When killing the innocent, the terrorist closes in on himself, undermining his freedom by deliberately turning away from God. This is an unacceptable price to pay for immediate political effectiveness.

Realists may be willing to pay this price, but at the end of the day, they understand only "one section of the truth." Alan Dershowitz and others may propose to torture terrorists in order to extract information from them, but in doing so, they arbitrarily subordinate spiritual values to material ones, capitalizing on the desperation of people in extreme situations. Responding to this constriction of value, John Paul II recognizes the importance of both material and spiritual values. Throughout his long career, he has emphasized our obligation to meet the material needs of suffering people in the world but has always ranked spiritual values above them. Political realism focuses on an absolutely essential but narrow range of values. Once we abandon its limited theory of value, its counsel to base political ethics on calculating consequences collapses into a dangerous arbitrariness.

At the end of *Our God's Brother,* the Stranger abandons Adam, concluding that he is an irresponsible artist who will never help the poor. The play ends with violence erupting in the streets. Surveying this impending disaster, Adam ends the play by saying: "I know for certain, though, that I have chosen the greater freedom" (Wojtyla 1987, 266). This statement brilliantly captures what is at stake in the debates about an ethic of consequences. With Kaplan, Weber, Hobbes and many other realists, we can elevate physical security and political order to the highest place in a hierarchy of values. We can embrace torture and other horrors that can undoubtedly produce short-term benefits. We can simply ignore other values or maintain that the material values are prerequisites for developing them. Or, with John Paul II, we may recognize the central importance of order and security but refuse to make them our highest values. It is the pope's contention that the greater freedom for humanity lies in taking this second path.

John Paul II and Moderate Realism

Many Roman Catholics may see John Paul II's criticisms of consequentialism as a welcome repudiation of a morally bankrupt ethic. However, they may also overlook how it challenges elements of Roman Catholic political thought. To illustrate this point, I turn to Weigel's work on the just war tradition. Weigel presents a nuanced form of Christian realism

called moderate realism, which assumes that sin infects politics, maintains that exercising political power is unavoidable, and rejects moralism. However, it also affirms that politics is the "arena of rationality and
moral responsibility," refusing to see it as entirely fallen (Weigel 1987,
43). Weigel embraces natural law thinking, arguing that we can grasp
through reason an "ought" in politics" (ibid.). He also resists equating
power and violence, arguing that power is the capacity to achieve corpo-
rate purposes. Finally, embracing the just war tradition, he insists that
it includes a concern for peace, understood as *"tranquillitas ordinis,"* a
"stability that allows social life to grow and develop" (ibid., 44). Peace is
never simply the absence of conflict but is instead a social order valuing
the dignity of the person.

Weigel's moderate realism is deeply attractive, because it does justice to important elements of the Christian tradition. Moreover, it is
neither utilitarian nor proportionalist, and Weigel is quite critical of
both positions. Nevertheless, he selectively adopts the consequentialist
reasoning of the realist tradition. For example, he defends the just war
tradition's *jus ad bellum* criterion of proportionality, which requires that
before going to war, a statesperson must weigh the values and disvalues
of military action. The criterion of proportionality, Weigel maintains,
states that the "good to be attained must be reasonably supposed to be
greater than the certain evils, material and spiritual, which war entails"
(Weigel 1987, 41). It constitutes a key form of moral reasoning that
should guide our decision to use military force, and Weigel has applied
it to different military conflicts. He strongly defended the moral legitimacy of the 1991 Persian Gulf War, criticizing those who argued that
modern warfare is, in principle, disproportionate. He noted that "modern
weapons technology makes "proportionate" and "discriminate" use of
armed force" far more possible than in the Second World War (Weigel
1991, 64). He also maintains that a nation can direct proportionality
and discrimination toward a just peace. The theory of statecraft implicit
in the just war tradition, he writes, "requires that the proportionate
and discriminate use of armed forces be ordered to the pursuit of peace
in all its component parts: freedom, justice, security and order" (ibid.,
71). He describes the just war tradition as a "moral calculus" oriented
toward these goals (ibid., 87). He has also discussed the 2002 American
war against terrorism in Afghanistan, arguing that it qualifies as a just

cause (Weigel 2002). Finally, he repeatedly argued that going to war against Iraq in the Second Gulf War was morally justifiable.[42] In all of these discussions, he appears to adopt a selective consequentialism that balances values and disvalues.

A natural response to Weigel's proposals is to ask how he can perform the complex "moral calculus" he proposes. How can we possibly have the vast political and military knowledge necessary to measure the consequences of our action? What is the time span involved in considering them, and which moral agents do we include in our calculus?[43] These questions suggest the enormity of the task Weigel sets before us, but they are not the ones I think are central. Instead, I think Weigel faces deeper problems because he presupposes that we can measure spiritual values. Notice that when discussing proportionality, he includes spiritual values in his moral calculus. Yet both John Paul II and Scheler maintain that such values are indivisible, and therefore we cannot easily measure them. How, then, can the statesperson ascertain precisely how military action will damage spiritual values?

Perhaps we might see the criterion of proportionality as primarily a brake on rash action. Rather than providing precise knowledge, it prevents us from rushing into a disaster. For example, during the Cold War, the United States refused to intervene to prevent the Soviet Union from invading Czechoslovakia in 1968. Such rash action might have precipitated a nuclear war, with incalculable damage to material and spiritual values. Those making this judgment need not have calculated the value of protecting the people of Czechoslovakia from tyranny versus the disvalues of starting a nuclear conflagration. Instead, they could have invoked the immeasurable horror of nuclear war in order to thwart rash action. Thus, we might declare that military force will damage material values greatly, and take an incalculable toll on spiritual values, without offering any more precise judgment. But this is not what Weigel offers. Instead, he believes that proportionality provides precise guidance for the policy-maker. Yet if John Paul II is right about the indivisibility of spiritual values, Weigel's confidence in the principle of proportionality is misplaced.

Weigel's problematic judgments about the first Persian Gulf War illustrate the weaknesses in his position. In several articles, he confidently asserts that this war was morally legitimate. Systematically, he considers the just war tradition's criteria, arguing that the coalition forces met their requirements. When he turns to the proportionality criterion of the *jus ad bellum*, Weigel acknowledges the difficulties in ascertaining if the First Gulf War was proportionate. Looking back at the war, he states that "we cannot measure the amplitude of the good that has been achieved to date" (Weigel 1992, 23). However, he notes that we could know "with clarity, even in the fall of 1990, that a failure to check Iraqi aggression would have serious consequences for the region and the world" (ibid., 23). Saddam Hussein was a vicious dictator who would have effectively liquidated Kuwaiti society. Moreover, by controlling a significant portion of the world's oil supply, he would have been in a position to develop weapons of mass destruction. In Weigel's view, "ejecting Iraq from Kuwait, and checking Saddam Hussein's drive for regional hegemony, were morally justified ends according to the 'war-decision' criterion of proportionality" (ibid.).

These are complex judgments, as Weigel acknowledges, and I happen to share his view that military force against Saddam Hussein in 1991 was morally defensible. Moreover, I think some rough calculations of consequences using material values supports this judgment. However, I cannot accept Weigel's embrace of proportionality, because he bases it on an untenable calculation of values. Unlike consequentialists, he insists that spiritual values be included in this calculus but never tells us how to perform it, and therefore offers little guidance for statespeople struggling to decide whether to go to war. Weigel never confronts this fundamental objection to his position.

Perhaps, however, by focusing on calculating consequences, I am misunderstanding the principle of proportionality. Finnis, John Boyle, and Grisez offer an intriguing argument that distinguishes between legitimate and illegitimate uses of proportionality. They acknowledge that if we think about it as a way of calculating values in order to ground moral norms, proportionality succumbs to conceptual difficulties. Rather than a form of consequentialist reasoning, however, they argue that it makes moral assessments by using moral standards that exist independent of any calculation. For example, we can use a principle of fairness to differentiate the "impartial from the biased acceptance of harmful side-effects of military action" (Finnis, Boyle, Grisez 1987, 264). Fairness disallows discriminate bombing of one community and indiscriminate bombing of another. Unlike consequentialism, proportionality in this case presupposes the truth of fairness rather than grounding it in a calculation of consequences. This use of proportionality is, therefore, "formed and tested by moral standards" arrived at in a nonconsequentialist manner (ibid., 266). Finnis, Boyle, and Grisez also recognize that people may use both this objective standard and feelings to commensurate values. Everyone, they write, "carries out this commensuration by an intuitive awareness of his or her own differentiated feelings towards various goods and bads as concretely remembered, experienced or imagined" (ibid., 265). However, they do not use these subjective feelings to *ground* moral norms.

Finnis, Boyle, and Grisez develop a subtle distinction between using consequentialist reasoning to ground moral norms and calculating consequences within a nonconsequentialist moral framework. They allow us to consider the consequences of our actions in moral reasoning, without descending into an incoherent and dangerous consequentialism. John Paul II shares this concern for consequences, acknowledging that calculating them is important. Like Finnis, Boyle, and Grisez, he allows for calculating with material values or only one spiritual value. For example, a state government might calculate that requiring parents to put their children in automobile seatbelts would save hundreds of lives. It makes this calculation with the value of life in mind, without trying to compare the cost of saving lives with the cost of restricting parental freedom. This would require it to measure the spiritual value of freedom, something that is obviously difficult to do. We may support public policies enabling persons to develop spiritually or oppose those that stifle spiritual development. In neither case must we calculate spiritual goods. We might oppose laws sanctioning physician-assisted suicide, arguing that they embody a deeply mistaken understanding of suffering. Empirically, we could be wrong about how the policy shapes our religious lives. However, rather than making a mistake of calculating material and spiritual values, in this case, we would be misunderstanding how a law affects our spiritual life.

In contrast, Weigel mistakenly promises objective guidance grounded in a calculation of values, an obviously flawed approach to war and peace. At most, he should urge the statesperson to use proportionality in the way Finnis, Boyle, and Grisez propose. This would yield very tentative and fallible judgments. Anything more must either arbitrarily ignore spiritual values or devolve into problematic calculi of what cannot be calculated. Weigel seems oblivious to the problems in measuring spiritual values, confidently asserting that particular military actions promote greater value over disvalue. Like so many other contemporary thinkers, he shows little awareness of how John Paul II uses phenomenology. If he understood the depth of the pope's philosophical project, he would have to acknowledge that it challenges his understanding of the just war tradition. If John Paul II is correct in arguing that we cannot measure spiritual values, we must reconceive the traditional just war criterion of proportionality. Proportionality becomes an important, but imperfect, ethical tool, providing caveats about using excessive force. It can prevent rash and dangerous action, but it cannot deliver on what just war theorists promise.[44]

During the Vietnam War, Protestant theologian Paul Ramsey gave a passionate sermon in Washington, D.C., articulating the proper role for the principle of proportionality in the just war tradition. Noting the difficulties in calculating the consequences of our actions, he maintained that the principle of proportionality first excludes "deliberately imprudent decisions—resulting from fear or passion or lethargy or inflexibility or prejudice or from the power of slogans like 'why not victory?'" (Ramsey 1983, 524). Second, it prohibits the *"uncharitable* exercise of political wisdom which in counting the good to be done did not cast its net widely enough, and so let out some of the common good of other peoples or some of the common good of all mankind which might have been effectively congruent with the interests and common good of one's own nation" (ibid.). With these two ideas in mind, Ramsey suggests that proportionality disallows a first or quick recourse to arms and proscribes continuing a war at all costs. However, beyond these two important ideas,

> no certain means can be assigned to the maxim that there should be a *reasonable* hope of a *reasonable* victory, or to the principle of proportion requiring the statesman to be constantly assessing, amid the encounters he is always going to meet, the relations of costs to *obtainable* benefits, or requiring him to review whether the great evil he chose in the beginning is not, in fact, turning out to be greater than the "greater evil" he first undertook to prevent. (Ramsey 1983, 528)

Ramsey was deeply skeptical about our capacity to make proportionate judgments before and during a war.[44] To make them, we need to engage in absurd calculations of spiritual and material values or to disregard spiritual values altogether, embracing a narrow cost-benefit analysis. Unfortunately, too many contemporary thinkers fail to think clearly about the indivisibility of spiritual values, and thus hubristically promise what they cannot deliver.

Conclusion

In an age in which scientific and technical knowledge often dominate discussions of ethics and public policy, an ethics of consequences is very appealing. It promises to address difficult moral issues by calculating benefits and harms in an objective fashion. In a pluralistic world, it seems to prevent protracted and unpleasant debates about values. Finally, it seems like the ethic of responsible people, who must face daily conflicts of values and cannot take refuge in moral absolutes. Those who oppose it in military decisions appear irresponsible, people whose ideas are not "relevant" to a complex modern or postmodern world. These cultural trends present critics of consequentialism with an uphill battle.

Despite these difficulties, I think that consequentialism's promise is illusionary. It rests on an arbitrary preference for material values or on specious arguments about our capacity to commensurate spiritual and material values. Undoubtedly, rough calculations of consequences are inevitable and even necessary in many arenas of human life. Nothing in John Paul II's work suggests otherwise. Recognizing this dimension of our moral life, however, is a far cry from consequentialism, which promises to develop moral norms by calculating consequences. Unless it can clearly indicate how to calculate spiritual values, consequentialism provides no support for moral norms. Instead, it falls back on arbitrary preference or culturally relative practices corrupted by perverse loves.

In his critique of consequentialism, John Paul II carefully uses both Thomistic and phenomenological resources. Unfortunately, many critics ignore or caricature how he uses phenomenology, failing to understand the depth of his engagement with Scheler and other twentieth-century thinkers. This is particularly the case with proportionalists and basic goods theorists who draw on Anglo-American philosophy. As Sokolowski argues, most of

> the misunderstandings of phenomenology come from interpretations that are still caught up in the problems and positions of modern thinking, still so trapped by the Cartesian and Lockean tradition that they fail to grasp what is new in phenomenology. Phenomenology calls for a major readjustment in the understanding of what philosophy is, and many people cannot make this change because they cannot free themselves from their background and cultural context. (Sokolowski 2000, 62)

In contemporary debates about consequentialism, too many people fail to move beyond their "background and cultural context." Both proportionalists and basic goods theorists ignore the possibility of apprehending the radical difference between spiritual and material values. Basic goods theorists fail to understand how John Paul II defends his hierarchy of value. Proportionalists acknowledge a hierarchy of values, but falsely assume we can maximize spiritual goods or values. Just war thinkers like Weigel and J. Bryan Hehir show little understanding of our experience of value and hierarchies of value. Consequently, many contemporary thinkers misunderstand John Paul II's radical challenge to their positions.

Realists like Machiavelli and Kissinger have urged the statesperson to embrace an ethic of consequences. However, if John Paul II is right about the indivisibility of spiritual values, this is bad advice. It encourages the statesperson to ignore essential dimensions of human life or to falsely claim he can commensurate the spiritual and the material. Neither of these approaches is satisfactory. Therefore, despite its extraordinary power to describe the darker dimensions of politics, political realism's normative project fails.

4

John Paul II and Participation in International Politics

The failure of the United Nations to prevent, and subsequently, to stop the genocide in Rwanda was a failure by the United Nations system as a whole. The fundamental failure was the lack of resources and political commitment devoted to developments in Rwanda and the United Nations presence there. There was a persistent lack of political will by Member States to act, or to act with enough assertiveness.[1]

> Report of the Independent Inquiry into the Actions of the United Nations during the 1994 Genocide in Rwanda

Hope and trust: these may seem matters beyond the purview of the United Nations. But they are not. The politics of nations, with which your Organization is principally concerned, can never ignore the transcendent, spiritual dimensions of the human experience, and could never ignore it without harming the cause of man and the cause of freedom.

> John Paul II[2]

When John Paul II appeared before the United Nations General Assembly in 1995, he confronted political realities drastically different from those he faced in 1979. At the United Nations in 1979, he spoke to a "bipolar" world divided between the United States and the Soviet Union. People referred to the "Third World," those political communities outside the orbit of the two superpowers. In 1995, this had all changed. The Soviet Union had collapsed, a host of new nation-states had emerged, and the United States became the sole superpower. In this new context, John Paul II urged the United Nations to promote international solidarity. In a compelling speech, he called upon nations to embrace a "civilization of love" that values the dignity of the human person. He insisted that the "United Nations organization needs to rise more and more above the cold status of an administrative institution and to become a moral centre where all the nations of the world feel at home and develop a shared awareness of being, as it were, a "family of nations" (1995UN, 14). Despite its moral and rhetorical power, however, there was something disturbing about John Paul II's speech. Coming on the heels of the United Nations' abject failure to prevent genocide in Rwanda, his comments about a family of nations had an air of unreality about them. The Member States of the UN showed little or no concern for members of their "family" on the African continent. Repeatedly, they stifled constructive responses to the Rwandan crisis, haggling over the definition of genocide while hundreds of thousands of people died. This terrible failure had little or no impact on John Paul II's speech to the United Nations. He mentions the Rwandan genocide, and clearly, some of his remarks about virulent nationalism apply to it. However, he never discusses why the so-called international community utterly failed to stop it. After so much post–World War II rhetoric about preventing genocide, this failure represented a moral stain on international relations. The contrasts between John Paul II's words about a family of nations and the realities of peacekeeping were stunning.

Undoubtedly, John Paul II understands the darker elements of politics, articulating a conception of sin that reduces utopian aspirations. He also undermines the ethical consequentialism so dominant in international politics. However, unlike many realists, John Paul II often ignores clashes between his ethical ideals. Realists emphasize the ambiguities of political choices, arguing that we often confront clashes of values that admit of no easy resolution. John Paul II develops rich conceptions of peace, human rights, democracy, and international relations, but often leaves the details of implementation to policy-makers. Unfortunately, this creates difficulties when he considers issues like humanitarian intervention. Humanitarian intervention presents the United Nations with seemingly intractable problems that drive many to despair. East Timor, Sierra Leone, Liberia, Somalia, the Congo, the former Yugoslavia, Kosovo, and Afghanistan have all seen humanitarian crises that seemed impossible to resolve. They brought responses from the international community, some successful but others utterly futile. These events provoked considerable ethical and political debate with important implications for a new century that has begun with terrorism and war.

In this chapter, I consider how John Paul II applies his ethic to humanitarian and military intervention. First, I outline the ethical issues in humanitarian intervention, describing realist and liberal approaches to it. On one hand, intervention may prevent genocide or mass starvation, embodying the virtue of solidarity. On the other hand, it may undermine state sovereignty, allowing intervening states to cavalierly override national self-determination. Second, I carefully outline John Paul II's understanding of participation, describing how it shapes his approach to international politics. Participation illustrates how he creatively uses the phenomenology of moral cognition to analyze international affairs. Third, applying the concept of participation to international politics, I explore John Paul II's account of the rights of nations, a civilization of love, and our duty to undertake humanitarian intervention. I suggest that prima facie, these elements of his political thought conflict, producing an acute clash between human rights and the right to national identity. Fourth, I discuss how some contemporary thinkers resolve such conflicts by invoking "moral blind alleys," the "lesser of two evils," and the just war principle of proportionality. I argue that these approaches succumb to the difficulties inherent in consequentialism. Fifth, I argue that John Paul II can address conflicts in his political thought by altering his concept of the rights of nations. As a personalist, he should attribute rights to nations only analogically, explicitly subordinating them to the value of the person. Finally, I maintain that John Paul II fails to apply his conception of sin to the United Nations. He urges it to cultivate deep knowledge of the person, but I argue that its response to

the Rwandan genocide indicates that it can barely promote knowledge
of our common humanity.

Should We Intervene?
The Dilemmas of Humanitarian Intervention

In the 1990s, the tragedies in the former Yugoslavia, Rwanda, and
Somalia led to a heated debate about morality and humanitarian intervention. It took place within the larger context of fundamental changes
in international politics. In the place of the two superpowers, the United
States emerged as the central military and economic power, with no serious
rivals. Regional powers like China and the European Union also developed.
Japan and other Asian countries confronted serious economic difficulties,
generating great uncertainty about the global financial system. Finally,
at the beginning of this century, terrorism emerged as a major threat
to industrialized nations. J. Bryan Hehir argues that such changes have
"eroded ideas once taken for granted in the discussion of world politics.
At stake in the process are the two key principles of international order:
the sovereignty of states and the norm of nonintervention" (Hehir 1995,
2). Often ignored practically, these ideas nevertheless played a central role
in international politics in the last three hundred years.

In recent years, support for them has waned, challenged by human
rights activists, international law, terrorism, preemptive military action,
and economic interdependence. Ignatieff details how in the 1990s, a "humanitarian internationalism" emerged, a vision of international politics
guided by "one set of minimum norms to which every regime in the
world formally subscribed" (Ignatieff 1997, 89).[3] Numerous organizations
created constituencies for international development, new human rights
regimes appeared, along with "newly globalized media like CNN to create a popular demand for international humanitarian intervention" (ibid.,
90). Ignatieff boldly claims that changes in media, information, and other
technologies made it increasingly impossible to restrict moral concern to
family, neighborhood, and province, thus changing "the modern moral
imagination" (ibid.). Many in industrialized democracies extended their
moral concern to people living far away from them. This concern, along
with the normal self-interested behavior of nations, led to the large-scale

humanitarian interventions of the 1990s. For humanitarian internationalists, these interventions proved to be a great disappointment. Unable
to fundamentally change the international system, in despair, many re-
treated from activism. Some in the United States and Western Europe
responded to perceived failures in Bosnia and Somalia by withdrawing
from internationalism and embracing forms of isolationism. Harshly
condemning these developments, Ignatieff nevertheless acknowledges
that the "internationalism of the early 1990s resembles less the creative
moment of 1945 than the failure of Wilsonian internationalism after
World War I" (ibid., 91). Echoing these comments at the end of the
1990s, Michael J. Smith called humanitarian efforts "global evangelism"
for a new international system, but noted that it "at best limps along, led
by a motley if erudite array of philosophers and human-rights activists"
(Smith 1999, 278).

Despite such developments, however, humanitarian internationalism
embodied ideas that remain important for international politics. To illustrate this point, I employ Smith's helpful distinction between liberal
and realist approaches to humanitarian intervention. Undoubtedly, the
liberal tradition has often rigidly supported the nation-state system but
also contains "a more universalist conception of human rights in which
sovereignty is a subsidiary and conditional value" (Smith 1999, 278).
On this view, according sovereignty an absolute value may support an
unjust status quo, perpetuated by extremist demagogues who allegedly
represent nations. To prevent this injustice, we ought to subordinate
sovereignty to human rights and occasionally intervene in the affairs of
other nations. The liberal conception of intervention assumes that the
moral standing of a society "rests on its ability to respect and to protect
the rights of its members and on their consent, explicit or implicit, to
its rules and institutions" (ibid., 288). For example, Saddam Hussein's
tyrannical regime in Iraq lacked moral legitimacy because it trampled
on the rights of its citizens. From a moral point of view, "we look at
social groupings formed by persons as derivative and constructed and
as drawing their legitimacy from the will and consent of these persons"
(ibid.). State sovereignty should never trump all other values, and it cannot immunize a state from outside intervention to stop ethnic cleansing,
genocide, or other crimes. Humanitarian intervention, therefore, may be
justified in order to override the sovereignty of an abusive state.

Smith also describes a realist approach to humanitarian intervention that emphasizes state sovereignty. Realists often maintain that humanitarian intervention represents little more than a fig leaf for the pursuit of national interest. Nation-states act entirely in their self-interest, and therefore, we ought to be wary of calls to help those suffering from famine or war. In international affairs, nations are well advised to pursue their national interests, rather than getting bogged down in overseas adventures that waste treasure and lives.[4] Henry Kissinger articulates this realist vision well, defending the Westphalian state system put in place by European powers in the seventeenth century (Kissinger 2001). This arrangement proscribed religious and political interference in the affairs of other states, producing the concept of noninterference in domestic politics. In Kissinger's view, this system maintained peace and order in international affairs for much of the nineteenth century. Although it did not prevent wars altogether, it limited them, preventing messianic interference in international relations.[5]

Kissinger sees the humanitarian interventions of the 1990s as disastrous departures from the Westphalian system that amount to "a revolution in the way the international system has operated for more than three hundred years" (Kissinger 2001, 235). Commenting on American interventions, he argues that "the new doctrine of humanitarian intervention asserts that humane convictions are so integral a part of the American tradition that both treasure and, in the extreme, lives must be risked to vindicate them around the world" (ibid., 253). For Kissinger, this doctrine embodies a moralism that ignores historical and political context. Moreover, it has an ad hoc character, driven by domestic politics and media attention. It is highly selective; American and European powers occupy Kosovo but disregard human rights violations in Chechnya, "intervene in Bosnia, but refuse to send military forces to Sierra Leone" (ibid., 257). Like many realists before him, Kissinger roundly condemns such selective moralism, accusing humanitarian internationalists of easing their consciences while ignoring widespread suffering.

With Kissinger, then, we see the elements of the realist approach to humanitarian intervention. For the realist, we should avoid making universal claims about a moral obligation to intervene, focusing instead on interventions serving a nation's national interest. We should pay careful attention to historical context, rejecting abstract principles that have little bearing on concrete political realities. Finally, we should be very attentive to how humanitarian interventions affect the nation-state system. The principle of nonintervention has served international politics well, preventing religious and political zealots from imposing their views on others. We should think hard before jettisoning it, particularly when confronting well-organized terrorist movements seeking to undermine world order.

This realist vision conflicts fundamentally with liberal approaches to humanitarian intervention. Liberals emphasize human rights before sovereignty, refusing to credit the Westphalian system with the benefits Kissinger ascribes to it. Instead of focusing on the national interest, they consider the rights of stateless populations and promote international human rights regimes. Instead of emphasizing the particulars of international politics, liberals embrace universal conceptions of human rights. Particular cases illustrate conflicts between liberal and realist principles. For example, early in the 1990s crisis in the former Yugoslavia, the Vatican and some European powers alienated Serbia by officially recognizing Croatia and Slovenia as nation-states.[6] On one hand, this seemed like a legitimate acknowledgment of the right to self-determination, an important element in the nation-state system. On the other hand, as both Serbia and later Croatia began committing terrible crimes within their new "nations," many Americans and Europeans called for NATO to stop them. National sovereignty and respect for human rights clashed, and few people at the time knew how to resolve this conflict.

Participation: The Key to Understanding International Politics

When approaching these kinds of problems, John Paul II draws heavily on the concept of participation, a product of his engagement with phenomenology. He develops this idea in order to capture the lived experience of communal action. By using it as opposed to the concept of intersubjectivity, he emphasizes how action reveals the person. *Intersubjectivity* is an important term for Husserl, describing the way in which multiple subjects shape consciousness by interacting. However, for John Paul II, it suggests primarily the "cognitive dimensions of intersubjectivity," rather than action as the "fundamental source for the cognition of man as person" (Wojtyla 1979, 315 n. 75).[7] Understanding cognition is indispensable for political life, but John Paul II thinks the acting person should be our focus. He also distinguishes his notion of participation from metaphysical understandings of the term, which Aquinas retrieved and developed from Neoplatonic sources.[8] Instead of developing a comprehensive participatory metaphysic, John Paul II analyzes how persons experience communal action.

Participation, John Paul II writes, is a "property of the person, a property that expresses itself in the ability of human beings to endow existence and action with a personal (personalistic) dimension when they exist and act together with others" (Wojtyla 1993, 237). Human beings often act and live together; however, this fact indicates "nothing about community, but speaks only of a multiplicity of beings, of acting subjects, who are people" (ibid., 238). A community, in contrast, denotes a "specific unity," a relation or sum of relations among individuals that is accidental to them (ibid.). Objectively, we can use the unity of persons to classify associations, but subjectively, we can also consider how a group affects its members' lived experience. In fact, the concept of participation involves a "positive relation to the humanity of others, understanding *humanity* here not as the abstract idea of the human being," but as "the personal self, in each instance unique and unrepeatable" (ibid., 237). Metaphysically, we define communities by focusing on beings and relations, and as a Thomist, John Paul II endorses this analysis. However, he also thinks that participation reveals elements of lived experience often absent in purely metaphysical analyses. As I noted in the last chapter, he presents a gradual movement from categorial knowledge of species-membership to knowledge of the person's particularity. Participation presupposes categorial knowledge of the person's value, an awareness that persons and things differ in value. Nevertheless, it is a preliminary step toward deeper knowledge of a person. John Paul II proposes that at the political level, we gradually come to know the irreducibility of persons.

To understand how such a radical change occurs, John Paul II describes dyadic structures of community. The first, the *I-thou* relationship, reflects the "interhuman, interpersonal dimension of community" (Wojtyla 1993, 241). I recognize another person as "one of many whom I could describe" (Wojtyla 1993, 243). I relate to her but am also potentially related to others. John Paul II emphasizes the *reflexivity* of this relationship, saying that when I relate to her, I acknowledge a "relation that somehow proceeds from me, but also returns to me" (ibid., 241). In this way, I partially constitute myself through my relations.[9]

In the I-thou relationship, two people "mutually become an *I* and a *thou* for each other and experience their relationship in this manner" (Wojtyla 1993, 243). By acting and reacting to each other, they constitute a unique form of human community. Factually, they come to know each other as personal subjects, but they also sense that they *ought* to "abide in mutual affirmation of the transcendent value of the persons (a value that may also be called *dignity*) and 'confirm' this in action" (ibid., 247). The "ought" thus enters into a factual relationship. In this analysis, I think we again see the limitations of the "is-ought" problem in twentieth-century ethics. What appears to be merely a fact, a relationship between persons, also contains a normative element that we uncover through lived experience. Summarizing the elements of the I-thou form of community, John Paul II says that it is "reducible to treating and really experiencing 'the other as oneself' (to use an expression taken directly from the Gospel)" (ibid., 244).

John Paul II contrasts the I-thou form of community with the *I-we* form, which he identifies with the traditional Roman Catholic concept of the common good. It differentiates social and interpersonal dimensions of community, highlighting how our relationships presuppose and form larger communities. The *we* in the dyad *I-we* refers "directly to multiplicity and indirectly to the persons belonging to this multiplicity" (Wojtyla 1993, 246). It originates when multiple persons become aware that they are united around a value, form a specific *we,* and partially constitute themselves by relating to it. The I-we link is also both a fact and a task because we *find* ourselves related to others in community, but must also *will* to foster this relationship. It takes on a normative character, because we feel the pull of an authentic community calling us to unite around a common value. Recasting a traditional teaching about the common good, John Paul II argues that it has a "greater fullness of value than the individual good of each separate *I* in a particular community" (ibid., 250). It is also "essentially free from utilitarianism," eliciting sacrifices that utilitarianism cannot explain (ibid., 251). Human persons grasp its great *spiritual* value, are often willing to sacrifice their lives for it, and eschew utilitarianism's myopic calculations of self-interest.

Importantly, John Paul II suggests that the common good can be "quantitatively diverse: two in the case of marriage (no longer just one + one, but a couple), several in the case of the family, millions in

the case of a particular nation, billions in the case of all humankind"
(Wojtyla 1993, 249). Subject to differentiation, it is an analogy of
proportionality. An analogy of proportionality exists when "the intrinsic similarity between analogates is expressed by a term that is
applied to all the analogates in its proper and literal meaning, but
with a proportional difference as found in each" (Clarke 2001, 49).
For example, we apply the concept of the common good "in accord
with the specific communal nature" proper to a community (Wojtyla
1993, 251). In different associations, persons realize it differently, but
each association must be a "clear reflection of the human *I*, of personal
subjectivity, rather than something opposed to this subjectivity. And
if it happens to be opposed, human beings as subjects must institute
reforms" (ibid.).

In this presentation of participation, I again see John Paul II's differences with Scheler. As a task, participation is a potentiality we must will
to actualize (Wojtyla 1993, 202–03). Referring specifically to Scheler,
John Paul II asks if the impulse toward participation is emotional and
spontaneous, suggesting that this is how Scheler understands it.[10] He
notes that emotions are "enormous resources, variously distributed
among people," and acknowledges that Scheler establishes a "basic,
innate disposition to participate in humanity as a value, to spontaneously open up to others" (ibid., 203). Nevertheless, Scheler mistakenly
thinks we can achieve participation by relying solely on emotion. This
is erroneous, John Paul II argues, because we must choose to affirm
one person among others. Emotional connections surely "facilitate this
choice," but by themselves, they are insufficient to actualize it (ibid.,
204). People may, for example, sympathize with those suffering from
famine, but unless they will to develop solidarity with them, this
emotion will pass, becoming just another crisis highlighted by media
outlets. In contrast, as they enter into complex relations, they can
realize that participation is a task they must undertake. Thus, when
discussing participation, John Paul II accentuates the will, which
he thinks is absent from Scheler's political thought. Both thinkers
emphasize lived experience as a central element in political life and
recognize how emotions shape our relations with others. However,
John Paul II insists that we must will to love in community, an idea
Scheler rejects vociferously.

The Problem of Alienation
and Inauthentic Attitudes

The will is particularly important because we often confront social situations that create alienation. Deftly adopting this concept from Marxism, John Paul II removes it from the purely economic sphere, applying it instead to "the realm of specifically human and interpersonal relations" (Wojtyla 1993, 205).[11] Undoubtedly, cultural and economic structures produce alienation, but at its core it "means the negation of participation, for it renders participation difficult or even impossible" (ibid., 206). Alienation undermines the community of persons by closing people in on themselves or subsuming them into collectives.[12] Like participation, it relates not merely to the person as a member of the human species, but also to the "human being as a personal subject" (ibid., 255). People continue to interact in alienating conditions, but the *we* in their relation is stifled and deformed. Alienation may, at times, even annihilate it, as in the case of totalitarianism. The family and other I-thou relationships can also promote an alienation that "subverts the lived experience of truth of the humanity, the truth of the essential worth of the person, in the human *thou*" (ibid., 256). A loved one or neighbor becomes a stranger or an enemy, negating what is particularly valuable in his personhood.

In addition to alienation, inauthentic attitudes like conformism and avoidance undermine participation. Conformism "denotes a tendency to comply with the accepted custom and to resemble others" in a servile way (Wojtyla 1979, 345). Naturally, complying with custom is indispensable for developing any community, but it often develops into passiveness, a failure to share in constructing community. It also reveals an incapacity to choose, making us merely subjects of what happens, rather than actors shaping our persons. Conformism produces indifference toward the common good that in its "servile form then becomes a denial of participation in the proper sense of the term" (ibid.). Avoidance, on the other hand, is "nothing but a withdrawal," originating when people simply turn away from participation because they find it too difficult (ibid.). In extreme circumstances, people may legitimately withdraw from an unjust social order. However, mere avoidance amounts to abandoning responsibility, denying the rich experience of participation.[13]

To summarize what John Paul II says about alienation and participation, these are opposed concepts capturing lived experience. Alienation exists when social structures destroy participation. Conformism and avoidance are attitudes that negate our responsibilities toward others. In contrast, participation is a property of persons enabling them to endow their interaction with others with a personalistic character. It moves the person from a categorial knowledge of the value of persons to the intuition of a *particular* and irreducible person. Persons do not automatically arrive at this insight but must will to actualize it. Finally, participation captures the lived experience of the common good, revealing how we actualize a value absent from our individual personhoods.

John Paul II at the United Nations: The Rights of Nations

Turning to how John Paul II applies this idea of participation to international politics, we see him confounding those who want to easily classify him. Recognizing changes in international politics in the aftermath of the Cold War, he embraces elements of both realism and liberalism. I noted in chapter 3 that in his 1995 speech to the United Nations, he defends the rights of nations, a traditional element of realism. Recall that he describes how the twentieth century saw terrible crimes in which nations and cultures were eliminated because they were considered inferior. In particular, he describes how the former Soviet Union annexed the Baltic States and Eastern Europe, eliminating their sovereignty under the guise of sham democracies (1995UN, 5). He also notes that the 1948 Universal Declaration of Human Rights says little about the rights of nations. The rights of nations raise "urgent questions about justice and freedom in the world today" (ibid.). John Paul II discusses these rights in terms of the universal and particular elements of human nature. Human beings find themselves between the universal "pole" of human nature and the particular "pole" of nation and ethnicity. We can never disregard the universal elements in human nature, for doing so plunges us into ethical and cultural relativism. Nevertheless, we also cannot forget the particular pole expressed by nations and ethnic groups. The word *nation,* with its Latin roots in the word *nasci,* "to be born," highlights how culture powerfully conditions our universal human nature. We are usually more intensely bound to particularity than to universality. As a fact, we find ourselves participating in the humanity of those sharing our language and culture. Usually, we must will to participate in a common humanity extending beyond this context.

This anthropological framework establishes the rights of nations, which John Paul II thinks are "nothing but 'human rights' fostered at the level of community life" (1995UN, 8). Naturally, we may have difficulty defining a particular nation's boundaries, because the nation and state are not isomorphic, and often the nation exists within a state arbitrarily created by external powers. This was particularly true during the Cold War, and when it ended, the bipolar political order disintegrated, spawning many new nations. With this context in mind, John Paul II cautiously attributes rights to nations. A nation has a right to exist, which "entails that no one—neither a State nor another nation, nor an international organization—is ever justified in asserting that an individual nation is not worthy of existence" (ibid.). This right differs from the modern concept of sovereignty, because various forms of political organization are compatible with nationhood. John Paul II also maintains that every nation enjoys a right to "its own language and culture," which it exercises through its educational system (ibid.). In an intriguing phrase, he says that it involves "spiritual sovereignty" that may even exist within the borders of a hostile state. Endorsing spiritual sovereignty is dangerous in a world that has seen ethnic cleansing, and John Paul II qualifies his claims by saying that a nation should shape its culture "according to its own traditions, excluding, of course, every abuse of human rights and in particular the oppression of minorities" (ibid.). Our common humanity should restrain how we express cultural or national identity. Here, John Paul II marshals his conception of human value as a counterweight against those who elevate the particular over the universal.

In addition to this familiar theme, John Paul II uses his conception of love to support cultural diversity (1995UN, 8). Different cultures, he maintains, are "but different ways of facing the question of the meaning of personal existence" (ibid., 9). Speaking to artists and intellectuals in the Republic of Georgia in 1999, he discussed love and transcendence, saying:

It is precisely in this movement of self-transcendence, of recognition of the other, of the need to communicate with the other, that culture is created. But this drive towards the other is possible only through love. Ultimately, it is love alone which succeeds in uprooting the tragic selfishness that lies deep within the human heart. It is love which helps us to place others and the Other at the centre of our lives. Christians have always sought to create a culture which is fundamentally open to the eternal and transcendent, while at the same time attentive to the temporal, the concrete, the human. Generations of Christians have striven to build and to pass on a culture, the goal of which is an ever more profound and universal fraternal communion of persons. Yet this universality is not one of oppressive uniformity. Genuine culture respects the mystery of the human person, and must therefore involve a dynamic exchange between the particular and the universal. It must seek a synthesis of unity and diversity. Love alone is capable of holding this tension in a creative and fruitful balance. (1999Culture, section 2)

Many of the elements of John Paul II's understanding of love appear in this speech, shaping how he approaches the rights of nations. Love is a movement toward others enabling us to move beyond our selfish orbits. It is a creative force drawing us toward higher values and undermining perverse ones. It enables us to embrace persons, forming a community in which persons commit themselves fully to others. Most importantly, it locates God at the center of our *ordo amoris*. Love, then, becomes a way to celebrate cultural diversity.

This subtle position is likely to engender misunderstanding, because it navigates between universality and particularity in a political context in which forces are moving in both directions. It celebrates difference, rejecting a homogenized global culture, while disciplining the accent on diversity by appealing to a universal human nature. Some might easily confuse it with cultural relativism, which accepts even the most appalling cultural practices in the name of diversity. However, John Paul II carefully rules relativism out by insisting that the "truth about man is the unchangeable standard by which all cultures are judged; but every culture has something to teach us about one or other dimension of that complex truth" (1995UN, 10). Rather than endorsing an ill-defined pluralism, he articulates a conception of human nature allowing for diverse cultural expressions.

Critics may also question why John Paul II thinks all cultures manifest some answer to transcendent questions. I think we see a deeper treatment of this idea in "Fides et Ratio," where he identifies fundamental questions that all cultures address, including "Who am I? Where have I come from and where am I going? Why is there evil? What is there after life?" (FR, 1).[14] In a controversial passage, he goes further, describing substantive metaphysical ideas that constitute "a core of philosophical insight within the history of thought as a whole" (FR, 4). This core includes not only logical principles like the principle of noncontradiction, but also the concept of a free person who can know God, beauty, truth and moral norms. This passage supports the value of cultural diversity.[15] Different cultures express diverse answers to fundamental metaphysical questions. To cut ourselves off from one of them robs us of important insight into the meaning of human life. John Paul II recognizes that participation occurs within a particular social and linguistic context that we should respect and enhance. The rights of nations protect nations from those seeking to destroy their particularity in the name of a universal culture. These rights, however, must never be used to violate human dignity. Participation obliges us to both acknowledge the irreducibility of persons and recognize cultural uniqueness.

The Civilization of Love

By defending the rights of nations, John Paul II bolsters the realist approach to humanitarian intervention. However, when he discusses the family of nations, he moves toward the liberal approach. The United Nations, he argues, must be more than simply a bureaucracy performing important functions in the international system. Instead, it must serve as a

> moral center where all the nations of the world feel at home and develop a shared awareness of being, as it were, a "family of nations." The idea of a "family" immediately evokes something more than simple functional relations or mere convergence of interests. The family is by nature a community based on mutual trust, mutual support and sincere respect. In an authentic family the strong do not dominate; instead, the weaker

members, because of their weakness, are all the more welcomed and
served. (1995UN, 14)

The international system should be neither a Hobbesian war of all against
all, nor simply a society tenuously held together by regimes or contracts.
Instead, it should be a family-like community that views cultural iden-
tities "as a common treasure belonging to the cultural patrimony of
mankind" (1995UN, 15). This requires nations not only to live with
others, but also to live for them by exchanging gifts. Rejecting the idea
that this vision is an "unattainable utopia," John Paul II urges the United
Nations to promote a family of nations (1995UN, 15). The dramatic
end of the Cold War illustrates how a vision that appears utopian can be
quite realistic, shaping international relations in profound ways.

To support a family of nations, John Paul II retrieves from Pope Paul
VI and others the concept of a "civilization of love." The United Nations,
he insists, should undertake a "common effort to build the civilization
of love, founded on the universal values of peace, solidarity, justice and
liberty" (1995UN, 18). The heart of this civilization should be "freedom
of individuals and the freedom of nations, lived in self-giving solidarity
and responsibility" (1995UN, 18). Invoking a familiar theme in his writings, John Paul II emphasizes that freedom is neither mere license, nor
simply the absence of tyranny. Instead, it is anchored in the truth about
the human person, a "creature of intelligence and free will, immersed
in the mystery which transcends his own being and endowed with the
ability to reflect and the ability to choose—and thus capable of wisdom
and virtue" (1995UN, 4). The civilization of love, then, requires nations
and persons to exercise freedom using this truth as a guide.

What are some of the other characteristics of the civilization of love? A
year before speaking to the United Nations, John Paul II described them
in his "Letter to Families," arguing that the word "civilization" refers to
human culture, which "answers man's spiritual and moral needs" ("Letter
to Families," 13).[16] Approaching the concept of the civilization of love
negatively and positively, John Paul II describes "two civilizations," one
marked by utilitarianism, the other characterized by self-giving love.
The utilitarian civilization suffers from a "crisis of concepts" because it
has lost any sense of what love, freedom, and the person mean. It reduces
these ideas to use and production, developing them in a "one-sided

way." It also violates the personalistic norm by using persons merely as instruments, and debases humanity by fastening on lower values, falsely identifying the truth with the "pleasant and useful." In fact, utilitarian happiness is "immediate gratification for the exclusive benefit of the individual, apart from or opposed to the objective demands of the true good." In sum, the utilitarian civilization promotes excessive individualism, ethical subjectivism, and a dehumanizing ethos of use. In contrast, the civilization of love creates and shares "the good of persons and of communities." It recognizes that love is demanding, requiring patience, endurance, and constant cultivation. In it, persons exert themselves to give to others selflessly. The civilization of love embodies the "radical acceptance of the understanding of man as a person who 'finds himself' by making a sincere gift of self."

I want to suggest that in this discussion of the civilization of love, John Paul II describes participation in theological language. Like participation, the civilization of love requires acknowledging the personhood of another in all its particularity. At its highest level, it manifests the reciprocal recognition of personhood. Finally, like participation, it requires effort and is demanding. By contrasting the two civilizations, John Paul II links his account of participation, his attack on utilitarianism, and his understanding of love. In the violent world of nations, he urges leaders to abandon narrow conceptions of the national interest in order to cultivate self-giving love. In doing so, he rejects the realist emphasis on national interest, urging nations to move beyond it to cultivate self-giving love in international affairs.

A Duty to Intervene

Such selflessness may require the strong to help the weak, lending support for humanitarian intervention. In fact, responding to the horrors of the 1990s, John Paul II adopted strong language about our obligation to intervene to prevent profound suffering. For example, addressing the United Nations Food and Agricultural Organization in 1993, he stated that

> the idea is maturing within the international community that humanitarian action, far from being the right of the strongest, must be inspired

by the conviction that intervention, or even interference when objective situations require it, is a response to a moral obligation to come to the aid of individuals, peoples or ethnic groups whose fundamental right to nutrition has been denied to the point of threatening their existence. (1993Food and Agriculture)

Speaking to those charged with alleviating starvation and malnutrition, he rejected simplistic understandings of famine, focusing instead on its root causes. Perhaps he had in mind cases like Somalia in 1992, where armed thugs interfered with food shipments, threatening thousands of people with starvation. In such circumstances, John Paul II suggests that we have a duty to intervene to help those in need.

In the first year of this century, John Paul II again affirmed humanitarian intervention as a duty, insisting that "an offense against human rights is an offense against the conscience of humanity as such, an offense against humanity itself" (2000Peace, section 7). Rejecting sovereignty as a buffer against external interference, he argued that crimes against humanity are never merely internal affairs within sovereign nations. They not only affect regional peace, but also invariably harm the innocent. With these words, John Paul II positions himself with liberal thinkers who reject sovereignty as an absolute value. He goes further, asserting that in the fluid and dangerous world of international politics, "there is a need to affirm the preeminent value of humanitarian law and the consequent duty to guarantee the right to humanitarian aid to suffering civilians and refugees. The duty to protect these rights extends beyond the geographical and political borders within which they are violated" (ibid.). Here, John Paul II asserts a right that seems to exceed what international law recognizes. As some contemporary thinkers note, international law restricts intervention severely, primarily because it originated within the nation-state system as an attempt to limit conflict. John Paul II proposes that we move away from this restrictive framework and embrace an obligation to help those suffering from famine or human rights abuses. The duty to intervene rests on the priority of the person to the collective. The "moral and political legitimacy" of the right to intervene is "in fact based on the principle that the good of the human person comes before all else and stands above all human institutions" (2000Peace, sec. 9). We ought to reject any proposal to subsume the person into an international collective.

To summarize how John Paul II approaches international politics, he adopts elements from both realist and liberal understandings of the international arena. To counter dangerous nationalism and value cultural diversity, he affirms the rights of nations. He also presents the civilization of love as a normative ideal for international politics. Finally, he articulates a duty to intervene to prevent humanitarian disasters. In all three of these areas, John Paul II's pre-papal understanding of participation plays an important role. Although he rarely mentions it, he presents it both theologically and philosophically in many of his speeches.

The Rights of Nations or Human Rights?

Commenting on one of John Paul II's early calls for humanitarian intervention, Weigel correctly notes that it "raised more questions than it answered" (Weigel 1999, 666). John Paul II rarely specifies to whom the obligation to intervene applies. The "international community," as Weigel notes, is a vague locution, more of a rhetorical device than a conceptual tool. Often, nations use it knowing full well that large powers do most of the work of the "international community." Without knowing which parties constitute it, we can make little sense of the idea of a duty to intervene to prevent humanitarian disasters. More importantly, by defending this duty, the rights of nations, and the civilization of love, John Paul II creates a conflict between ethical ideals. For example, in the 1990s, Serbia claimed the right to self-determination and nationhood. Yet, it pursued this goal through ethnic cleansing, a profoundly immoral policy. In such a case, should we endorse its right to nationhood? Or, do the rights of persons trump it? If so, what are the precise grounds for making this judgment? What does it mean to say that the right of nation is "trumped" or overridden by the concern for individual dignity? Are we allowed to simply deny self-determination in the name of humanitarian intervention, or must we give some credence to even the most unappealing forms of nationalism? These questions suggest some significant conflicts within John Paul II's approach to international politics.

These conflicts are particularly acute because John Paul II affirms a hierarchy of value ranking spiritual over material values. When analyzing globalization, he condemns untrammeled economic growth, arguing that it reflects a distorted hierarchy of value. He identifies a conflict between material and spiritual values, and then resolves it by making spiritual values preeminent. He confronts a different problem when the rights of nations and the dignity of the person conflict. In his words, nations have "spiritual sovereignty"; they not only protect a populace from external harm, and provide for material needs, but also embody answers to spiritual questions. However, we now have a conflict between spiritual values that we cannot resolve by affirming the preeminence of spiritual values. We seem to be at an impasse, confronting a conflict between spiritual values that all demand our respect.

At times, John Paul II seems to recognize these difficulties. For example, discussing peace, he notes that

> There is also the difficulty of combining principles and values which, however reconcilable in the abstract, can prove on the practical level to be resistant to any easy synthesis. In addition, at a deeper level, there are always the demands which ethical commitment makes upon individuals, who are not free of self-interest and human limitations. (2000Peace, sec. 3)

Because of its complexity, humanitarian intervention presents seemingly intractable conflicts. Unfortunately, John Paul II says little about how to resolve them. This is frustrating for those struggling to respond to humanitarian disasters. As pontiff, John Paul II often rightfully refuses to present detailed policy blueprints, arguing that the Church must avoid making precise policy recommendations. Nevertheless, when he offers guidance at the level of moral principles, we find diverse concepts that apparently clash. It is reasonable, therefore, to ask if we can resolve this conflict.

Consequentialism as a Guide?

Like realists in the past, some contemporary thinkers maintain that we cannot resolve it. For example, although they are not realists, Robert McNamara and James Blight argue that we cannot avoid doing evil when intervening to help others. They use philosopher Thomas Nagel's work in the 1970s to argue that humanitarian intervention presents us with "moral blind-alleys" (McNamara and Blight 2001, 122).[17] A moral blind alley is a situation in which "one cannot find a way to refrain from doing (or not doing) that which one believes is morally wrong" (ibid., 123). Any course of action we choose will be morally unacceptable. The post–Cold War international arena, McNamara and Blight argue, presents us with such inescapable moral blind alleys. Communal violence is driven by the "incompatible claims of self-determination and nationalist extremism," and in this climate, no one can retain clean hands (ibid.). In Liberia, Sierra Leone, Kosovo, Bosnia, and other places, the United Nations has confronted moral blind alleys in which doing evil was inevitable. Similarly, in the aftermath of the September 11 terrorist attacks on the United States, the United States attacked both the Taliban and al-Qaeda in Afghanistan. Using technologically sophisticated bombs that penetrated caves, American forces expelled the Taliban and al-Qaeda forces from numerous locations in Afghanistan. These bombs allowed Americans to avoid becoming mired in a vicious ground war that would have cost many lives. However, they also led to civilian casualties, and for some, this put the United States in a moral blind alley from which it could not exit.

Interestingly, McNamara and Blight criticize John Paul II and the United States Catholic bishops for suggesting that we might extricate ourselves from such moral blind alleys. Both, they suggest, mistakenly think we can intervene to prevent genocide and ethnic cleansing without doing evil. Discussing how the United Nations failed to prevent genocide in Rwanda, McNamara and Blight suggest that even if it had intervened, it would have confronted the possibility of hostage taking, and might have killed innocent civilians. They note that John Paul II

states that it is our *duty* to intervene in such cases. Yet in the case of Rwanda, it is not at all clear that an attempt to carry out this "duty" would have led to a morally satisfactory conclusion. Yet the inverse is also true; not intervening was clearly not morally satisfactory. (Ibid., 129)

With John Paul II in mind, McNamara and Blight warn "those who would embark on an intervention to correct an egregious evil" that "the morality of the outcome will be determined by far more than the intention to do good" (ibid., 131). Before pronouncing an intervention morally legitimate, we must weigh its probable consequences, knowing full well that we will commit evil acts.

The moral blind alley approach captures the horrors peacekeepers often face when intervening to prevent humanitarian disasters. Sometimes, it appears, they can only do evil. McNamara and Blight also legitimately criticize John Paul II for failing to carefully consider the quagmires of humanitarian intervention. Peacekeepers in Bosnia and Rwanda have confronted terrible situations. For example, in Rwanda in 1994, ten Belgian peacekeepers were brutally tortured and murdered while trying to prevent genocide. Their bodies were "so badly cut up that they had become impossible to count" (Power 2002, 332). Such events seemed to trap peacekeepers in impossible situations. Philosophically, McNamara and Blight capture this sense that peacekeeping involves moral blind alleys.

Despite its attractiveness, however, the moral blind alley approach suffers from conceptual confusions and creates political apathy. First, it offers us little guidance about how to act in the international arena. What do McNamara, Blight, and others propose we do when confronting a moral blind alley? They assume we have reason to intervene to prevent genocide, but if intervention and nonintervention both involve doing evil acts, I see no reason to intervene. Inaction and action both become legitimate choices. If we do have reason to intervene, as McNamara and Blight clearly think we do, then one choice is clearly preferable to another, and we are not in a moral blind alley. McNamara and Blight explicitly distinguish their position from the "lesser of two evils" approach, but as far as I can tell, it quickly becomes indistinguishable from it. Humanitarian intervention implies that it is in some way better than inaction and therefore suggests that we have chosen a lesser evil.[18] Additionally, this view undermines any motivation to intervene. American and European publics are notoriously reluctant to commit troops and treasure to goals only remotely connected to their nations' immediate national interest. Telling them that they confront a moral blind alley only bolsters this reluctance, undermining attempts to build international coalitions to prevent genocide, famine, or terrorism. In sum, there is little political or conceptual reason to endorse the "moral blind alley" approach to humanitarian intervention.

If the moral blind alley position amounts to choosing the lesser evil, why not embrace the idea of a "lesser evil"? Kaplan proposes that this is exactly what we should do. As I noted in the last chapter, he says that when dealing with "failed states," the best policy involves "doing or accepting a certain amount of 'evil' to make possible a proportionately greater amount of good" (Kaplan 2000, 121–22). Reviving the realist conception of national interest, Kaplan argues that when a large power confronts genocide or chaos, it must carefully decide if intervening will promote more good than evil. He declares that "dealing with bad people will always be necessary to prevent even greater evil" (ibid., 103). Leaders may have difficulty ascertaining which policies promote good over evil, but they must try to achieve some good in terrible circumstances.

Although it appears to offer more guidance than the "moral blind-alley approach," the "lesser evil" approach suffers from all of the arbitrariness endemic to consequentialism. Generally, those advocating it tell us that we must "balance" or "weigh" various goods and evils. However, this vague language offers no assistance to those responding to a humanitarian crisis. Which values should we "balance" or "weigh" when deciding whether to use force to feed the starving in Somalia? How can we measure how air attacks against Serbia affect the personhood of Belgrade's inhabitants? How do we ascertain how intervening in Bosnia affects the spiritual lives of Muslims and Orthodox Christians? How do we "balance" the risk of civilian casualties in Afghanistan over against the great benefits of freedom from the intolerant and oppressive Taliban regime? Usually, discussions about humanitarian interventions ignore these questions, arbitrarily focusing on tangible values. We are again back to what Scheler and John Paul II repeatedly say, that consequentialism is an unworkable ethical project. It provides us with no guidance about how to help those in need.

Some Roman Catholic thinkers reject the lesser-evil idea, proposing instead to resolve conflicts over humanitarian intervention by adopting the just war tradition's principle of proportionality. For example, Hehir carefully outlines criteria for humanitarian intervention (Hehir 1995). Insisting on multilateral authorization, he expands the idea of a just cause beyond genocide, and urges intervening forces to use just means. Like Weigel, he endorses the criterion of proportionality, proposing that it helps us intervene justly. For example, writing about NATO's 1999 air war in Kosovo, Hehir states that combatants must use the principle of proportionality before acting, continuously review it during a war, and consider it when assessing their conduct after a war (Hehir 1999). Writing about how the United States should respond to the September 11 attacks, he emphasizes that any response must adhere to the just war tradition's criterion of proportionality. Against how many states can the United States declare war, Hehir asks, "without being itself defined as a threat to international order?" (Hehir 2001).

Hehir rejects consequentialism as a way of developing ethical principles but employs it selectively when discussing proportionality. Unfortunately, in doing so, he also succumbs to arbitrariness. For example, putting on a tactician's hat, Hehir makes complex judgments about how to wage war in Kosovo, at one point stating that he would "drop some bridges (those carrying military supplies) at night and not turn off the lights" (Hehir 1999). Yet, in this analysis, it is entirely unclear what he is doing. Military planners and soldiers have a moral obligation to consider proportionality in order to avoid embarking on disastrous military adventures. They make proportionate judgments using a limited set of values involving lives and equipment lost. This is the kind of proportionate reason Finnis, Boyle, and Grisez identify as important and legitimate. In contrast, Hehir purports to provide a *moral* evaluation of the humanitarian intervention in Kosovo, and he cannot consider only one set of values. He says virtually nothing about spiritual values, focusing conveniently on military matters. For a religious and moral analysis, this simply will not do. Hehir arbitrarily ignores the spiritual values related to the person, failing to discuss how the war in Kosovo affected them. This is understandable, because if he were to consider them, his analysis would devolve into an incoherent attempt to calculate spiritual values. Like Weigel, Hehir employs a selective consequentialist reasoning that has little philosophical merit. We cannot, therefore, use it to resolve dilemmas in humanitarian intervention.

The Priority of Person over Collective: How John Paul II Can Address the Dilemmas of Humanitarian Intervention

Without adopting one of the positions I have discussed, can John Paul II resolve the ethical dilemmas of humanitarian intervention? Do the rights of nations take precedence over those suffering from famine or genocide? Or do the needs of persons supersede these rights, permitting us to override national sovereignty to help the needy? In my view, John Paul II cannot address these questions without altering his understanding of the rights of nations, which confuses the person and the collective. He creates this confusion by moving too easily from individual rights to the rights of nations. We cannot say, as he does in his 1995 United Nations speech, that the rights of nations are "nothing but 'human rights' fostered at the specific level of community life" (1995UN, 8). This quick conceptual move ignores John Paul II's own numerous warnings about attributing moral agency to collectives. We have already seen that when discussing structures of sin, he insists that we attribute sin to collectives only analogically. Institutions lack the inner life necessary to be sinful, and therefore, a "situation—or likewise an institution, society itself—is not in itself the subject of moral acts. Hence a situation cannot be good or bad" (RP, 16). Analogically, social structures can be sinful, but we should avoid attributing sin literally to "some vague entity or anonymous collectivity such as the situation, the system, society, structures or institutions" (RP, 16).

This argument applies not only to sin, but also to rights. In defending human rights, John Paul II grounds them in persons who possess an inner life, a capacity for self-determination, and the freedom to relate to truth. Things and collectives lack these characteristics and therefore cannot have rights. John Paul II tells us that when considering communities, we should speak

> of a "quasi-subjectiveness," rather than of a proper subject of acting. All the people existing and acting together are obviously exercising a role in a common action, but in a different way than when each of them performs an action in its entirety. The new subjectiveness is the share of all the members of a community, or, in a broader sense, of a social group. In fact, it is but a quasi-subjectiveness, because even when the being and acting is realized together with others it is the *man-person who is always its proper subject.* (Wojtyla 1979, 277)[19]

The acting person is always our guide in thinking about community, and when analyzing social units, we must avoid thinking about them as

subjects. I think this warning applies particularly to nations. Undoubtedly, they express unique cultures and understandings of the metaphysical
mysteries confronting human beings. However, they have no inner life in
any meaningful sense of this term and therefore cannot have the rights a
subject possesses. As a personalist, John Paul II cannot attribute rights
to them in anything more than an analogical or legal sense.[20]

Unfortunately, when speaking to the United Nations, John Paul II
conflates univocal and analogical uses of the term *right*. Unless he avoids
univocal language about the rights of nations, he cannot resolve the
dilemmas of humanitarian intervention. In a study of the language of
rights in the United States, Mary Ann Glendon warns that the "oc-
casions for conflict among rights multiply as catalogs of rights grow
longer" (Glendon 1991, 16), and this is a danger that John Paul II
ought to consider. He affirms a host of individual rights, taking the
1948 Universal Declaration of Human Rights as his guide.[21] In recent
years, critics of human rights language have argued that it ignores
our social responsibilities and presupposes an atomistic conception
devoid of a social nature. Needless to say, such criticisms hardly apply
to John Paul II, who locates human rights within his conception of
participation. Nevertheless, by expanding the scope of rights to nations in 1995, he created significant conflicts between the rights of
persons and the rights of nations. I cannot see how he can retain them
both as equally important.

John Paul II can resolve this conflict by emphasizing the univocal
character of language about the human person, as well as the analogical
character of language about collectives. The common good, as he tells us
when writing about participation, involves an analogy of proportion. By
emphasizing this analogy, he could avoid attributing rights to collectives,
in keeping with his work on structures of sin. Furthermore, he could still
indicate how vitally important culture is in forming the human person.
Finally, when nationalism and the value of the person conflict, he could
argue that the rights of the person take precedence over those of nations.
The nation always serves the person, and promoting it by harming her
is inherently contradictory. In fact, when discussing humanitarian intervention, John Paul II suggests, but does not develop, this approach.
For example, five years after his 1995 United Nations speech, he stated,
"the good of the human person comes before all else and stands above all

human institutions" (2000Peace, sec. 9). We ought to institutionalize this idea by seeking "a *renewal of international law and international institutions,* a renewal whose starting-point and basic organizing principle should be the primacy of the good of humanity and of the human person over every other consideration" (ibid., sec. 12.32). Such strong language provides ample ground for ranking the person's dignity above the rights of nations. Participation serves the person, and it should never be subordinated to the nation. When national and individual rights clash, we order our ethical principles by affirming the primacy of the person over the group. I think John Paul II's theory of value and his critique of consequentialism leave him no other option but to adopt this conclusion.

How Should we Intervene?
Criteria for Humanitarian Intervention

Concretely, what does it mean to prioritize the person over the nation? Realists and nonrealists understandably worry that setting this priority may undermine the nation-state system, authorizing interventions that create disorder in international politics. For example, Hehir argues that we ought to be very careful before overriding national sovereignty. The international system, he correctly notes, contains "enormous differences of power and potential" between states, and large states often use humanitarian intervention "for reasons of power politics" (Hehir 1995, 8). Consequently, the "wisdom of Westphalia should be heeded. Intervention may be necessary, but it should not be made easy. Hence the need to sustain the presumption against it" (ibid.). Hehir's remarks reflect a genuine worry about how recent attacks on nonintervention may legitimize new forms of imperialism and coercion.[22]

In the wake of the September 11 terrorist attacks, many nations have become particularly worried about this problem, for they perceive in U.S. foreign policy a new unilateralism. Some maintain that it is a form of imperialism, while others worry that the United States often tragically overreaches when trying to help other countries.[23] In an eloquent essay entitled "The Seductiveness of Moral Disgust" (written before the September 11 attacks), Ignatieff articulates these worries, describing the negative consequences and hypocrisy of humanitarian interventions in the 1990s. Purporting to be postimperial, interventions in Bosnia and other places were often instead haunted by "ambitions, follies, and ironies of an imperial kind" (Ignatieff 1998, 92–93). As Ignatieff puts it, we "intervened not only to save others, but to save ourselves, or rather an image of ourselves as defenders of universal decencies" (ibid., 95). Intervening powers illegitimately assumed that they "had the power to do anything. This assumption of omnipotence often stood between indignation and insight, between feeling strongly and knowing what it was possible to do" (ibid., 96). Such excessive ambitions and aspirations produced great disillusion, creating an unwillingness to intervene to prevent future humanitarian disasters.

Ignatieff overstates his case, sometimes ignoring the dedicated activists and aid workers who struggled to respond to humanitarian disasters. Nevertheless, he reveals the dangers of uncritically pursuing policies that value the person over the nation. John Paul II recognizes these dangers, and offers criteria for when and how to intervene.[24] He identifies those to whom the obligation applies, mentioning international agencies, regional bodies, religious institutions, and humanitarian organizations (2000Peace, sec. 10). He discusses the *means* they should use, insisting that they initially include nonviolent mediation and negotiations. Additionally, he legitimizes armed intervention, noting that "when a civilian population risks being overcome by the attacks of an unjust aggressor and political efforts and non-violent defence prove to be of no avail, it is legitimate and even obligatory to take concrete measures to disarm the aggressor" (ibid., sec. 11). Violence is not only morally legitimate to defend the innocent, but at times it may be *obligatory.* Despite his deep sympathies for nonviolence, therefore, John Paul II rejects a pacifist position proscribing violence in humanitarian interventions. He also carefully sets conditions for using violence, insisting that interventions "must be limited in time and precise in their aims. They must be carried out in full respect for international law, guaranteed by an authority that is internationally recognized and, in any event, never left to the outcome of armed intervention alone" (ibid.). Peacekeepers may use violence, but only under strict conditions that limit it.[25]

In his understanding of humanitarian intervention, John Paul II joins others who develop criteria for humanitarian intervention. For example, Hehir calls for a multinational approach to humanitarian intervention guided by the principles of the just war tradition (Hehir

1995). McNamara and Blight argue that state sovereignty is not an absolute value and insist on multinational action for humanitarian interventions (McNamara and Blight 2001, ch. 3). Finally, Smith calls for carefully restraining humanitarian intervention, insisting that it be measured and careful (Smith 1999). Therefore, John Paul II is part of a growing trend to rethink humanitarian intervention on multinational and ethical grounds. Because he understands the value of a nation, he retrieves elements of a realist approach to humanitarian intervention. However, he also shares with liberals a commitment to the priority of the human person. What he adds to the discussion is a sophisticated account of participation that values collective life without denigrating the person. He shares with many the language of human rights, but at the end of the day, he always returns to the acting person.

At this point, those committed to consequentialism might rightfully ask how John Paul II arrives at his criteria for humanitarian intervention. Does he calculate the consequences of various policies, thus falling prey to his own criticisms of consequentialism? Some in the contemporary debate defend their views this way. For example, Kissinger maintains that the "ultimate dilemma of the statesman is to strike a balance between values and interests, and, occasionally, between peace and justice" (Kissinger 2001, 286). Scathingly, he argues that United States failed to achieve this balance in its humanitarian interventions in the 1990s. The language of "balance" here clearly indicates Kissinger's commitment to consequentialism. Among contemporary scholars, it is not difficult to find similar consequentialist defenses of principles of humanitarian intervention.

John Paul II rarely defends his criteria for humanitarian intervention, but I think he can without appealing to consequentialism. For example, he might agree with McNamara and Blight, who defend multilateralism by arguing that it has cognitive and perceptual advantages over unilateralism (McNamara and Blight, 2001, 132–50). Humanitarian intervention presents enormously complex problems that few leaders can understand without assistance from others. Similarly, intelligence-gathering is a vital part of battling terrorism, and no nation can rely solely on its own intelligence agencies. Acting multilaterally, therefore, provides indispensable information. For example, the United States military won a quick victory over Iraq in the Second Gulf War in 2003. However, it encountered significant difficulties after the war, incurring casualties and criticism for its failure to account for various contingencies. Many countries maintained that a multilateral approach would have enabled the United States to construct a more effective post-war policy in Iraq. When a great power consults others, it also reduces the perception that it is bullying or initiating some kind of neocolonialism. In the intense debates at the United Nations prior to the Second Gulf War, many diplomats opposed an invasion of Iraq by appealing to the perceptional and informational benefits of multilateralism. Such justifications for multilateralism avoid balancing spiritual goods in an incoherent fashion. They involve fallible judgments and cannot establish absolute rules about when to intervene. Sometimes, nations may have to intervene unilaterally. Nevertheless, the cognitive and perceptual advantages of multilateralism give us good reason to generally prefer it to unilateralism. Similarly, John Paul II can use the person's value to justify his strictures on violence in humanitarian intervention. It provides ample warrant for saying that we ought to seek nonviolent solutions before resorting to violence. Violence destroys the person and should only be a last resort. Reaching this conclusion requires no computation of spiritual values. Finally, John Paul II can also support his appeal to a public authority by maintaining that we need an agent to promote the common good. He might maintain that the very idea of the common good requires an agent to promote it.

In such reflections, I have provided a very sketchy nonconsequentialist defense of criteria for humanitarian intervention, and going further would require a separate essay on this issue. I simply want to indicate that it is mistaken to think that without consequentialism we are ethically lost when intervening in troubled parts of the world. Statespeople often adopt consequentialism when intervening but are not required to do so. Undoubtedly, by prioritizing the value of the person over the nation, John Paul II creates great potential for disorder and abuse of power in international relations. However, he is attentive to this danger, cautiously endorsing armed, multilateral intervention, guided by international law and clear military and political objectives.

The Sinfulness of the United Nations

With this ethical vision clear, however, I want to close this chapter by arguing that in his writings on international politics, John Paul II confuses the aims of associations and fails to apply his conception of sin to the United Nations. To address the first point, I think John Paul II confounds the aims of transnational institutions with those of the family, mistakenly asserting that international relations should be a "family of nations." He tells us that in an objective sense, we classify communities by identifying the common value their members pursue. Persons form a "community of acting," defined by the "aim that brings men to act together" (Wojtyla 1979, 279). Subjectively, we classify communities by considering how they help persons fulfill themselves. Using these ways of classifying social entities, I think it is obvious that nation-states and families differ substantially in subjective and objective ways. The family, in John Paul II's writings, forms a community of persons, serves life, participates in developing society, and shares in the life and mission of the church.[26] It cultivates deep emotional bonds between persons, providing them with unique opportunities to develop their personhood. We need not endorse a Hobbesian conception of international politics to see that these features are simply absent from the world of nation-states. Size is the obvious dissimilarity between families and nations. Moreover, we have to institutionalize political life in a nation-state, producing impersonal bureaucracies unlike anything we find in the family. Operated by these bureaucracies, nation-states lack a moral center. When we apply concepts like self-gift, trust, and solidarity to them, who exactly is the moral agent?

In his 1995 speech to the United Nations, John Paul II recognizes this problem when urging the United Nations to rise above the "cold status" of a bureaucracy and move toward "mutual trust, mutual support, and sincere respect" (1995UN, 14). However, he overlooks the possibility that an association may reach a size that renders it incapable of performing particular functions. Ideally, family members know each other very well and address problems in an intimate and effective way. This is not true in the world of nations. Reinhold Niebuhr makes this point convincingly, arguing that nations "do not have direct contact with other national communities, with which they must form some kind of international community. They know the problems of other peoples only indirectly and at second hand" (Niebuhr 1983, 85). Famously, Niebuhr distinguishes between interpersonal and political ethics, a distinction I reject. Nevertheless, he highlights important differences between nations and other associations that too many people today have forgotten. Niebuhr reminds us of the unpleasant truth that we rarely treat those living far from us with familial empathy. The transition from the interpersonal to the international realm is extremely difficult to make.

Niebuhr wrote his famous work on the immorality of nations years before the United Nations came on the international scene, and John Paul II is correct in saying that today it serves as an important forum for promoting contact between nations. However, he also underestimates sin's power over it. For example, I believe its failure to prevent genocide in Rwanda exemplified a sinful indifference to the fate of those living in countries with little power or influence in international politics. Analysts disagree about whether the United Nations could have prevented the genocide, but it never seriously tried to do so. A damning 1999 Independent Inquiry into the United Nations action concluded that Member States showed an appalling unwillingness to commit resources and displayed terrible paralyses of will that stifled attempts to prevent genocide.[27] General Romeo A. Dallaire, commander of the United Nations Observer Mission (UNAMIR) before and during the genocide, writes despairingly about how the United Nations ignored his pleas for assistance in preventing it. It failed to provide his troops with adequate equipment and support, created inefficient command and control systems, and disregarded repeated requests for further assistance.[28] The Report of the Independent Inquiry agrees with this assessment, concluding that the "fundamental capacity problems of UNAMIR led to the terrible and humiliating situation of the UN peacekeeping force almost paralyzed in the face of a wave of some of the worse brutality humankind has seen in this century" (United Nations 1999, "Conclusions," section 1). General Dallaire concludes that those who could effectively stop the genocide refused, while contingents from poor nations valiantly battled it. Poor nations "shamed the world by doing the right thing," while others procrastinated, obfuscating the truth of what was happening in Rwanda (Dallaire 1998, 85).

This shameful episode illustrates perfectly the inauthentic attitudes of avoidance and conformism. United Nations representatives evaded their responsibilities to their own forces, never mind the people of Rwanda. Avoiding a deeper involvement in Rwanda became "a kind of substitute or compensatory attitude for those who find solidarity or opposition too difficult" (Wojtyla 1979, 347). Member States in the United Nations refused to admit that genocide was occurring. To again quote the Independent Inquiry, "the lack of will to act in response to the crisis in Rwanda becomes all the more deplorable in light of the reluctance of key members of the International Community to acknowledge that the mass murder being pursued in front of global media was a genocide" (United Nations 1999, "Conclusions," sec. 5). Linda Melvern notes that in Rwanda, the "incitement to genocide was broadcast via a radio station and the people were psychologically prepared for months, and were ordered and coerced to carry out the extermination" (Melvern 2000, 4).[29] Despite the transparency of the genocide, members of the international community exhibited willful ignorance about what was happening before their eyes. To admit that genocide was occurring would have required them to take action under the 1948 Convention on the Prevention and Punishment of the Crime of Genocide, so they played semantic games to avoid their responsibilities.[30] Additionally, many in America and Europe ignored what was happening in Rwanda, conforming to prevailing attitudes about the United Nations. Ill-informed politicians denigrated it, adopting popular and mistaken conceptions of its failures in Somalia and elsewhere. The sins of conformism and avoidance produced structures of sin that impeded a constructive response to genocide.

In writing about structures of sin, John Paul II mentions other sins that are relevant here, the "very personal sins of those who cause or support evil or who exploit it; of those who are in a position to avoid, eliminate or at least limit certain social evils but who fail to do so out of laziness, fear or the conspiracy of silence, through secret complicity or indifference; of those who take refuge in the supposed impossibility of changing the world and also of those who sidestep the effort and sacrifice required, producing specious reasons of higher order" (RP, 16). This catalog of sins of omissions and commissions goes beyond bureaucratic inefficiency. It includes failures of the will, an important element in the Rwandan tragedy. To again quote Melvern, what happened in Rwanda "showed that despite the creation of an organization set up to prevent a repetition of genocide—for the UN is central to this task—it failed to do so, even when the evidence was indisputable" (Melvern 2000, 5). Nation-states took refuge in "specious reasons of higher order" to evade their moral responsibilities. Philip Gourevitch, a journalist who witnessed the terrible aftermath of the Rwandan genocide, captures the significance of these sins, noting bitterly that

> Rwanda had presented the world with the most unambiguous case of genocide since Hitler's war against the Jews, and the world sent blankets, beans, and bandages to camps controlled by the killers, apparently hoping that everybody would behave nicely in the future. The West's post-Holocaust pledge that genocide would never again be tolerated proved to be hollow, and for all the fine sentiments inspired by the memory of Auschwitz, the problem remains that denouncing evil is a far cry from doing good. (Gourevitch 1998, 170)

Sadly, John Paul II rarely discusses this terrible failure of will and what it suggests about the United Nations and the civilization of love.

Can the United Nations Respond to Distortions in Globalization and Nationalism?

Despite such failures in the area of humanitarian intervention, however, perhaps the United Nations can address the spiritual distortions in globalization and nationalism. Often, John Paul II suggests that it is the proper vehicle for this kind of work. For example, considering globalization, he notes that that the United Nations has the opportunity to

> contribute to the globalization of solidarity by serving as a meeting place for States and civil society and as a convergence of the varied interests and needs—regional and particular—of the world at large. Cooperation between international agencies and non-governmental organizations will help to ensure that the interests of States—legitimate though they may be—and of the different groups within them, will not be invoked or defended at the expense of the interests or rights of other peoples, especially the less fortunate. Political and economic activity conducted in a spirit of international solidarity can and ought to lead to the voluntary limitation of unilateral advantages so that other countries and peoples may share in the same benefits. In this way the social and economic well-being of everyone is served. (2000UN, sec. 3)

In this passage, John Paul II provides a detailed account of how the United Nations can respond to globalization's distortions. In his view, it can serve as an umbrella organization under which nongovernmental organizations can meet. It can provide indispensable checks on nation-state power and foster cooperation between states and nongovernmental agencies, leading nations to voluntarily limit their pursuit of narrow national interest.

Undoubtedly, dialogue among nations and nongovernmental organizations can prevent terrible disasters. However, why does John Paul II think that by itself, it can alter value distortions in international affairs? If we recall the central elements of his understanding of sin, such scenarios seem unlikely. Sin is an intentionality toward using others, grounded in a distorted *ordo amoris*. It is an *axiological reduction,* diminishing our relationship to values. It reflects our alienation from God, which is particularly acute today because of modernity's "ways of denial." Those promoting the narrow interests of a nation-state often reflect these dynamics. They relate only to a narrow set of values, ignoring the needs of persons in other countries. They receive emotional and other support for this willful ignorance from domestic constituencies. Dialogue and cooperation seem unlikely to alter such fundamental distortions. For example, in 2002–2003, the United States, France, Russia, and other countries failed to reach any agreement about how to respond to Iraq. Extensive dialogue yielded only recriminations and anger that many observers of the United Nations believe significantly damaged its credibility. Michael J. Glennon goes so far as to declare that the United Nations' "grand attempt to subject the use of force to the rule of law had failed" (Glennon 2003). Even if we do not share his dour assessment of what happened before the Second Gulf War, it should be clear that dialogue failed utterly to change anyone's mind about this war. Similarly, we have little reason to believe that the United Nations can counter the powerful economic and social forces promoting a homogenized global culture. Undoubtedly, it can make important structural changes in areas like international finance and debt relief that can reduce the negative elements of globalization. In some countries like Cambodia and Namibia, the United Nations has also exerted important cultural influences on the populace. However, in others, it has little or no influence, particularly in those countries where people have access only to state-controlled media. In these settings, it is hard to see how the United Nations can fulfill the cultural mandates John Paul II accords to it.

John Paul II's own experiences with the international conferences in Cairo and Beijing in the 1990s suggest that the United Nations may, in fact, impede positive responses to globalization.[31] These conferences focused on population growth, poverty, and women's rights in the developing world. Both witnessed sharp, public conflicts between the Vatican, the United Nations, and various nongovernmental organizations over issues like contraception, the family, and limiting population growth. John Paul II harshly criticized draft documents for these conferences, accusing them of undermining the value of human life and the family. Immediately before the Cairo conference in 1994, he penned a strongly worded letter to U.S. President Clinton. Discussing the draft document, he stated that

> the idea of sexuality underlying this text is totally individualistic, to such an extent that marriage now appears as something outmoded. An institution as natural, fundamental and universal as the family cannot be manipulated by anyone. Who could give such a mandate to individuals or institutions? The family is part of the heritage of humanity! Moreover, the Universal Declaration of Human Rights clearly states that the family is "the natural and fundamental group unit of society" (Art. 16.3). The International Year of the Family should therefore be a special occasion for society and the state to grant the family the protection which the universal declaration recognizes it should have. Anything less would be a betrayal of the noblest ideals of the United Nations. (1994Clinton)

In writing about these developments, John Paul II maintains that a minority of activists and United Nations officials wrested control of the population conferences in order to impose an ideological agenda on them. These attempts represented more than simply the incapacity to rise above a cold bureaucracy. They also went beyond forms of conformism and avoidance. Some who advocated for abortion rights and different models of the family rejected John Paul II's conception of a proper *ordo amoris*. Their disagreement was not simply intellectual, but revealed deep-seated affective orientations. In "Evangelium Vitae," John Paul II analyzes these orientations with great eloquence, famously describing them as a "culture of death." He details the institutional support for the culture of death, uncovering its deep roots in a culture that rejects the dignity of the human person. He recognizes that changing the culture of death requires not only deep institutional changes, but also a profound change in our orientation toward values. Unfortunately, when he writes about the United Nations, John Paul II departs from this powerful message, maintaining that dialogue alone will alter axiological distortions. I see a glaring and inexplicable contrast between his speeches before the United Nations and his writings on the culture of death.

Much to the dismay of some participants at the Cairo and Beijing conferences, the Vatican successfully opposed key elements of conference agendas. However, as Weigel shows, it did so by shrewd political maneuvers that failed to alter the ideological commitments of others.[32] In fact, many activists went away from these experiences embittered and entrenched in their ideological positions. Weigel describes John Paul II's interventions during these conferences as moral victories that stifled attempts to internationalize a right to abortion and coercive population policies. I agree with this assessment but think that there is a substantial difference between prevailing politically and cultivating a civilization of love. The battles over the Cairo and Beijing conferences illustrate how forces within the United Nations can embrace and cling to value-distortions. Sadly, they leave us little reason to believe that the United Nations can overcome ideological differences, promote international solidarity, and correct globalization's distortions.

These dynamics should also generate skepticism about the idea that the United Nations can successfully combat virulent nationalism. John Paul II's own careful analysis of virulent nationalism suggests just how difficult a challenge it presents. Virulent nationalism reflects a distorted *ordo amoris* that embraces the nation as the highest value. It is a form of deep-seated idolatry that perverts the proper order of values. Finally, it is often impervious to change, solidifying distortions even under severe pressure to change. Ignatieff gives us some sense of how difficult it is to alter these dynamics. Reflecting on the war in the former Yugoslavia, he describes how such conflicts originate when a state holding various nationalities together disintegrates, terrible Hobbesian fear takes hold, and nationalist paranoia emerges (Ignatieff 1997, 45). Often, these dynamics lead people to dehumanize those outside of their group. For example,

Ignatieff tells us that in the former Yugoslavia, media outlets "were readying their populations to think of the other side as vermin, insects, dogs, and other noisome creatures" (ibid., 56).[33] A deep intolerance emerged, a "willed refusal to focus on individual difference, and a perverse insistence that individual identity can be subsumed in the group" (ibid., 63). Cognitive illusions shaped perverse willing, leading people to see the world entirely in terms of group membership. What is wrong with this form of nationalism, Ignatieff writes, is "not the desire to be master in your own house, but the conviction that only people like yourself deserve to be in the house" (ibid., 59).

The United Nations can also do very little when virulent nationalists deliberately undermine the emotional bonds conducive to participation. They actively oppose recognizing the irreducible in others, choosing instead to classify them according to group membership. They employ epistemological devices to deny the uniqueness of the individual. They place excessive importance on minor differences that allegedly locate persons in fixed groups.[34] Despite its power, the United Nations cannot easily counter these destructive forces, because it plays little role in cultivating emotional bonds between persons. Member States like the United States repeatedly refuse to allow it to act in their stead, creating hostility toward it among some segments of their populations. The United Nations' well-known failures and incompetence further diminish its credibility as an effective cultural force. Nationalist and terrorist movements demonize it, disdaining it as invader and occupier. In the face of such powerful resistance, the emotional prerequisites for participation are simply absent. Perhaps, however, we need not develop emotional bonds in order to respond to virulent nationalism. I cannot ascertain if John Paul II thinks emotional resources are a necessary condition for participation.[35] Perhaps he believes that even absent emotional bonds, persons can will to acknowledge the personhood of others.

I think the United Nations is an unlikely vehicle for realizing such a project, and John Paul II should lower his aspirations for it.[36] In recent years, large nation-states like the former Soviet Union have collapsed, and similar developments may occur in other parts of the world. The war on terrorism may aggravate existing ethnic or regional conflicts, producing further disorder. The divisive debates over the Second Gulf War have also substantially weakened the United Nations. Nevertheless, if it is wise, it may be able to serve as a crucial third party that alleviates the Hobbesian fear fueling nationalist movements. Given the forces arrayed against it, perhaps all we can hope for is that it cultivates knowledge of a common human nature. This would be a major accomplishment, because claims about the universality of human nature are under siege in many parts of the globe. Philosophically, a host of contemporary thinkers deny that we share a common nature, derisively dismissing this idea as "essentialism." Politically, demagogues of all political persuasions are only too happy to valorize ethnic difference and demonize those outside of their groups. In light of such philosophical and political developments, it is a major achievement simply to retain knowledge of a common human nature.

The United Nations can cultivate this knowledge by promoting policies fostering the person's development and by refraining from endorsing those that promote the culture of death. These important steps, however, differ from those enhancing the *eidetic intuition* of the irreducibility of the other. Most people in the world have little or no contact with the United Nations. The little contact they have bears no resemblance to the intense interaction they experience in families or churches. To again bring Niebuhr into this discussion, "what lies beyond the nation, the community of mankind, is too vague to inspire devotion" (Niebuhr 1983, 85). Local forces are much more likely to develop participation than is an enormous international organization. Events like the Rwandan genocide support this conclusion. In 1994, most of the populations of the industrialized world completely ignored the Rwandan genocide. Members of the human species were systematically slaughtered and dismembered; yet many people simply disregarded this horror as something happening far away on a continent with unsolvable problems. They not only lacked any insight into the uniqueness of persons in Rwanda, but also ignored their species membership and value. Similarly, those who murdered several thousand innocent people in New York and Washington, D.C., in 2001 effaced their knowledge of our common humanity, deliberately using innocent human beings merely as tools for their projects. They appeared to lack any sense of our common humanity. Naturally, we should never exclude the possibility that we can actualize the ideal of participation for all persons in a global community. To do so ignores the power to change that John Paul II has embodied in his public life. He is right to point to the events in Poland during the Cold War as illustrating the capacity to develop participation.[37] Nevertheless, on this matter, the political realists have wisdom that John Paul II ignores. The world of nation-states is *not* a family, and its political apathy, disorder, and nationalism produce profound alienation. Entities like the family and church must promote participation, and we should be grateful if the United Nations manages to retain awareness of our common humanity.

Conclusion

The sudden and unexpected collapse of the Soviet Union at the end of the last century fundamentally altered international politics. It opened up large parts of the world to democracy and economic freedom, creating extraordinary opportunities for people denied them for too long. Globalization holds wonderful promise for human beings around the world. However, increased fragmentation has accompanied it, producing ethnic wars, terrorism, and other kinds of disorder. This fragmentation presents the United Nations and other transnational organizations with acute moral and political dilemmas. Ethnic cleansing, genocide, global terrorism, the phenomenon of "failed states"—all demand some response, and recent failures of humanitarian intervention have significantly altered ethical thinking about international relations. Realists appealing to the importance of state sovereignty ignore how the nation-state system often perpetuates and validates criminal behavior and profound injustice. Liberals demanding that we override state sovereignty to help those in need neglect the sobering limitations of military and humanitarian intervention.

John Paul II has entered these debates frequently and eloquently, using elements from both the realist and liberal approaches. I have argued that participation is the key to understanding his complex position. It reflects John Paul II's engagement with Scheler, for it captures the lived experience of acting together. It requires persons to acknowledge both a shared human nature and the uniqueness and irreducibility of the person. Participation demands that we become deeply involved in the lives of others, gradually grasping their uniqueness. It also opposes all social structures that subsume the person into the collective or deny that she has communal obligations. In responding to post–Cold War developments in international politics, John Paul II has applied this idea of participation in key ways. He defends the rights of nations as a way to value cultural diversity, which he thinks reflects divine creativity. He calls upon the United Nations to promote a civilization of love, a culture of participation embodying self-giving love. Finally, he articulates an obligation to help those in need, repeatedly supporting humanitarian intervention. These elements of his political ethic, I have argued, conflict, and unlike many in contemporary thought, John Paul II cannot resolve this conflict by appealing to consequentialism. Instead, he must make the value of the person preeminent and order his ethical and political principles to foster it.

I have also argued, however, that John Paul II pays insufficient attention to how sin infects the United Nations. Its size and value-distortions give us little reason to believe that it can cultivate participation in international politics. It can and must proclaim and institutionalize the knowledge of our shared human nature, which prohibits us from using others instrumentally. However, knowledge of a common human nature differs significantly from the deeper knowledge of the uniqueness of each person. I think the difficulty here is not that John Paul II lacks an adequate conception of the human fault. Theologically and philosophically, he understands how human beings distort their relationships to values and evade their responsibilities toward God. A realist cannot legitimately argue, then, that he underestimates human depravity, an odd thing to say of someone who battled communism for many years. Instead, I think John Paul II simply fails to apply his conception of sin to the United Nations, overestimating its capacity to alter value-distortions in international affairs.

In his astute analyses of humanitarian intervention, Ignatieff reminds us of how excessive aspirations may undermine what is possible, producing cynicism, despair, and the unwillingness to do what we know is right. He suggests that American and European powers might have been able to limit some of the horrors of the 1990s if they had understood that "we can always do less than we would like, that we may be able to stop horror, but we cannot always prevent tragedy" (Ignatieff 2000, 96). Sadly, John Paul II fails to heed Ignatieff's wise words. This failure does not, in my mind, undermine the pope's insights about the rights of nations and participation in international politics. Instead, it means we ought to apply his rich conception of the human fault more consistently. In the context of political realism, more consistency on this matter poses significant dangers. Realists maintain that if we fully understand human sinfulness, we must inevitably adopt an ethic of consequences. Otherwise, the forces of disorder and darkness will destroy us. This is the power and logic of the realist position. I recognize its appeal, but I believe that John Paul II's rich conception of the human person provides the resources to resist it.

Conclusion

In his *Discourses on the First Ten Books of Titus Livius,* Machiavelli astutely analyzes the dangers of changing political regimes. Recognizing that new leaders confront intransigent forces stifling positive change, he advises them to retain as much of the old regime as possible. However, when profound disorder makes developing legal mechanisms and civic habits impossible, Machiavelli argues, we need extreme measures to create order. A new leader, he says, may need to "build new cities, to destroy those already built, and to move the inhabitants from one place to another far distant from it; in short, to leave nothing of that province intact, and nothing in it, neither rank, nor institution, nor form of government, nor wealth, except it be held by such as recognize that it comes from you" (Machiavelli 1970, I.26). This advice to leaders is horrifying in our age, which has seen ethnic cleansing, the policy of violently driving out populations in order to create an ethnically pure state. Fully aware of this horror, Machiavelli ends his commentary by noting:

> Such methods are exceedingly cruel and repugnant to any community, not only to a Christian one, but to any composed of men. It behooves, therefore, any man to shun them, and to prefer rather to live as a private citizen than as a king with such ruination of men to his score. None the less, for the sort of man who is unwilling to take up this first course of well doing, it is expedient, should he wish to hold what he has, to enter on the path of wrong doing. Actually, however, most men prefer to steer a middle course, which is very harmful; for they know not how to be wholly good nor yet wholly bad. (Ibid.)

In this passage, Machiavelli captures political realism's descriptive and normative elements. Descriptively, realists see political life as dangerous, violent, and disordered, and they maintain that order is always precarious. They emphasize that political action is deeply ambivalent, leaving us with little certainty that we are doing the right thing.

This is a compelling understanding of politics, and those who reject it often naively ignore political disorder. For much of the twentieth century, political realists attacked those who refused to acknowledge political realities. Facing Nazi and communist tyrannies, they exposed the foolishness of those who disregarded the pursuit of political power. Revived briefly at the end of the Cold War, political idealism has confronted serious challenges. Genocide, ethnic cleansing, extreme nationalism, worldwide terrorism, and the military and economic power of the United States have all dashed hopes that the twenty-first century would see the end of power politics. In today's dangerous world, where suicidal terrorists have no moral qualms about killing thousands of innocent people, those who reject political realism's descriptive account of politics have little to offer as an alternative.

Normatively, realists have always maintained that this descriptive account of political life requires us to adopt an ethic of consequences. If political life is indeed a violent struggle for power, clinging to moral principles at all costs brings nothing but disaster. The unscrupulous take full advantage of moral absolutists, and evil ultimately triumphs. Those who think otherwise exhibit a dangerous form of selfishness that values individual virtue over the common good. For realists, it is irresponsible to emphasize character development and absolute moral rules when facing extermination. As Machiavelli puts it, "with princes, there is no court of appeal, we must look at the final result," and good character has little value if the final result is tyranny or extermination (Machiavelli 1964, ch. 18). Machiavelli's words are as relevant today as they were in sixteenth-century Italy, and they demand a response from those who thoughtlessly criticize realism.

Unfortunately, contemporary debates about political realism often produce only frustrating conceptual impasses. For example, in recent years, we have witnessed repeated clashes between human rights activists and political realists over the morality of economic sanctions. The United States uses economic sanctions against countries like North Korea and

Cuba, maintaining that these countries are "rogue states" (see Gordon 1999). Human rights activists maintain that sanctions are profoundly immoral because they deny food and medicine to the innocent. Political realists argue that they are necessary to curb rogue states attempting to obtain weapons of mass destruction. Human rights activists respond by condemning an ethic of consequences as immoral. In turn, realists reject the absolute character of human rights, arguing that human rights activists adhere too strongly to them. This clash of ethics has produced little but disappointing and unenlightening exchanges of charge and countercharge.

This debate illustrates well Alasdair MacIntyre's argument several decades ago that contemporary ethical thinkers retain only the "fragments of a conceptual scheme, parts which now lack those contexts from which their significance derived" (MacIntyre 1981, 2). Clinging to these fragments, contemporary ethics gets bogged down in interminable debates in which participants cannot even agree on what would constitute agreement. MacIntyre exaggerated his account in order to uncover distortions in late twentieth-century ethics. Nevertheless, it is very instructive and applicable to contemporary disputes about political consequentialism. Lacking metaphysical and historical sophistication, they offer little more than shallow ethical analysis.

John Paul II's philosophical project provides the conceptual resources to move beyond such impoverished analysis. By retrieving elements of modern phenomenology within a Thomistic philosophy of being, it challenges some of the basic presuppositions of contemporary ethics. Its Thomistic metaphysical framework is evident in much of what John Paul II writes. Without it, he maintains, we will succumb to one of the species of relativism crowding the contemporary philosophical landscape. Thomistic concepts such as act and potency, the will, and truth are indispensable for any contemporary ethics. In this way, John Paul II finds common cause with Jacques Maritain, Etienne Gilson, and others who expose the deficiencies of strands of modern philosophy that reject a realist metaphysic. However, what makes him so intriguing is that he also recognizes that modern phenomenology is important in a world that values subjectivity and interiority. For him, modernity's move toward subjectivity is fraught with dangers, many of which have taken social and political forms. Nevertheless, it also has much to teach us about consciousness and human action. John Paul II's philosophical project holds great promise because it retrieves the best of modern thought within a Thomistic realism.

Some Thomists resist this attempt to use phenomenology, but they often ignore modern phenomenology's complexity. Understandably, they worry about uncritically marrying two complex philosophical traditions. They also identify underdeveloped areas in John Paul II's philosophical project. Finally, correctly, they note that on key philosophical issues, Thomism has to depart from modern phenomenology. Nevertheless, much of their criticism reflects ill-defined understandings of this modern philosophical movement. Too often, Thomists identify phenomenology with philosophical idealism, focusing excessively on Husserl's 1913 writings. Or they equate it with what Heidegger and his followers produced. However, these are selective readings of the phenomenological movement. It is no accident that phenomenology often attracted Roman Catholic thinkers. Retrieving intentionality, they developed sophisticated responses to Cartesian skepticism and modern subjectivism. Engaging Husserl's early work, Scheler, von Hildebrand, Stein, and others developed a realist epistemology and metaphysic. We can neither dismiss their work as philosophical idealism nor declare that it is in principle incompatible with Thomism. In fact, many of these realist phenomenologists are very interested in engaging Thomism and share some of its philosophical concerns. This is particularly true in epistemology, where Scheler, Stein, and von Hildebrand develop theories of knowledge with important links to medieval thought.

In pursuing his goal of using phenomenology within Thomism, John Paul II chose Scheler as his central source for phenomenological insights. Exegetically, I have argued that Scheler's influence on him is more extensive than most people recognize. John Paul II departs significantly from Scheler by emphasizing the will, intellect, and self-determination. As a Thomist, he rejects Scheler's idea that love is a form of cognition acting independently from the intellect. Finally, he argues that Scheler's hierarchy of value offers insufficient guidance, because Scheler rejects the moral law as an essential part of ethics. Nevertheless, he also shares much with Scheler. The first idea these thinkers embrace is our intentional relationship to values. Beginning with Brentano and Husserl, modern phenomenology retrieved and developed the concept of intentionality prominent in medieval philosophy. John Paul II resists making it the sole basis for analyzing consciousness, but uses it to capture our lived experience of values. What he and Scheler share differentiates them sharply from many in contemporary ethics. For example, debates over human rights and consequentialism often arbitrarily ignore lived experience. They rely on unexamined epistemological prejudices about how the mind, social contracts, or cultures construct values. Both Scheler and John Paul II expose just how impoverished these ideas are. They refuse to identify experience with sense impressions that we must organize with mental or cultural categories. They also deny that it is limited to observation, induction, or deduction. Instead, they argue that we experience objects confronting us as wholes. Among these are values that attract and move us. Both Scheler and John Paul II believe that philosophy can reveal how this relationship to values shapes who we are.

Like Scheler, John Paul II also maintains that love is movement toward values and defends a hierarchy of value. Masterfully exploring kinds of love, he describes how they affect our interaction with others. Departing from Scheler by emphasizing the will and effort, John Paul II creates a moral imperative to enter into loving relationships. Persons must will to develop a *communio personarum,* or a community of persons, characterized by self-giving love and the gracious acceptance of others as gifts. Finally, like Scheler, John Paul II uses intentionality and love to develop a hierarchy of value. He distinguishes between material and spiritual values, arguing that spiritual values are preeminent over material ones. Spiritual values are enduring and indivisible, making them superior to material ones. In defending this hierarchy, John Paul II differentiates between the spiritual value of the person and the value of things. This becomes the basis for his personalistic norm, which proscribes using persons merely as a means. As a Thomist, he defends the axiological distinction between persons and things by arguing that unlike things, persons have an inner life and a capacity to relate to truth. Phenomenologically, he maintains that we perceive the person's value, understanding that persons are more valuable than things or animals. However, this perception provides only a basic knowledge of personhood that lacks depth. To arrive at deeper knowledge, we must contemplate the acting person until we gradually intuit who she is.

These three ideas, our intentional relation to value, love, and the hierarchy of value, provide the conceptual tools John Paul II uses to respond to political realism. First, they enable him to counter charges that he has naïve view of human nature that ignores its darker elements. Despite what some contemporary Roman Catholic and Protestant thinkers believe, John Paul II has a rich conception of sin. When considering international politics, he carefully uses the ideas he retrieves from Scheler to analyze the human fault. Globalization and nationalism have characterized international politics after the Cold War, and both have brought important benefits to the oppressed and powerless. However, they can also embody profound axiological distortions. Both developments may elevate material over spiritual values, creating sinful situations that trap people in distorted loves. They may also exacerbate our ruptured relationship with God, leading us to embrace idols of the market and nation. These dynamics may lead some to violently reject globalization, producing nihilistic terrorism. When responding to such developments in international politics, John Paul II demonstrates that like political realists, he is fully aware of the pursuit of political power. Thus, he blunts realism's challenge by embracing its descriptive account of the darker sides of political life.

However, his philosophical project also undermines realism's normative claims. It does little good to respond to consequentialism by claiming that it cannot accurately calculate consequences and harms the weak. Historically, consequentialists have answered such charges, defending rules that help calculate consequences and insisting that it is moral absolutists who harm the innocent. Too often, opponents of consequentialism play its conceptual game, entering into the complex calculations of consequences endemic to rational choice theory, economics, health care policy, and other fields enthralled with scientific rationality. Rather than becoming a player, John Paul II challenges the game's legitimacy. For John Paul II, consequentialism is an unworkable ethical project, because it claims to be able to calculate qualitatively different values. However, this is extremely difficult, because spiritual values are indivisible and therefore cannot figure into a calculation of consequences. Historically, political realists have focused heavily on power, measuring it in terms of geography and military and economic capabilities. Sometimes they emphasize how this power cultivates civic values. For example, when advising leaders to use brutality, Machiavelli argues that it can sustain a political order promoting civic republicanism. Similarly, Kaplan argues for a contemporary pagan ethics that values courage and civic responsibility. However, both thinkers never tell us how to compute values such as courage, citizen involvement, and community ethos. Moreover, they fail to indicate how material values relate to pagan values.

Invariably, realists fall back on the judgments of individual states-people, or employ culturally specific norms to guide how they calculate consequences. However, these are notoriously vague and subjective, and ignore the universal dimensions of ethics. Consequently, they either validate contemporary value-perversions or imply some form of cultural or historical relativism. The key issue here, as John Finnis and contemporary basic goods theorists maintain, is that consequentialism requires an ethical currency with which to compute values. However, spiritual and material values differ fundamentally and therefore cannot be put on the same scale.

I have argued, however, that John Paul II differs from both basic goods theorists and proportionalists because he defends our intentional relationship to values and embraces a hierarchy of value. The debate between these two schools of thought focuses on important questions about action theory, but it occurs within a constricted philosophical climate that begs a host of epistemological and metaphysical questions. Both basic goods theorists and proportionalists deny that we directly apprehend values, mistakenly dismissing such an idea as intuitionism. They exaggerate the modern "is-ought" gap, ignoring how we experience value and oughtness in the natural world. Finally, they reject the idea of a hierarchy of value, raising superficial objections to it that John Paul II easily counters.

By employing Scheler's ideas about the indivisibility of spiritual values, John Paul II presents a serious challenge to political consequentialism. Political actors must often calculate the consequences of economic or other policies. These calculations may involve one or more material values that we can statistically measure. However, political realism demands something more from political leaders. It argues that the disorderly world of international politics requires us to replace interpersonal ethical ideas with calculations of consequences. This necessarily means that we must either arbitrarily ignore indivisible spiritual values or make problematic calculi. Few political realists or consequentialists recognize this challenge, and John Paul II has done an invaluable service in mounting it. Confronting a tyrant without moral scruples, we may find an ethic of consequences very attractive. Encountering economists, medical researchers, and military strategists promising to make precise calculations of consequences, we may have difficulty resisting them. When we face violent terrorists without a moral conscience, torture may seem like a legitimate means of obtaining vital intelligence. However, despite such an ethic's allure and the importance of scientific and social-scientific rationality, modern-day consequentialists embrace myopic and historically ill-informed axiologies. Through his writings and his persona, John Paul II shows how to resist them.

John Paul II also applies this ethic to international relations, making participation a central element of his analysis. Participation is a property of persons enabling them to gradually and reciprocally come to understand the depth of each other's personhood. This becomes an ideal for the world of nations, and John Paul II uses it to defend the rights of nations, the civilization of love, and the duty to intervene and help the needy. At key points in the 1990s, he entered debates about humanitarian intervention, urging international institutions to intervene to prevent famine and other calamities. Initially offering ill-defined conceptions of intervention, he gradually articulated criteria for intervention, including a multinational response and careful use of force. He joined a number of recent thinkers who emphasize multinational solutions to grave international problems.

Unfortunately, when considering the United Nations, John Paul II applies his understanding of human sinfulness inconsistently. Neglecting his own counsel to avoid applying moral concepts univocally to impersonal entities, he ascribes rights to nations, creating acute conflicts between human rights and rights to national identity. Additionally, when urging the United Nations to develop a family of nations, he confuses the aims of the family and nation-state. Finally, he fails to see that the United Nations exerts little influence on the lived experience of people around the globe and is often corrupted by value distortions. The failure of the so-called international community to prevent genocide in Rwanda in 1994 illustrates vividly how the United Nations can be profoundly distorted. However, despite his own negative experiences with it during its conferences on population, John Paul II clings to the idea that it can enhance global participation.

This inconsistency, I believe, is not fatal to John Paul II's conception of international politics. Instead, it requires that we emphasize realism's descriptive project much more seriously than John Paul II does. International politics is not a family. At its best, it is a society tenuously held together by legal and other regimes that enable us to recognize our common humanity. The United Nations can certainly curb some of the disorder of international politics and foster the knowledge of our universal human nature. However, large and often corrupt international institutions are unlikely to move us from this knowledge to a deep participation in the personhood of others. Emphasizing the sinfulness of international institutions exerts greater pressure on us to adopt an ethic of consequences. When they fail to prevent large-scale violence and oppression, we are often tempted to adopt it for the sake of short-term order. This is particularly true in the face of terrorism, which targets the innocent in order to instill fear. Understandably, victims and potential victims of terrorism may embrace an ethic of consequences, endorsing torture, indiscriminate bombing, and other horrors. Machiavelli, Hobbes, Kissinger, and many other realists urge such a response on us, and I recognize its attractiveness. Nevertheless, I have argued that it is both conceptually problematic and spiritually impoverished. For John Paul II, the dignity of the person is what is centrally important, and we cannot legitimately disregard it for short- or even long-term political effectiveness.

In a famous passage in *The Republic,* Socrates discusses the relationship between philosophy and power. Speaking to his follower Glaucon, he says,

> Cities will have no respite from evil, my dear Glaucon, nor will the human race, I think, unless philosophers rule as kings in the cities, or those whom we now call kings and rulers genuinely and adequately study philosophy, until, that is, political power and philosophy coalesce, and the various natures of those who now pursue the one to the exclusion of the other are forcibly debarred from doing so. (Plato 1974, book 5, 473c)

The problem of how to relate philosophic wisdom to the brutal world of power politics preoccupies Plato throughout this great work. Those who love wisdom, he notes, are the least likely to enter the political life, while those exercising power are unlikely to care about philosophy. Centuries later, Machiavelli addressed this same problem in a radically different way. He rejected philosophical speculation about the ideal political community, arguing that it is a dangerous distraction that has

no place in political life. In a celebrated part of *The Prince,* he writes
that in politics it is

> more appropriate to pursue the effectual truth of the matter rather than
> its imagined one. And many have imagined republics and principalities
> that have never been seen or known to exist in reality; for there is such a
> gap between how one lives and how one should live that he who neglects
> what is being done for what should be done will learn his destruction
> rather than his preservation; for a man who wishes to profess goodness at
> all times must fall to ruin among so many who are not good. Whereby it
> is necessary for a prince who wishes to maintain his position to learn how
> not to be good, and to use it or not according to necessity. (Machiavelli
> 1964, ch. 15)

One of the most important expressions of political realism, this passage
suggests that we abandon the attempt to apply philosophy to politics,
embracing instead an ethic of consequences that effectively maintains
order. Anything else is irresponsible speculation leading to political
destruction.

Undoubtedly, John Paul II rejects Machiavelli's counsel to "learn how
not to be good." However, he also differs from Plato in his response to
the perennial problem of relating philosophy and politics. As a political
actor, he participated in some of the twentieth century's central events.
He lived through the two great totalitarian regimes of that century
and contributed to ending the Cold War, one of the most stunning and
unexpected events in recent memory. He has also been an important
actor in the political order that has emerged at the end of the Cold War,
representing a worldwide church in countless places around the globe.
Despite this intense political involvement, however, John Paul II is not a
philosopher-king. He neither uses the violence Plato associates with ruling
nor represents a particular political community. As Weigel notes in an
insightful lecture about the papacy and power, "the 'political' impact of
this pontificate, unlike that of Innocent III, has *not* come from deploying
what political realists recognize as the instruments of political power.
Rather, the Pope's capacity to shape history has been exercised through
a different set of levers" (Weigel 2001, 18). These levers include public
witness, discussions with political leaders, and institutions that shape

culture. John Paul II has shown the extraordinary power of these modes of acting. He has developed a different modal for engaging political life, one that is a "reminder of the ethical dimension of the exercise of power and a check on the absolutist tendency built into all modern politics. By reminding the world of power that it is not sovereign over all aspects of life, the papacy, engaged diplomatically, performs an invaluable service to the world of power" (ibid., 25).

This alternative mode of relating philosophy and power makes John Paul II's philosophical project deeply attractive. Its central themes are always clear: the value of the person, the importance of Thomistic metaphysics, and the vital role of our experience of values and God. Yet, John Paul II always uses these concepts creatively, whether it is in battling tyranny, exposing the negative effects of globalization, fighting virulent nationalism, or calling for humanitarian intervention. Too often, philosophers apply philosophical concepts to political life crudely, ignoring political power and the complex circumstances that confront political actors. Likewise, politicians and amateur political philosophers often abuse philosophy, perverting it for political ends or jumping to superficial philosophical conclusions without engaging in careful intellectual labor. In contrast, John Paul II links thought and action carefully, recognizing the dangers and difficulties of engaging public life philosophically. Moreover, in connecting reflection and an extraordinary public persona, he provides a powerful witness against political realism. In politics, Machiavelli does not have the last word, and necessity does not require us to do evil to achieve good. Political realism often emerges as an important and compelling response to political disorder. When it does, we need both a careful philosophical response to it and acts of public witness showing that its ethical claims are false. John Paul II offers an extraordinary vision that we should return to again and again to meet the challenges of the twenty-first century.

Notes

Introduction

1. Thucydides 1982, book 5, 89.

2. Adam Chmielowski is the principal character in Karol Wojtyla's play *Our God's Brother*, in Karol Wojtyla, *The Collected Plays and Writings on Theatre* (Berkeley and Los Angeles: University of California Press, 1987).

3. Recently, Mary Ann Glendon has insightfully analyzed the Melian Dialogue, opening her book on the United Nations and human rights by discussing it. See Glendon 2001.

4. It is important to recognize that the Athenians may not represent Thucydides' own position. Too often, contemporary realists uncritically equate the two, ignoring how Thucydides subtly criticizes the Athenians. For an excellent recent treatment of this issue, see Johnson 1993. Johnson argues that Thucydides is highly critical of the Athenian position at Melos.

5. Political realism differs from metaphysical realism, the thesis that a world exists independently of our capacity to think or talk about it. For a good discussion of different kinds of realism, see Lovin 1995.

6. I have learned a great deal from Robert Gilpin's work on realism, and I draw particularly on it for my definition of political realism, see Gilpin 1986.

7. For a recent discussion of Augustine's political realism, see Elshtain 1995.

8. For an excellent treatment of these dynamics in Thucydides, see Rahe 1985.

9. This was the subject of Niebuhr's famous early work *Moral Man and Immoral Society* (Niebuhr 1983).

10. See Waltz 1979. Waltz's position is known as "structural realism," because it emphasizes how the structure of the international system shapes state behavior. *Neorealism* is another term often used to characterize this position. For a good reader on neorealism, see Brown, Lynn-Jones, and Miller 1995. Often, contemporary realists contrast neorealism with "classical realism," which they argue emphasizes human nature rather than structures. For them, Hans Morgenthau represents classical realism. For

a number of reasons, I find this contrast unsatisfying, but I will not discuss it here. I intend my definition of realism to include all forms of realism. For an account of the neorealism–classical realism contrast, see Forde 1995.

11. For example, see Walzer 1977. For an excellent selection of articles reflecting fresh thinking about political realism, see Frankel 1995/96.

12. Some scholars argue that Winston Churchill was an amoralist. For one discussion of his realism, see Kaufman 1997.

13. For these texts, see Jeffreys 2000.

14. See Grene 1950.

15. See Weber 1958.

16. This doctrine of preemption has provoked considerable debate among just war theorists, who recognize that it raises difficult questions for the just war tradition. Michael Walzer has been particularly thoughtful about this issue; see Walzer 2002. For an excellent set of articles on this topic, see *Ethics and International Affairs* 17, no. 1 (spring 2003).

17. Importantly, McCormick denies that he is a consequentialist, refusing to equate proportionalism and consequentialism. Nevertheless, at key points in his thinking, he appeals to consequences to settle ethical conflicts.

18. These are two well-known examples in Anglo-American ethics.

19. See Walzer 1974.

20. Weigel discusses this visit in detail; see Weigel 1999, 790–92, 805–14.

Chapter 1: John Paul II and the Experience of Values

1. Quoted in Nota 1983, 18.

2. Buttiglione makes this point. See his excellent discussion of the dissertation on St. John of the Cross and experience (Buttiglione 1997, ch. 3).

3. See Williams 1981, 116.

4. For one of the best summaries of John Paul II's differences with Scheler, see Kupczak 2000, 143–46. See also Schmitz 1993, chapter 2; Buttiglione 1997, chapter 3; and Williams 1981, chapter 5.

5. This habilitation thesis is available in Polish and German, but an English translation is no longer available. I have read the German translation, made by Manfred Frings. See Wojtyla 1980.

6. For excellent essays devoted to various elements of John Paul II's philosophical project, see McDermott 1991. Mary Shivanandan also explores how John Paul II uses Scheler, focusing on how it shapes his theology of the body. Her recent book is an excellent treatment of his writings on marriage and sexuality; see Shivanandan 1999.

7. George Hunston Williams notes the ambiguity of the term *experience,* suggesting that we use the term *lived experience* instead (Williams 1981). I will follow Williams in using this term.

8. For a different narrative about the person, see Clarke 2001. Although Clarke agrees with the idea that Thomas Aquinas pays insufficient attention to the person, he believes his work has the resources to provide a fuller account.

9. Discussing phenomenology, Kupczak makes this same point, saying that phenomenology can "discover and describe many aspects of the human phenomenon which otherwise would be unknown to a metaphysician" working solely within Thomism (Kupczak 2000, 146).

10. For a further discussion of this method, see Kupczak 2000. John Paul II is not alone among twentieth-century Thomists in linking phenomenology and Thomism. In addition to the Lublin Thomists, the Louvain Thomists embraced elements of phenomenology. For example, see Steenberghen 1949, 1952, and Raeymaeker 1954. W. Norris Clarke, S.J., also develops a rich personalism by drawing on phenomenology; see Clarke 1993.

11. In the early years of his papacy, John Paul II gave several insightful addresses on Thomas Aquinas and modernity. For one such lecture, see "Method and Doctrine of St. Thomas in Dialogue with Modern Culture," in Schall 1982.

12. Buttiglione offers an excellent discussion of this influence; see Buttiglione 1997.

13. See Kupczak 2000, 49–58.

14. See "Fides et Ratio," section 74.

15. In "Fides et Ratio," John Paul II advises philosophers to avoid philosophical eclecticism, advice he has carefully followed over the years. For this discussion, see "Fides et Ratio," section 86.

16. In considering Scheler's influence on John Paul II, I focus on those texts John Paul II has clearly read. It is difficult to ascertain with precision how much of Scheler's work he has read. However, I have gone through the habilitation thesis and his other works, noting the texts he discusses. One of the difficulties in considering Scheler is that he altered his positions over the course of his career. Scheler scholars talk about his early years in which Rudolf Eucken influenced him, and divide his work into two periods, his middle years that draw heavily on Augustine and Pascal, and his final years, during which he moved away from Christian theism. John Paul II draws almost entirely from Scheler's middle period, 1912–22, and some of the works he uses are: *Formalism in Ethics and Non-Formal Ethics of Values*, *The Nature of Sympathy*, *Ressentiment*, *On the Eternal in Man*, *The Rehabilitation of Virtue*, and *On Shame*.

17. See Kupczak 2000.

18. This is the case in most of Rawls's writings, including his recent history of ethics and his response to critics on the idea that justice is political, not metaphysical. For discussions of intuitionism, see Rawls 2000, 2001.

19. Rawls defends this conception against critics in Rawls 2001.

20. Richard Rorty refuses to respond to questions about justification. For one example, see Rorty 1991.

21. Martha Nussbaum is an important exception. In a recent book, she argues that emotions are intentional, and maintains that contemporary ethics ignores their importance (Nussbaum 2001).

22. In citing Dennett, I in no way endorse his materialistic understanding of intentionality, which I think is false and ethically problematic.

23. I have learned a great deal from Robert Sokolowski's very clear introduction to phenomenology (Sokolowski 2000).

24. In his habilitation thesis, John Paul II recognizes the links between medieval and modern understandings of intentionality, focusing on Brentano in particular. See Wojtyla 1980, 43.

25. See Husserl 2001, investigation 5, chapter 2. In this part of the *Logical Investigations*, Husserl responds to his teacher Brentano, who identifies intentionality as the chief characteristic of the mental. For Brentano's discussion of intentionality, see Brentano 1995, book 2, chapter 1.

26. See "Husserl's Phenomenology and the Philosophy of St. Thomas Aquinas: Attempt at a Comparison" (Stein 1997).

27. See Hayen 1939. I am greatly indebted to W. Norris Clarke, S.J., for this reference and for conversations about intentionality.

28. Buttiglione also recognizes this point. See Buttiglione 1997, 270–78.

29. Schmitz notes how this language of mirroring harks back to medieval accounts of the mind and its illumination, a very interesting point that I will not explore here. See Schmitz 1993, 71–72.

30. This worry about idealism appears often in the pope's discussion of phenomenology, but it is hard to understand exactly what worries him. Without a clear definition of idealism, saying that it is dangerous tells us little. For example, what exactly is idealism? Why is it so dangerous? I have benefited greatly from conversations with Gilbert T. Null, who made me aware of the controversies regarding applying the term *idealism* to Husserl's work.

31. A good statement of this point appears in a footnote in *The Acting Person*, where the pope insists that "strictly speaking, consciousness, as here conceived, has no intentionality and so the term, as we use it, has only a secondary and derived meaning owing to the intentional acts of knowledge or self-knowledge as real faculties" (Wojtyla 1979, 303).

32. Kupczak makes this point; see Kupczak 2000, 149. For a discussion of John Paul II's worry about consciousness and reifying the person, see Schmitz 1993, 66–68.

33. In his habilitation thesis, John Paul II clearly affirms the value of phenomenology for uncovering our intentional relation to value, while simultaneously criticizing its limitations. See Wojtyla 1980, 97–101.

34. In private correspondence, Manfred Frings has suggested to me that Scheler focuses primarily on the person, with intentionality serving as a tool for developing his personalism. I am grateful to Frings for his insights and comments.

35. I have learned a great deal about this topic from W. Norris Clarke, S.J., and am grateful for extended conversations with him about different kinds of being. For

his treatment of this topic, see Clarke 2001, chapter 2. See also Finance 1960, 67–70, 277–79.

36. For example, see his comments about this issue in "Ordo amoris" and his essay "Idealism and realism." Both essays are in Scheler 1973b.

37. For one of von Hildebrand's extensive discussions of intentionality, see von Hildebrand 1953, 17. I thank John F. Crosby for suggesting I read this fascinating chapter.

38. Although I am focusing only on Scheler here, I also doubt whether Buttiglione is correct about Husserl. The early Husserl affirmed the existence of "ideal objects," which retain an independence from how the mind constructs them. For example, see the "Prolegomena" and first two investigations in the *Logical Investigations* (Husserl 2001).

39. Mieczyslaw A. Krapiec, Karol Wojtyla's colleague and president-rector of the University of Lublin, wrote carefully about Thomism and intentionality. Attentive to Thomism's differences with modern phenomenology, his work is worth considering in the debate about Thomism and intentionality. For his discussion of intentionality, see *I-Man: An Outline of Philosophical Anthropology* (Krapiec 1983, 172–84).

40. For a discussion of how understanding permeates all experience, see "The Problem of the Theory of Morality," in Wojtyla 1993, 128.

41. In developing his ideas about the will, John Paul II critically engages Kant and Hume. For one such engagement, see "On the Directive or Subservient Role of Reason in Ethics in the Philosophy of Thomas Aquinas, David Hume, and Immanuel Kant," in Wojtyla 1993, chapter 4.

42. See Schmitz's work for a more detailed presentation of John Paul II's theory of action (Schmitz 1993). See also Kupczak's book. Kupczak is very a very helpful guide for those of us who do not read Polish, for he explains key Polish terms in John Paul's work on action.

43. In *The Acting Person*, John Paul II develops an account of choice and forms of willing. For his discussion, see Wojtyla 1979, 128–48.

44. I have learned a great deal from Woznicki's excellent work.

45. This encyclical is, in part, an extended argument about why love is more important than justice. For another discussion of love and justice, see 1986Liberation, section 57.

46. For an excellent discussion of this topic, see Frings 1997, 68–69.

47. For good discussions of Scheler and love, see Spader 2002, chapter 4, and Edward V. Vacek, S.J., "Scheler's Phenomenology of Love" in *Journal of Religion* 62 (April 1982): 156–77.

48. In my view, Scheler misinterprets Pascal, ascribing too much to feeling, and ignoring what Pascal says about the heart and reason. However, I will pass over this exegetical issue.

49. Interestingly, John Paul II is also drawn to this phrase from Pascal, using it several times in *Sign of Contradiction* to analyze divine love. See Wojtyla 1979b, 22, 47.

50. See also Wojtyla 1980, 169.

51. For example, see Wojtyla 1960, 299–300 n. 35–36.

52. Spader carefully discusses Wojtyla's critique of Scheler on emotion and reason, see Spader 2002, 264–66.

53. When discussing marital love, John Paul II uses the term "betrothed love." As far as I can tell, self-giving love is the larger category, and the betrothed love of marriage is one of its instantiations.

54. Many commentators have considered how John Paul II develops the idea of a *communio personarum,* and I only rehearse what some of them say about it.

55. The pope develops these ideas by analyzing the Book of Genesis. For years, this text has been important for his thinking. In *Sign of Contradiction*, he states that "it may sound a trifle strange, but I think it is true, that today one cannot understand either Sartre or Marx without having first read and pondered very deeply the first three chapters of Genesis" (Wojtyla, 1979b, 24).

56. For other discussions of love as self-gift, see Wojtyla 1979b, chapter 7.

57. Ultimately, what makes it so important is that it mirrors the divine Trinity. The Trinity is the supreme exemplar of self-giving love.

58. The idea that the *ordo amoris* shapes our lives is one of the reasons Scheler develops his concept of "model persons." He emphasizes that we cannot change our *ordo amoris* simply by willing a change. Instead, we change it by following a person who exemplifies particular moral values. For his discussion of model persons, see Scheler 1973a, 572–83. Spader does an excellent job of exploring why model persons are important for Scheler; see Spader 2002, 140–43.

59. For this quote from Troeltsch, see Deeken 1974, 20. Scheler appreciates but is very critical of Nietzsche. He criticizes him for making vital values preeminent and for misunderstanding Christianity.

60. Here, I draw heavily on Spader's work; see Spader 2002.

61. Joseph de Finance, S.J., affirms this same idea, offering a fascinating assessment of Scheler and Dietnich von Hildbrand from within a Thomistic metaphysic. See Finance 1991, 81–105.

62. Drawing on Brentano, Scheler develops formal axioms to rank values. For example, one axiom states, "the existence of a positive value is itself a positive value" (Scheler 1973a, 82).

63. For his uneasiness about the concept of "criterion," see Scheler 1973a, 93. For a later discussion of this issue, see "Idealism and Realism," in Scheler 1973b. For a good discussion of Scheler and criteria, see Spader 2002, 72.

64. My own view is that such claims are simplistic and false.

65. Naturally, this method makes it imperative that we develop a theory of error, an understanding of how people misunderstand or distort values. Scheler is perfectly aware of this need, presenting his well-known account of *ressentiment* and developing an understanding of cognitive error. One of his most interesting essays on cognitive error is "The Idols of Self-Knowledge." See Scheler 1973b, chapter 1. I am grateful to Gilbert T. Null for conversations about the need for a theory of error.

66. Scheler offers, among other criteria, the *foundation* of values that helps us rank them. One value, *A*, is the foundation of another, *B*, if "a certain value A can only be given on

the condition of the givenness of a certain value B, and this by virtue of an essential lawful necessity" (Scheler 1973a, 94). In this case, *A* is a higher value than *B*. For example, useful values are founded on agreeable values because usefulness can only be given on the basis of agreeableness. Something is useful because it is a means to an agreeable value.

67. I have learned a great deal about Scheler and Wojtyla from John F. Crosby. W. King Mott briefly compares Scheler and John Paul II on hierarchies of value in his work on the pope and economics. Unfortunately, he analyzes only one of Scheler's works, a later book that in my view does not represent Scheler's most important philosophical work. See Mott 1999, chapter 1.

68. Weigel astutely notes that this play is "Karol Wojtyla's first exercise" in liberation theology (Weigel 1999, 114). For background on this play, see Weigel 1999, 112–16, and Schmitz 1993, 8–12.

69. Some speculate that the Stranger in this play is Lenin.

70. Weigel provides an excellent account of the context of the 1979 speech. For this discussion, see Weigel 1999, 346–50.

71. Avery Dulles has written extensively on John Paul II and culture; see Dulles 1999.

72. This essay is in Wojtyla 1993. Although neglected, it has recently received welcome attention. For an excellent discussion of it, see Buttiglione 1997, 292–306.

73. This discussion of praxis obviously reflects John Paul II's engagement with Marxist thought. However, I agree with Buttiglione that although Marxism prompts him to consider important issues, there is little evidence that it influences his thought in any significant way. For Buttiglione's discussion, see Buttiglione 1997, 292–305. Throughout his papacy, John Paul II has addressed artists and intellectuals, and emphasized the importance of developing the inner life of the person through the arts. For two good examples, see his 1999 "Address to the World of Culture" in the Republic of Georgia, and his "Letter of His Holiness Pope John Paul II to Artists," April 4, 1999.

74. For an excellent discussion of Scheler and Kant, see Blosser 1995.

75. For one example, see "Salvifici Doloris," section 29.

Chapter 2: John Paul II and Political Disorder

1. Niebuhr 1983, xx.

2. *Radiation of Fatherhood,* in Wojtyla 1987, 335.

3. Similar charges of utopianism are not difficult to find. For example, Stanley Hauerwas, in a sharp critique of "Laborem Exercens," argues that John Paul II neglects power relations in the economic order. See Hauerwas 1983, 53–54.

4. John Paul II's debt to Kant here is clear, and he acknowledges it. In his *Foundations of the Metaphysics of Morals*, Kant offers a version of the categorical imperative that states that "man and, in general, every rational being exists as an end in himself and not merely as a means to be arbitrarily used by this or that will" (Kant 1959, 46). Kant's justification for this principle differs significantly from John Paul II's, because he focuses more on rationality than on love.

5. He rejects what he calls the "puritanical" approach to sexuality, which denies the value of pleasure. See Wojtyla 1960, 57–60.

6. In these talks, he focuses on biblical exegesis, reflecting on the Book of Genesis, the Gospels, and Pauline texts.

7. All of the references in this and the next paragraph are from Wojtyla 1980, 148–51.

8. In this context, John Paul II describes the biblical prohibition against adultery not simply as negative, but also as a positive invitation to relate to goodness, truth, and beauty. See Wojtyla 1980, 168–71.

9. See also Wojtyla 1960, 297 n. 27.

10. The denial of God was a theme in many of John Paul II's early lectures to university students, particularly to those in France. For one excellent example, see his "Raise Your Eyes toward Jesus Christ," in Schall 1982.

11. For many years, John Paul II had a deep friendship with Henri de Lubac, and in reading this analysis of the Tower of Babel story, one cannot help but think of Lubac's masterful analysis of modern atheism, *The Drama of Atheist Humanism* (De Lubac 1950). In this work, de Lubac analyzes Dostoevsky's use of the image of the tower as symbolic of modern atheism.

12. All references in the rest of this paragraph are to "Reconciliation and Penance," sections 14–15.

13. In his 1986 document on liberation theology, he states that "by denying or trying to deny God, who is his Beginning and End, man profoundly disturbs his own order and interior balance and also those of society and even of visible creation"; see 1986Liberation, section 38.

14. For another account of this causality, see 1986Liberation, section 39, which states that idolatry is "an extreme form of disorder produced by sin. The replacement of adoration of the living God by worship of created things falsifies the relationships between individuals and brings with it various kinds of oppression. Culpable ignorance of God unleashes the passions, which are causes of imbalance and conflicts in the human heart. From this there inevitably come disorders which affect the sphere of the family and society: sexual license, injustice and murder."

15. All references in this paragraph will be to SR, 36. For good articles on this encyclical, see Baum and Ellsberg 1989 and Berger and Myers 1988.

16. I will return to the issue of solidarity in my last chapter. For a good treatment of it, see Doran 1996.

17. All references in this paragraph will be to "Reconciliation and Penance," section 16.

18. Scheler focused heavily on collective guilt after the First World War. A strong supporter of the German war effort, he came to see the war as a turning point in European civilization. For his discussions of guilt, love, and civilization, see "Repentance and Rebirth," "Christian Love and the Twentieth Century: An Address," and "The Reconstruction of European Culture," all in Scheler 1960.

19. For some of this discussion of corporations and responsibility, see Beauchamp and Bowie 2000.

20. This emphasis on the person leads Scheler to develop his fascinating classification of "value-persons" who incarnate values. For example, the saint embodies the values of the holy, while the genius incarnates spiritual values.

21. For example, see J. Bryan Hehir, S.J., "Reordering the World," Hehir 1992.

22. In this context, John Paul II develops the subsidiarity principle, the idea that higher-order communities should not interfere with the functioning of lower-order ones, see *Centesimus Annus, 48.*

23. In considering this account of work, I have found essays in Houck and Williams 1983 particularly helpful.

24. For good discussions of this encyclical, see Berger and Myer 1988. In this volume, Berger is particularly good on some of the deficiencies of the document, which makes a number of controversial empirical claims.

25. John Paul II cites Gabriel Marcel as source of this distinction.

26. For another example of this movement, see "Pastores Dabo Vobis," section 9.

27. For several excellent examples of this engagement, see Schall 1982. Schall collects a number of John Paul II's early addresses to university audiences, many of which emphasize linking science and personalism.

28. For a recent and very controversial account of the Asian financial crisis, see Stiglitz 2003. In this discussion of Southeast Asia, I draw on my own experience living in Thailand in 1998–1999.

29. For Stanley Hoffmann's astute analysis of international politics and nationalism, see Hoffmann 1998, chapters 12–15.

30. These remarks are obviously shaped by John Paul II's own experiences in Poland, and he explicitly mentions this experience in his address. For an intriguing discussion of the role of the nation in John Paul II's theology, see Krolikowski 1998.

31. For an excellent discussion of how Hobbesian fear created violent nationalism in the Balkans, see Ignatieff 1997.

32. In this speech to the United Nations (1995UN, 9), John Paul II also links virulent nationalism to utilitarianism, a discussion to which I will return in a later chapter.

33. In chapter 4, I will explore in greater detail the metaphysical and ethical support for this idea.

Chapter 3: An Ethic of Responsibility Is neither Responsible nor Feasible

1. Niebuhr 1960, xi.

2. 1995UN, section 13.

3. See Morgenthau 1970.

4. For good discussions of action theory and intrinsically evil acts, see Porter 1999 and Finnis 1991.

5. For one example, see J. C. Smart's essay in Smart and Williams 1973.

6. For a discussion of trolley problems, see Thompson 1976, 1985.

7. For an excellent account of the impractical character of consequentialist calculations, see Finnis 1991, chapter 1, section 5.

8. For comments on utilitarianism, see Scheler 1973, 179.

9. See Scheler 1961.

10. This is a major theme in *Love and Responsibility*. See Wojtyla 1960, 128.

11. This is part of Crosby's subtle analysis of the incommunicability of the person, to which I have not done justice here.

12. John Paul II may be mistaken in his interpretation of Aquinas. A full treatment of this issue would require me to consider Finnis's work on Thomas. See Finnis 1998.

13. In writing this section, I have benefited from conversations with Robert P. George.

14. For a careful discussion of this contrast, see Crosby 1996, 82–83, 115. Crosby draws heavily on this distinction to illuminate the nature of the self.

15. For an excellent philosophical defense of this position, see Clarke 2001, chapter 15.

16. In several intriguing footnotes, Kupczak suggests that Wojtyla may be drawing from Jacques Maritain's work; see Kupczak 2000, 70 n. 61, 71 n. 63. For an excellent treatment of Thomistic epistemology that focuses on lived experience, see Steenberghen 1949.

17. There is much more to say on these matters, but I forgo a longer discussion. I find Crosby's work to be very helpful for exploring the deeper issues about our cognition of value; see Crosby 1996. I have also learned a great deal from Dietrich von Hildebrand's work on ethics; see von Hildebrand 1953. In the *Acting Person*, John Paul II acknowledges that he is "fully aware that dealing specifically with the theory of value and knowledge can be considered only against a broad background of investigations dealing specifically with the theory of value and knowledge (the cognitive experience of value)" (Wojtyla 1979, 311 n. 50). He cites Dietrich von Hildebrand and Nicholas Hartmann as sources for his thought.

18. Edith Stein offers one of the most interesting discussions of intuition I have ever read. In an article entitled "Husserl's Phenomenology and the Philosophy of St. Thomas Aquinas: Attempt at a Comparison," she compares intuition in Thomism and phenomenology; see Stein 1997. I have learned much about Stein from conversations with Sarah Borden at Wheaton College.

19. This may or may not depart from the Aristotelian concept of induction, but I will forgo investigating this matter, and for clarity's sake, limit the range of the concept of induction.

20. Naturally, this account of categorial intuition raises many philosophical questions that I cannot address here. Sokolowski explores them well in his work (Sokolowski 2000).

21. For Husserl, eidetic intuition involves a complex process called "imaginative variation" through which we come to know essences. I will not explore this idea.

22. For phenomenologists, "species" is an ontological rather than a biological concept, denoting the lowest level of classification.

23. I owe this reference to Kupczak's work.

24. Spader points out that the German word *Anschauung* should be translated not as "intuition," but as "seeing." For Scheler, the word bears no resemblance to W. D. Ross's use of it. For Spader's comment, see Spader 2002, 56 n. 7. I have learned a great deal from Spader's excellent book on Scheler.

25. See von Hildebrand 1953, chapter 1. I thank John F. Crosby for alerting me to this important chapter on intentionality and value. In using von Hildebrand, I am not suggesting that he and John Paul II are in accord on all philosophical issues. I see close similarities in their thought, but showing them would require much more work on my part. Here, I am being suggestive, rather than demonstrative. For a good comparison between Karol Wojtyla and Dietrich von Hildebrand, see Crosby 1995.

26. Here, I draw on von Hildebrand's account of perception in *What Is Philosophy?* (von Hildebrand 1960, chapter 6). Blosser insightfully notes that "so long as we keep in mind the 'pathic' nuances of Scheler's particular notion, the term 'perception' is perfectly appropriate to use. The ordinary signification of 'perception' is by no means restricted to the five senses, but includes mental awareness (or intuition) that is independent of these, and is certainly broad enough to include the sense of Scheler's expression" (Blosser 1995, 119 n. 1).

27. In thinking about this concept, I have found Josef Seifert's work helpful; see Seifert 1981.

28. I have learned from Crosby's discussion of John Paul II's thought on this matter; see Crosby 1996, chapter 3.

29. What this implies metaphysically is a difficult matter to ascertain. What, exactly, do we grasp when we grasp the form of the person? Crosby argues the persons have "individual essences" that we gradually come to know. I am unable to ascertain if John Paul II agrees, but if he does, he would be departing from the Thomistic tradition on a key point. My own view is that we can retrieve his position within an *esse*-essence framework, without embracing the idea of an individual essence. In private conversation, Schmitz noted that by using the term "eidetic insight," John Paul II does not necessarily commit himself to the idea of individual forms. I agree entirely, but wish that John Paul II made this point clearly. I thank Kenneth Schmitz for his insightful comments and observations at the 2003 Annual Meeting of the American Catholic Philosophical Association.

30. For one example, see Finnis 1984, 22.

31. For this discussion, see Scheler 1973a, 171–77, 295–317. Scheler's treatment of relativism is one of most sophisticated discussions of this topic I have ever read.

32. For George's discussion, see George 1999, 69–75.

33. For example, see "The Basis of the Moral Norm," in Wojtyla 1993, 85.

34. See sections 36–50 for an extensive discussion of this issue. Obviously, this brief treatment of the moral law raises complex questions about how John Paul II uses natural law, a topic I will not consider in this book. For good discussions of natural law, see Curran and McCormick 1991.

35. Finnis is particularly good on this matter; see Finnis 1984, 33–55.

36. For one place where Finnis discusses the is-ought issue, see Finnis 1984, 33–38.

37. I owe this reference to Peter Simpson's book; see Simpson 2001, 30.

38. John Paul II shows a great deal of interest in Scheler's idea of "exemplars," types of persons who move us to alter our *ordo amoris*.

39. This is only one axiom in a complex presentation.

40. True to his uneasiness with willing, Scheler presents preferring as a form of cognition that occurs "in the absence of all conation, choosing, and willing" (Scheler 1973a, 87).

41. In a chapter in *Christian Moral Reasoning: An Analytic Guide*, Hallett devotes a chapter to a hierarchy of values. He raises a number of important questions about hierarchies of value, and his discussion is insightful. However, he only briefly and superficially discusses Scheler. See Hallett 1983, chapter 7.

42. For one example, see "The Just War Case for the War," *America* 188, no. 11 (March 31, 2003): 7–12.

43. For a discussion of some of these issues, see Griffiths and Weigel 2002. On this topic, I have learned much from discussions with Paul J. Griffiths.

44. My criticisms of Weigel may remind readers of twentieth-century debates about proportionality between thinkers like Paul Ramsey, John Courtney Murray, and Robert W. Tucker. Specifically, they most resemble the positions Ramsey took in his many writings about the just war tradition. Tucker was a sharp critic of proportionality, distinguishing between proportionality of effectiveness and proportionality of values. The former simply requires statesmen to exercise prudence and effectively pursue political ends. The latter requires them to proportionate values. In an extended footnote, Tucker hints at some of the difficulties in measuring values that I have considered in this book. For this discussion, see Tucker 1966, 18–19. For Ramsey's response, see Ramsey 1983, chapter 17. I have learned a great deal from this debate between Ramsey and Tucker. James Turner Johnson has been a consistent critic of Ramsey, arguing that he misunderstands the history of the just war tradition and neglects its *jus ad bellum* criteria. For one particularly good discussion, see Johnson 1991.

Chapter 4: John Paul II and Participation in International Politics

1. United Nations 1999, introduction.

2. "Address of His Holiness Pope John Paul II to the Fiftieth General Assembly of the United Nations Organization," section 16.

3. For a discussion of the optimism about international politics that was so powerful after the Cold War's end, see Melvern 2000, chapter 8.

4. For Smith's discussion of realism, see Smith 1999, 280–83.

5. Kissinger's arguments about the merits of the Westphalian system are deeply controversial, and I will not assess them. My own view is that they ignore how the

Westphalian system had detrimental consequences for political communities outside of Europe. For one critical discussion of Kissinger, see Smith 1987.

6. For a discussion of the Vatican, see Weigel 1999, 652–53.

7. For a good introduction to the concept of intersubjectivity, see Sokolowski 2000, chapter 10. Edith Stein was deeply interested in this concept. In her dissertation written under Husserl, she focused on empathy and intersubjectivity; see Stein 1989.

8. For these understandings of participation, see Cornelio Fabro's famous work on Thomas Aquinas and participation (Fabro 1950).

9. John Paul II notes that metaphysically, this relationship is an accident, because relating to a particular person is an accidental property. However, as a lived experience it occurs between "fully constituted, separate, personal subjects, along with all that comprises the personal subjectivity of each of them" (Wojtyla 1993, 242).

10. I will not evaluate the accuracy of this interpretation, but I think Scheler's position is more complex than John Paul II describes.

11. I agree with Buttiglione and others who argue that Marxism has little influence on how John Paul II uses this concept; see Buttiglione 1997, chapter 8.

12. These are the two forms of alienation John Paul II identifies at the end of *The Acting Person*, which he calls individualism and totalism. See Wojtyla 1979, 328–22.

13. John Paul II's reflections on alienation and participation are clearly shaped by his experiences living in Communist Poland and his historic work with Solidarity. For background on these experiences, see Weigel 1999, chapters 10–12.

14. For an excellent collection of essays devoted to this encyclical, see Smith and McInerny 2001.

15. With others, I believe that some of the substantive concepts in this core are not, in fact, universal, but are culturally particular. I have learned a great deal about this issue from conversations with Paul J. Griffiths.

16. All references in this paragraph will be to "Letter to Families," sections 13–14.

17. For Nagel's work, see Nagel 1974.

18. Here, I pass over some questions about ethical conflicts that figure prominently in contemporary ethics. In the last several decades, Martha Nussbaum (Nussbaum 1988), Bernard Williams (Williams 1985), and others have explored situations of moral conflict. A key question in this debate is whether moral agents can find themselves in a situation where they must do evil, out of no fault of their own. For an excellent but neglected treatment of these issues, see Santurri 1987.

19. See also "The Person: Subject and Community," in Wojtyla 1993, 238.

20. I recognize that to say more about this topic, I would have to develop the idea of analogy, applying it to political thought. I am grateful to Paul J. Griffiths for his comments about analogy and collectives.

21. For example, see 1979UN, section 13.

22. For one discussion of imperialism, see Ignatieff 2002.

23. For excellent discussions of what the United States action in the Second Gulf War means for the international system and international law, see Rubenfield 2003; Slaughter 2003; Glennon 2003; and Hathaway 2003.

24. I do not want to criticize Weigel for missing these speeches, because he published his work in 1999.

25. John Paul II made similar arguments when opposing the U.S. action in the Second Gulf War. See the "Address of His Holiness John Paul II to the Diplomatic Corps," section 4, January 13, 2003.

26. See "Familiaris Consortio," section 17.

27. See the *Report of the Independent Inquiry into the Actions of the United Nations during the 1994 Genocide in Rwanda*. For a riveting account of what happened in Rwanda, see Gourevitch 1999, 40. For a good discussion of General Dallaire's actions, see Power 2002, 335–45.

28. In her book on the Rwandan genocide, Melvern offers considerable evidence showing that international aid agencies, the United Nations, and individual nation-states like the United States all willfully ignored or even contributed to the genocide. I find her arguments not only persuasive but profoundly depressing.

29. Samantha Power describes how the Clinton administration opposed using the term *genocide* to describe what was happening in Rwanda, see Power 2002, 358–364.

30. For the text of this convention, see Melvern 2000, Appendix 2.

31. For a good account of these conferences, see Weigel 1999, 715–19, 766–71.

32. See Weigel 1999, 715–27, 766–71.

33. This is a well-documented phenomenon in studies of genocide. For example, in Rwanda, the state-run radio repeatedly broadcasted hate messages that portrayed the Tutsi in dehumanizing ways. Melvern does an excellent job of discussing this vile institution; see Melvern 2000, chapter 7.

34. See Ignatieff's essay, "The Narcissism of Minor Differences" in Ignatieff 1997.

35. Scheler undoubtedly believed this to be the case; see Scheler 1973a, 526–61.

36. Power carefully discusses why the "international community" has so often failed to adequately respond to genocide; see Power 2002, chapter 14. As I do, she hopes that it will not reproduce its failures in Rwanda and the former Yugoslavia.

37. For a beautiful discussion of the role of spiritual forces in bringing the Cold War to an end, see "Centesimus Annus," 24–25.

Works Cited

Augustine of Hippo, St. 1986. *Concerning the city of God against the pagans*. Translated by Henry Bettenson, with an introduction by John O'Meara. New York: Penguin.

Baseheart, Catherine, S.C.N. 1997. *Person in the world: Introduction to the philosophy of Edith Stein*. Dordrecht: Kluwer Academic.

Baum, Gregory, and Robert Ellsberg. 1989. *The logic of solidarity: Commentaries on Pope John Paul II's encyclical* On social concern. Maryknoll, N.Y.: Orbis Books.

Beauchamp, Tom L., and Norman E. Bowie, eds. 1983. *Ethical theory and business*. Englewood Cliffs, N.J.: Prentice-Hall.

Berger, Peter L., and Kenneth A. Myers. 1988. *Aspiring to freedom: Commentaries on John Paul II's encyclical* The social concerns of the church. Grand Rapids: Eerdmans.

Blosser, Philip. 1995. *Scheler's critique of Kant's ethics*. Athens: Ohio University Press.

Brandt, Richard. 1974. Utilitarianism and the rules of war. In T. M. Scanlon, Marshall Cohen, and Thomas Nagel, eds., *War and moral responsibility: A philosophy & public affairs reader*. Princeton, N.J.: Princeton University Press.

Brentano, Franz. 1995. *Psychology from an empirical standpoint*. Edited by Oskar Kraus. With a new introduction by Peter Simons. Translated by Antos C. Rancurello, D. B. Terrell, and Linda L. McAlister. New York: Routledge.

Brown, Michael E., Sean M. Lynn-Jones, and Steven E. Miller. 1995. *Perils of anarchy: Contemporary realism and international security*. Cambridge: MIT Press.

Buttiglione, Rocco. 1997. *Karol Wojtyla: The thought of the man who became Pope John Paul II*. Grand Rapids: Eerdmans.

Clarke, W. Norris, S.J. 1993. *Person and being*. Milwaukee: Marquette University Press.

———. 2001. *The one and the many: A contemporary Thomistic metaphysic*. Notre Dame, Ind.: University of Notre Dame Press.

Conley, John J., S.J., and Joseph W. Koterski, S.J., eds. 1999. *Prophecy and diplomacy: The moral doctrine of John Paul II*. New York: Fordham University Press.

Crosby, John F. 1995. Karol Wojtyla on the objectivity and the subjectivity of moral obligation. In *Christian humanism: International perspectives*. Edited by Richard Francis and Jane Francis. New York: Peter Lang, 27–36.

———. 1996. *The selfhood of the human person*. Washington, D.C.: Catholic University Press of America.

———. 1997. Max Scheler's principle of moral and religious solidarity. *Communio* 24 (Spring): 110–27.

Curran, Charles E., and Richard A. McCormick, S.J. 1991. *Natural law and theology (readings in moral theology 7)*. Mahwah, N.J.: Paulist Press.

———. 1998. *John Paul II and moral theology*. New York: Paulist Press.

Dalliere, Romeo A. 1999. The end of innocence: Rwanda 1994. In *Hard choices: Moral dilemmas in humanitarian intervention*. Edited by Jonathan Moore, with a foreword by Cornelio Sommaruga. Lanham, Md.: Rowman and Littlefield.

Deeken, Alfons. 1974. *Process and permanence in ethics: Max Scheler's moral philosophy*. New York: Paulist Press.

Dennett, Daniel. 1997. *Kinds of Mind: Toward an Understanding of Consciousness*. New York: Basic Books.

Dershowitz, Alan M. 2002. *Why terrorism works*. New Haven: Yale University Press.

Doran, Kevin P. 1996. *Solidarity: A synthesis of personalism and communalism in the thought of Karol Wojtyla/Pope John Paul II*. New York: Peter Lang.

Dulles, Avery, S.J. 1999. *The splendor of faith: The theological vision of Pope John Paul II*. New York: Crossroad.

Elshtain, Jean Bethke. 1995. *Augustine and the limits of politics*. Notre Dame, Ind.: University of Notre Dame Press.

Fabro, Cornelio. 1950. *La nozione metafisica di partecipazione secondo S. Tomasso d'Aquino*. Torino: Società editrice internazionale.

Finance, Joseph de, S.J. 1960. *Être et agir dans la philosophie de S. Thomas*. Rome: Università Gregoriana.

———. 1991. *An Ethical Inquiry*. Rome: Editrice Pontificia Università Gregoriana.

Finnis, John. 1980. *Natural law and natural rights*. Oxford: Clarendon.

———. 1991. *Moral absolutes: Tradition, revision, and truth*. Washington, D.C.: Catholic University Press of America.

———. 1998. *Aquinas: Moral, political, and legal theory*. Oxford: Clarendon.

Finnis, John, Joseph M. Boyle, and Germain Grisez. 1987. *Nuclear deterrence, morality, and realism*. Oxford: Clarendon.

Fletcher, Joseph F. 1966. *Situation ethics: The new morality*. Philadelphia: Westminster.

Forde, Steven. 1995. International realism and the science of politics: Thucydides, Machiavelli, and neorealism. *International Studies Quarterly* 39, no. 2 (June): 141–61.

Formicola, Jo Renee. 2002. *Pope John Paul II: Prophetic politician*. Washington, D.C.: Georgetown University Press.

Frankel, Benjamin, ed. 1995. *Security Studies, Special Issue: Roots of Realism* 5, no. 2 (Winter).

———. 1996. *Security Studies, Special Issue: Realism: Restatements and Renewal* 5, no. 3 (Spring).

Frings, Manfred S. 1997. *The mind of Max Scheler*, vol. 14. Milwaukee: Marquette University Press.

Gaddis, John Lewis. 1992/93. International relations theory and the end of the Cold War. *International Security* 17, no. 3 (Winter): 5–58.

George, Robert P. 1999. *In defense of natural law*. Oxford: Clarendon.

Gilpin, Robert G. 1986. The richness of the tradition of political realism. In *Neorealism and its critics*. Edited by Robert O. Keohane. New
York: Columbia University Press.

————. 2000. *The challenge of global capitalism: The world economy in the
21st century*. With the assistance of Jean Millis Gilpin. Princeton, N.J.:
Princeton University Press.

Glendon, Mary Ann. 1991. *Rights talk: The impoverishment of political
discourse*. New York: Free Press.

————. 2001. *A world made new: Eleanor Roosevelt and the universal declaration of human rights*. New York: Random House.

Glennon, Michael J. 2002. Terrorism and the limits of the law. *Wilson
Quarterly* 26, no. 2 (Spring): 12–20.

————. 2003. Why the Security Council failed. *Foreign Affairs* 82, no.
3 (May/June): 16–36.

————. 2003. Sometimes a great notion. *Wilson Quarterly* 27 (Autumn):
45–49.

Gordon, Joy. 1999. A peaceful deadly remedy: The ethics of economic
sanctions. *Ethics and International Affairs* 13: 123–42.

Gourevitch, Philip. 1998. *We wish to inform you that tomorrow we will be
killed with our families: Stories from Rwanda*. New York: Farrar, Straus,
and Giroux.

Gregg, Samuel. 1999. *Challenging the modern world: Karol Wojtyla/John
Paul II and the development of Catholic social teaching*. Lanham, Md.:
Lexington Books.

Grene, David. 1950. *Greek political theory: The image of man in Thucydides
and Plato*. Chicago: University of Chicago Press.

Griffin, Leslie C. 1983. Moral teaching as moral criticism. In *Co-creation
and capitalism*. Edited by John Houck and Oliver F. Williams, C.S.C.
Lanham, Md.: University Press of America.

Griffiths, Paul J., and George Weigel. 2002. Just war: An exchange.
First Things 122 (April): 31–36.

Habermas, Jürgen. 1990. *Moral consciousness and communicative action*.
Translated by Christian Lenhardt and Shierry Weber Nicholsen. Introduction by Thomas McCarthy. Cambridge: MIT Press.

Hallett, Garth, S.J. 1983. *Christian moral reasoning: An analytical guide.* Notre Dame, Ind.: University of Notre Dame Press.

———. 1995. *Greater good: The case for proportionalism.* Washington, D.C.: Georgetown University Press.

Hardin, Russell. 1988. *Morality within the limits of reason.* Chicago: University of Chicago Press.

Hathaway, Oona A. Two cheers for international law. *Wilson Quarterly* 27 (Autumn): 50–54.

Hauerwas, Stanley. 1983. Work as co-creation: A remarkably bad idea. In *Co-creation and capitalism: John Paul II's* Laborem exercens. Edited by John W. Houck and Oliver F. Williams, C.S.C. Lanham, Md.: University Press of America.

Hayen, André. 1939. L'intentionalité de l'être et métaphysique de la participation. *Revue néoscolastique* 42:385–410.

Heath, Peter. 1975. The idea of a phenomenological ethics. In *Phenomenology and philosophical understanding,* edited by Edo Pivčević. Cambridge: Cambridge University Press.

Hehir, J. Bryan, S.J. 1992. Reordering the world. In *A new worldly order: John Paul II and human freedom*, edited by George Weigel. Washington, D.C.: Ethics and Public Policy Center.

———. 1995. Intervention: From theories to cases. *Ethics & International Affairs* 9:1–13.

———. 1999. Kosovo: The war of values and the values of war. *America* 180 (May 15): 7–12.

———. 2001. What can be done? What should be done? *America* 185, no. 10 (October 8): 9–12.

Hobbes, Thomas. 1991. *Leviathan.* Edited by Richard Tuck. Cambridge: Cambridge University Press.

Hoffmann, Bruce. 2002. A nasty business. *Atlantic Monthly* 289, no. 1 (January): 49–52.

Hoffmann, Stanley. 1998. *World disorders: Troubled peace in the post–Cold War era.* Lanham, Md.: Rowman & Littlefield.

Hollenbach, David, S.J. 1983. Human work and the story of creation: Theology and ethics in Laborem exercens. In *Co-Creation and capitalism:*

John Paul II's Laborem Exercens, edited by John W. Houck and Oliver
F. Williams, C.S.C. Lanham, Md.: University Press of America.

Houck, John W., and Oliver F. Williams, C.S.C.. 1983. *Co-creation and
capitalism*. Lanham, Md.: University Press of America.

————. 1991. *The making of an economic vision: John Paul II's* On social
concern. Edited by John W. Houck and Oliver F. Williams, C.S.C.
Lanham, Md.: University Press of America.

Husserl, Edmund. 2001. *Logical investigations*, vols. 1–2. New York:
Routledge.

Ignatieff, Michael. 1998. *The warrior's honor: Ethnic war and the modern
conscience*. New York: Metropolitan Books.

————. 2002. How to keep Afghanistan from falling apart: The case
for a committed American imperialism. *New York Times Magazine*,
July 28.

————. 2003. The American empire (get used to it). *New York Times
Magazine*, January 5.

Jeffreys, Derek S. 2000. Unfaithfulness and disorder in Calvin's political
thought. *Review of Politics* 62, no. 1 (Winter): 107–29.

Johnson, James Turner. 1991. Just war in the thought of Paul Ramsey.
Journal of Religious Ethics 19, no. 2 (Fall): 183–205.

Johnson, Laurie M. 1993. *Thucydides, Hobbes, and the interpretation of realism*. DeKalb: Northern Illinois University Press.

Kant, Immanuel. 1959. *Foundations of the metaphysics of morals and What is
enlightenment?* Translated with an introduction by Lewis White Beck.
Indianapolis: Bobbs-Merrill.

Kaplan, Robert D. 2000. *The coming anarchy: Shattering the dreams of the
post–Cold War*. New York: Random House.

————. 2002. *Warrior politics: Why leadership demands a pagan ethos*. New
York: Random House.

————. 2003. Supremacy by stealth. *Atlantic Monthly* 292, no. 1 (July/
August): 66–80.

Kaufman, Robert G. 1995. E.H. Carr, Winston Churchill, Reinhold
Niebuhr and us: the case for principled, prudential democratic realism. *Security Studies, Special Issue: Roots of Realism* 5, no. 2 (Winter):
314–54. Edited by Benjamin Frankel.

Kissinger, Henry. 2001. *Does America need a foreign policy?: Toward a diplomacy for the 21st century*. New York: Simon and Schuster.

Krapiec, Mieczyslaw A. 1983. *I-Man: An outline of philosophical anthropology*. New Britain, Conn.: Mariel Publications.

Krolikowski, Janusz. 1998. "My homeland and my nation": The theology of the nation in the teaching of John Paul II during his first visit in Poland (June 2–10, 1979). *Logos: A Journal of Catholic Thought and Culture* 1, no. 2: 56–75.

Kupczak, Jaroslaw. 2000. *Destined for liberty: The human person in the philosophy of Karol Wojtyla/Pope John Paul II*. Washington, D.C.: Catholic University Press of America.

Kwitny, Jonathan. 1997. *Man of the century: The life and times of Pope John Paul II*. New York: Henry Holt.

Langan, John, S.J. 1991. Solidarity, sin, common good, and responsibility for change in contemporary society. In *The making of an economic vision: John Paul II's* On social concern. Edited by John W. Houck and Oliver F. Williams, C.S.C. Lanham, Md.: University Press of America.

Lovin, Robin. 1995. *Reinhold Niebuhr and Christian realism*. Cambridge: Cambridge University Press.

Lubac, Henri de. 1950. *The drama of atheist humanism*. Translated by Edith M. Riley. New York: Sheed & Ward.

McCann, Dennis P. 1991. The unconstrained vision of John Paul II or How to resist the temptation of an economic counterculture. In *The making of an economic vision: John Paul II's* On social concern. Edited by John W. Houck and Oliver C. Williams, C.S.C. Lanham, Md.: University Press of America.

Machiavelli, Niccolò. 1964. *The prince*. Translated and edited by Mark Musa. New York: St. Martin's Press.

————. 1970. *The discourses*. Edited with an introduction by Bernard Crick. Translated by Leslie J. Walker, S.J. New York: Penguin Books.

MacIntyre, Alasdair. 1981. *After virtue: A study in moral theory*. Notre Dame, Ind.: University of Notre Dame Press.

McCormick, Richard A., S.J. 1978. Commentaries on the commentary. In *Doing evil to achieve good: Moral choice in conflict situations*, edited by Richard McCormick and Paul Ramsey. Chicago: Loyola University Press.

McDermott, John, S.J., ed. 1991. *The thought of John Paul II: A collection of essays and studies*. Chicago: Loyola University Press.

McNamara, Robert S., and James G. Blight. 2001. *Wilson's ghost: Reducing the risk of conflict, killing, and catastrophe in the 21st century*. New York: Public Affairs.

Melvern, Linda. 2000. *A people betrayed: The role of the West in Rwanda's genocide*. London: Zed Books.

Mill, John Stuart. 1979. *Utilitarianism*. Edited with an introduction by George Sher. Indianapolis: Hackett.

Morgenthau, Hans. 1970. *Truth and power: Essays of a decade, 1960–70*. New York: Praeger.

Morgenthau, Hans. J., and Kenneth W. Thompson. 1985. *Politics among nations: The struggle for power and peace*. 6th ed. New York: Knopf.

Mott, King W., Jr. 1999. *The third way: Economic justice according to John Paul II*. Lanham, Md.: University Press of America.

Nagel, Thomas. 1974. War and massacre. In *War and moral responsibility: A philosophy & public affairs reader*, edited by T. M. Scanlon, Marshall Cohen, and Thomas Nagel. Princeton, N.J.: Princeton University Press.

National Security Strategy of the United States of America. Available online at http://www.whitehouse.gov/nsc/nss.html

Niebuhr, Reinhold. 1953. Augustine's political realism. In *Christian realism and political problems*. Fairfield, Conn.: A. M. Kelley.

———. 1983. *Moral man and immoral society*. New York: Macmillan.

Nota, John H., S.J. 1983. *Max Scheler, the man and his work*. Translated by Theodore Plantinga and John H. Nota, S.J. Chicago: Franciscan Herald Press.

Nussbaum, Martha C. 1986. *The fragility of goodness: Luck and ethics in Greek tragedy*. Cambridge: Cambridge University Press.

———. 2001. *Upheavals of thought: The intelligence of emotions*. Cambridge: Cambridge University Press.

Pettit, Philip. 1991. Consequentialism. In *A companion to ethics*. Edited by Peter Singer. Oxford: Blackwell.

Plato. *The republic*. 1974. Translated by G.M.A. Grube. Indianapolis: Hackett.

Porter, Jean. 1995. *The moral act of Christian ethics*. Cambridge: Cambridge University Press.

———. 1996. Direct and indirect in Grisez's moral theory. *Theological Studies* 57, no. 4 (December): 611–33.

Posner, Richard A. 1981. *The economics of justice*. Cambridge: Harvard University Press.

Power, Samantha. 2002. *"A problem from hell": America and the age of genocide*. New York: Basic Books.

Raeymaeker, Louis de. 1954. *Philosophie de l'être*. Louvain: Editions de l'Institut Supérieur de Philosophie.

Rahe, Paul. 1985. Thucydides' critique of realpolitik. *Security Studies* 5 (Winter): 105–42.

Ramsey, Paul. 1983. Counting the costs. In *The just war: Force and political responsibility*. Lanham, Md.: University Press of America.

Rawls, John. 2000. *Lectures on the history of moral philosophy*. Edited by Barbara Herman. Cambridge: Harvard University Press.

———. 2001. *Justice as fairness: A restatement*. Edited by Erin Kelly. Cambridge: Harvard University Press.

Rorty, Richard. 1991. *Objectivity, relativism, and truth: Philosophical Papers*, vol. 1. Cambridge: Cambridge University Press.

Rubenfield, Jeb. 2003. The two world orders. *Wilson Quarterly* 27 (Autumn): 22–36.

Sacco, Colombo. 1998. *John Paul II and world politics: Twenty years of a search for a new approach, 1978–1998*. Canon Law Monograph Series, no. 2. Leuven, Belgium: Peeters.

Santurri, Edmund N. 1988. *Perplexity in the moral life: Philosophical and theological considerations*. Charlottesville: University of Virginia Press.

Schall, James V., S.J. 1982. *The church, the state, and society in the thought of Pope John Paul II*. Quincy, Ill.: Franciscan Press.

Scheler, Max. 1957. *The nature of sympathy*. Translated by Peter Heath. New Haven: Yale University Press.

————. 1960 *On the eternal in man.* Translated by Bernard Noble. New York: Harper and Brothers.

————. 1961. *Ressentiment.* Translated by William W. Holdheim. Edited by Lewis A. Coser. New York: Free Press of Glencoe.

————. 1973a. *Formalism in ethics and non-formal ethics of values: A new attempt toward the foundation of an ethical personalism.* Translated by Manfred S. Frings and Roger L. Funk. Evanston, Ill.: Northwestern University Press.

————. 1973b. *Selected philosophical essays.* Translated by David R. Lachtermann. Evanston, Ill.: Northwestern University Press.

————. 1980. *Person and self-value: Three essays.* Edited and partially translated by Manfred S. Frings. Edited by Kenneth W. Stikkers. London: Routledge & Kegan Paul.

Schmitz, Kenneth L. 1993. *At the center of the human drama: The philosophical anthropology of Karol Wojtyla/Pope John Paul II.* Washington, D.C.: Catholic University Press of America.

Seifert, Josef. 1981. Karol Cardinal Wojtyla (Pope John Paul II) as philosopher and the Cracow/Lublin school of philosophy. *Aletheia* 2: 130–199. Available at www.iap.li/oldversion/site/research/Aletheia/Aletheia_II/Aletheia2.pdf.

Shivanandan, Mary. 1999. *Crossing the threshold of love: A new vision of marriage in the light of John Paul II's anthropology.* Washington, D.C.: Catholic University of America Press.

Simpson, Peter. 2001. *On Karol Wojtyla.* Belmont, Calif.: Wadsworth/Thomson Learning.

Singer, Peter. 1996. *Rethinking life and death: The collapse of our traditional ethics.* New York: St. Martin's Press.

Slaughter, Anne-Marie. 2003. Leading through law. *Wilson Quarterly* 27 (Autumn): 37–44.

Smart, J. C., and Bernard Williams. 1973. *Utilitarianism: For and against.* Cambridge: Cambridge University Press.

Smith, Michael Joseph. 1987. *Realist thought from Weber to Kissinger.* Baton Rouge: Louisiana State University Press.

———. 1999. Humanitarian intervention: An overview of the issues. In *Ethics and international affairs: A reader.* 2d ed. Edited by Joel H. Rosenthal. Washington, D.C.: Georgetown University Press.

Smith, Timothy L., and Ralph McInerny, eds. 2001. *Faith and reason: The Notre Dame Symposium, 1999.* Chicago: St. Augustine's.

Sokolowski, Robert. 2000. *Introduction to phenomenology.* Cambridge: Cambridge University Press.

Spader, Peter H. 2002. *Scheler's ethical personalism: Its logic, development, and promise.* New York: Fordham University Press.

Steenberghen, Fernand van. 1949. *Epistemology.* Translated by the Reverend Martin J. Flynn. New York: J. F. Wagner.

———. 1952. *Ontology.* Translated by the Reverend Martin J. Flynn. New York: J. F. Wagner.

Stein, Edith. 1989. *On the problem of empathy.* Washington D.C.: ICS.

———. 1997. Husserl's phenomenology and the philosophy of St. Thomas Aquinas. In *Person in the world: Introduction to the philosophy of Edith Stein,* by Mary Catharine Baseheart, S.C.N. Dordrecht: Kluwer Academic.

Stiglitz, Joseph. 2003. *Globalization and its discontents.* New York: W. W. Norton.

Therrien, Michael. John Paul II's use of the term *neo-liberalism* in *Ecclesia in America.* Based on a paper delivered at the Pontifical College Josephinum, April 8, 2000. Available online at http://www.acton.org/cep/pubs/papers/neoliberalism.html

Thompson, Judith Jarvis. 1976. Killing, letting die, and the trolley problem. *Monist* 59:204–17.

———. 1985. The trolley problem. *Yale Law Journal* 94:1395–1415.

Thucydides. 1982. *The Peloponnesian War.* Translated by Richard Crawley. Revised, with an introduction by Terry E. Wick. New York: McGraw-Hill.

Tucker, Robert W. 1966. *Just war and the Vatican Council II: A critique.* New York: Council on Religion and International Affairs.

United Nations. *Report of the independent inquiry into the actions of the United Nations during the 1994 genocide in Rwanda.* Available online at http://www.un.org/News/dh/latest/rwanda.htm

Vacek, Edward, S.J. 1982. Scheler's phenomenology of love. *Journal of Religion* 62 (April 1982): 156–77.

———. 1985. Proportionalism: One view of the debate. *Theological Studies* 46:287–314.

Vatican website, http://www.vatican.va/holyfather/John Paul II/

von Hildebrand, Dietrich. 1953. *Christian ethics*. New York: D. McKay.

———. 1991. *What is philosophy?* With an introductory essay by Josef Seifert. London: Routledge.

Waltz, Kenneth. 1979. *Theory of international relations*. New York: WCB/McGraw Hill.

Walzer, Michael. 1974. Political action: The problem of dirty hands. In *War and moral responsibility: A philosophy & public affairs reader*, edited by T. M. Scanlon, Marshall Cohen, and Thomas Nagel. Princeton, N.J.: Princeton University Press.

———. 1977. *Just and unjust wars*. New York: Basic Books.

———. 2002. No strikes: Inspectors yes, war, no. *New Republic* (September 30): 19–22.

Weber, Max. 1958. Politics as a vocation. In *From Max Weber: Essays in sociology*. Edited by C. Wright Mills and Hans H. Gerth. Oxford: Oxford University Press.

Weigel, George. 1987. *Tranquillitas ordinis: The present failure and future promise of American Catholic thought on war and peace*. Oxford: Oxford University Press.

———. 1992. From last resort to endgame: Morality, the Gulf War, and the peace process. In *But was it just?: Reflections on the morality of the Persian Gulf War*. Edited by David E. Crosse. New York: Doubleday.

———. 1999. *Witness to hope: The biography of Pope John Paul II*. New York: Cliff Street Books.

———. 2001. Papacy and power. *First Things* 110 (February): 18–25.

———, ed. 1992. *A new worldly order*. Washington, D.C: University Press of America.

———. The just war case for the war. *America* 188, no. 11 (March 31, 2003): 7–12.

————, and James Turner Johnson. 1991. *Just war and the Gulf War*. Washington, D.C.: Ethics and Public Policy Center.

Williams, Bernard. 1982. *Moral luck*. Cambridge: Cambridge University Press.

Williams, George Hunston. 1981. *The mind of John Paul II: Origins of his thought and action*. New York: Seabury.

Williams, Thomas D. 1997. Values, virtue, and John Paul II. *First Things* 72 (April): 29–32.

Wojtyla, Karol. 1960. *Love and responsibility*. Translated by H. T. Willetts. New York: Farrar, Straus, and Giroux.

————. 1976. Special contribution to the debate: The intentional act and the human act, that is, act and experience. In *The crisis of culture: Steps to reopen the phenomenological investigation of man*. Analecta Husserliana 5. Dordrecht: D. Reidel.

————. 1979a. *The acting person*. Translated by Andrzej Potocki. Dordrecht: D. Reidel.

————. 1979b. *Sign of contradiction*. New York: Seabury.

————. 1980. *Primat des Geistes*. Edited by Manfred S. Frings. Stuttgart: Seewald Verlag.

————. 1987. *The collected plays and writings on theatre*. Translated by Taborski Boleslaw. Berkeley and Los Angeles: University of California Press.

————. 1993. *Person and community: Selected essays*. Translated by Teresa Sandok. New York: Peter Lang.

————. 1997. *The theology of the body: Human love in the divine plan*. With a foreword by John S. Grabowski. Boston: Pauline Books & Media.

Woznicki, Andrew N. 1980. *A Christian humanism: Karol Wojtyla's existential personalism*. New Britain, Conn.: Mariel Publications.

Yoder, John Howard. 1983. The conditions of countercultural credibility. In *Co-creation and capitalism*, edited by John W. Houck and Oliver F. Williams, C.S.C. Lanham, Md.: University Press of America.

Index